Washington's Hidden Tragedy

Washington's Hidden Tragedy

The Failure To Make Government Work

Frederic V. Malek

 THE FREE PRESS
A Division of Macmillan Publishing Co., Inc.
NEW YORK

Collier Macmillan Publishers
LONDON

The Free Press
A Division of Macmillan Publishing Co., Inc.
866 Third Avenue, New York, N.Y. 10022

Collier Macmillan Canada, Ltd.

Library of Congress Catalog Card Number: 77–18430

Printed in the United States of America

printing number

1 2 3 4 5 6 7 8 9 10

Library of Congress Cataloging in Publication Data

Malek, Frederic V
   Washington's hidden tragedy.

   Includes index.
   1. United States—Politics and government.
I. Title.
JK421.M34   353'.009'046   77–18430
ISBN 0-02-919790-2

Excerpts and adaptations from Frederic V. Malek, "Mr. Executive Goes to Washington," *Harvard Business Review,* Sept.–Oct. 1972, pp. 63–68, copyright © 1972 by the President and Fellows of Harvard College. All rights reserved. Reprinted by permission. *See pp. 43–59.*
   Excerpts and adaptations from Frederic V. Malek, "Assessment of Management Quality: A Guide for Outsiders," *Business Horizons* (Graduate School of Business, Indiana University), April 1968, pp. 23–28, copyright © 1968 by The Foundation for the School of Business at Indiana University. Reprinted by permission. *See pp. 202–207.*

Contents

Preface

I entered government service in 1969 after a brief but reasonably productive career as a professional executive in business. I came with no political background and was bound by no political ideology. I came with the assumption, considered somewhat naive by many, that the job of my colleagues and me was to cause government to be more effective in serving the American people.

It was something of a shock to learn that many players in the very political arena that comprises the top levels of government cared not so much about how well government worked as about how well it appeared to be working. It was equally shocking to see how little attention was actually focused on gaining the best possible performance from government and how limited were the tools available to do so. Without the orientation or the tools, there was little wonder that efforts were limited, and the results even more so.

Largely because of my particular background, my assignments in government were generally more concerned with managing and with making government perform more effectively, as opposed to developing policy initiatives. During my five and a half years of government service, progress was made in making government work better in some areas and setbacks were sustained in others. The whole of my experience convinced me that government was not delivering acceptable performance and that this inability to perform constituted a major tragedy in our country. I also became convinced, however, that while the major problems have persisted for decades, and will most likely endure for many more, government performance can be vastly improved with increased consciousness and a more determined application of proven principles. Thus, the decision to write this book.

The purpose of this book is to raise the consciousness of concerned citizens and government officials toward the need and the challenge to make government deliver at a higher level, and to offer observations of how to accomplish this to those who share my view that government must be made to work better.

Reflecting my own experience, this book is written from the point of view of the executive branch of government. Therefore, without in any way negating the critical role of the Congress in making government work better, I have chosen to limit my analysis and recommendations for the most part to that which is within the purview of the executive branch.

This book is not intended as a treatise or a work of deep research. Rather, it represents studied reflections on the problems that exist and on what can be done about them, by one who has worked at the business of making government work in a major department, in the White House, and in the Office of Management and Budget. I have tried to distill from my experience and from that of some of my colleagues those key lessons and principles that, if applicable, can in the aggregate have a serious, long-lasting impact on the effectiveness of government.

I am indebted to a number of former colleagues for their patience in reviewing and commenting on various segments of this book. They have been generous with their time and perceptive with their recollections, and, as in times past, it has been a joy to work with them.

I would like to express particular gratitude to Roy Ash, Jim Edwards, Don Ogilvie, and Tony Turner, who reviewed the entire manuscript and whose comments and insights were invaluable. Finally, I would like to single out Noel Koch and David Gergen, whose critique and suggestions strengthened both the style and the substance of this book.

I am aware that there will be some who question that any lasting value can be derived from the Nixon years or that any attempts were made during that period to better government performance, other than those that were politically motivated. However, it is historical fact that tens of millions of Americans voted for a change in 1968 and confirmed this desire in 1972, and thousands of dedicated people went to Washington to help cope with our nation's problems and opportunities. Watergate and its related scandal touched only a small and atypical group; the remaining thousands worked arduously and proficiently, albeit largely unnoticed, to make government work effectively both before and during those troubled times. It is to those unsung public servants whose fine efforts and accomplishments were overshadowed by the tragedy of Watergate that this book is dedicated.

Chapter One

A Government That Doesn't Deliver

Virtually every candidate for political office in America campaigns on the theme that government must be made to "work better." The precise meaning of the term—if there can be one—will vary according to the constituency addressed. It may mean smaller government, more efficient government, more responsive government, or even bigger government.

That such rhetoric is obligatory suggests a deep-seated, pervasive concern among American voters about such things as the size, cost, and effectiveness of their government. That it is perennial shows, however, that promises to make government "work better" are rarely kept. Granting good faith to the candidates and recognizing that there are a great number of constraints and impediments to improving the way government functions, the least considered and perhaps most important fact is that government does not work well because it is not managed well.

It is commonplace to observe that many Americans have lost confidence in their government. Frequently, the blame is heaped upon Vietnam and the revelations of government misconduct in the mid-seventies. Much of the concern about government, however, stems from a popular feeling that despite its vast size and enormous expense, government just doesn't deliver. That feeling is well founded.

Even the most ardent advocates of big government are frequently disillusioned. They concede the failures of many Great Society programs and wonder what went wrong. They have come to recognize, as have conservatives, that there are many reasons why government no longer commands the full sympathies or respect of the American people. It is now widely agreed that the government has undertaken many activities that it can't do well, that it has undertaken some activities that it can't do at all, and that it has failed to undertake other activities that it should be doing better. It is also recognized that the recurring deadlock between the legislative and executive branches of the government has inhibited the effective performance of government. But it has not been widely understood that another major factor contributing to the shortcomings of government is its lack of managerial discipline. That is the subject we shall examine here.

There have been many changes during the postwar years that make government more difficult to manage today. For one thing, government has grown substantially in size. About one person in six in our current work force works for government at some level—federal, state, or local. While most of the recent growth in personnel has occurred at the local level, there has also been a large increase in federal personnel working on social programs, offset to some degree by a decrease in those concentrating on national defense and security. Correspondingly, government spends far more money than it did in the early postwar years, so that government managers must deal with much larger budgets. Government spending at all levels is now over a third of the gross national product, compared to about 10 percent just before the New Deal. Moreover, Washington has assumed far greater authority for the way local and state governments perform. With every grant from Washington to Walla Walla comes a mound of red tape and oversight responsibilities that tax the administrative skills of federal bureaucrats to the hilt. Finally, there has also been a substantial increase in the authority of the federal government over the lives of individual Americans and individual enterprises, expressed most vividly in the explosion of federal regulations. This growth in authority has progressed in spurts from the New Deal to the present, partly as the result of a growing ambition for power within the executive branch, but mostly in response to the needs or desires of the country as expressed through the political process.

During the 1970s, the birth and development of the Federal Energy Administration illustrates perhaps better than any other example the misplaced impetus behind government growth as well as a number of the managerial shortcomings endemic to government. In the early 1950s it became clear to many observers that the United States was heading toward an energy crunch. Producers, economists, and even study commissions warned that the demand for energy was rapidly increasing but production was faltering. Drilling for new natural gas peaked in 1961, and domestic production actually began a downward spiral in 1970. The country that had once been a prime exporter was becoming dangerously dependent on foreign oil sources. Yet the government turned a blind eye toward the pending shortages. There were few institutional arrangements to head off the crisis, and policies were actually pursued that discouraged production and encouraged demand. And then when the crisis was almost upon us, the government's response was fitful, haphazard, and tragically inadequate.

The first significant response occurred in the spring of 1973 when four men moved into a small room on the second floor of the Old Executive Office Building across from the west wing of the White House. They were the nucleus of a group of about a dozen people whose responsibility it was to prepare the United States for the possibility that foreign producers might turn off the oil spigots.

The group was led by Charles DiBona, an Oxford-trained

economist recruited by Treasury Secretary George Shultz and assisted by a team from the Office of Management and Budget (OMB). DiBona was a skillful analyst who, in addition to his own considerable abilities, brought to the task a cadre of able young men from his most recent post as head of the Center for Naval Analysis. They set to work to identify all factors contributing to a possible energy crisis, to design a contingency program, and to implement the program when and if the crisis came. Most of official Washington doubted, or acted as though it doubted, that the time would come. Meanwhile, the businesslike approach of the DiBona group ignored the fact that in Washington a problem solved is a political opportunity forfeited. Many political figures in Washington are simply less interested in finding workable solutions than in milking political capital from the problem.

Within a matter of weeks a general energy program took shape. As complex as the problem was, the solutions fell into two easily definable areas: conservation of demand and expansion of supply. On the conservative side, several months before the crisis hit, the DiBona group prepared recommendations covering lower speed limits, lower temperatures in the winter and higher ones in the summer, less extravagant lighting (the national Christmas tree was to be dim that year), car pooling, limited rationing systems (odd/even days for gas purchases, five-dollar maximums, gas stations that simply ran out of gas), cold showers (Great Britain advocated that friends bathe together), no distant vacations, and similarly imaginative steps. These measures were not in themselves sufficient during the embargo, but they did help to produce a remarkable, though short-lived, decline in the amount of energy consumed in the United States.

On the supply side, the options were less plentiful and the time required for implementation much longer. Secondary and tertiary recovery techniques for drawing ad-

ditional crude out of the "dry" wells involved costly technology that could add little to existing supplies and at much
greater expense. The Alaskan pipeline was funded, but it
was not expected to bring in North Slope oil until 1978. The
Naval Petroleum Reserves were a possible source, if the
House Armed Services Committee would approve opening
them; it declared it would not. Regulated natural gas prices
made it unprofitable for the gas industry to explore and
bring in new gas fields, yet pro-consumer groups in the Congress were adamant that these natural gas prices not be
deregulated. The outer continental shelf might contain considerable petroleum reserves, but the people of the coastal
states didn't want anyone drilling off their shores. Exotic recovery technologies might exploit wind, tides, and sun, but
not soon enough. Coal was the obvious immediate answer,
but the environmentalists did not propose to lose their hard-
won victories to a prospective energy crisis. President Nixon
interrupted a meeting in the Cabinet Room to tell Environmental Protection Agency Administrator Russell Train that
two of his brothers had contracted fatal pulmonary diseases
from being cold and that if a choice had to be made he,
Nixon, wasn't coming down on the side of clean air and
cold homes.

On April 18, 1973, culminating the work of the DiBona
group, President Nixon unveiled a comprehensive energy
program for the nation. It was the first time in history that
a President had proposed so sweeping a program. The program provided as many options as possible for executive
action, but most of it required congressional action; and the
Congress knew a political football when it saw one.

Congress refused to provide the President with the authority to act and at the same time flailed him for not
acting. In the face of congressional resistance President
Nixon and his staff decided that the energy issue needed a
more publicly visible effort. On June 29, President Nixon
replaced DiBona with the incumbent governor of Colorado,

John A. Love, and announced that Love would be responsible for formulating and coordinating energy policies in a new agency, the Energy Policy Office.

DiBona was asked to remain since he had already formulated the program and understood it. The talented men he had brought to the White House were loyal to him and might be expected to leave if he left. Though undoubtedly disappointed, DiBona stayed on as Love's deputy.

John Love was deliberate, phlegmatic, decent, and totally lacking in all jugular instincts. These virtues would serve him poorly in his new job. As the American people became more aware of the energy crisis, its political utility continued to grow, as did the desirability of being identified with efforts to cope with it. Many saw it as an opportunity; few acted with the proper concern for the gravity of the situation.

In October of 1973 the Arab nations launched their long-anticipated strike at Israel. The United States began a major airlift to supply the beleaguered Israelis, who were soon able to counterattack, crossing the Suez Canal on the western front and throwing Syrian forces back toward Damascus in the east. Before the month was out the Arab nations declared an embargo on petroleum shipments to the United States and its allies. What many in the press and among consumer groups had persisted in calling a "phony crisis" had quickly become very real indeed. Warning lights in the White House, which had been flashing orange, suddenly went red. Despite the best efforts of the energy planners, the nation was not really prepared to meet the crisis.

In November, President Nixon established the Energy Emergency Action Group and announced to the nation that he would chair it himself. Shortly thereafter, however, Nixon turned his attention to other matters, and, without his strong leadership, the group soon fell into disarray. John Love simply didn't have the personal force or the internal support to lead it, and the group became a bear pit with its members spending their greatest energies jockeying for position rather than dealing imaginatively with the substantive issues. Rogers Morton wanted to head a proposed new cabinet post, the Department of Energy and Natural Resources, which would replace the Department of Interior. And Deputy Treasury Secretary William Simon wanted a platform to demonstrate his considerable abilities, as well as a hedge against the possibility of their not being rewarded with the position of Secretary of Treasury.

Finally, the undermining and jockeying against the leadership of the Office of Energy Policy reached a crescendo, and Nixon decided to send in still another team to pull together the country's energy policies. Love and DiBona were cashiered, and in their place Nixon put Simon and John Sawhill, OMB's Associate Director for Energy and Natural Resources.

With a virtuoso display of political skills and organizational understanding, Simon and Sawhill designed the Federal Energy Office, selected and assigned the key members, and laid out an agency for action. Where DiBona and then Love had labored under budgetary constraints, territorial disputes, and factional jealousies, all branches of the establishment bowed to the wishes of Simon and Sawhill. Unlike DiBona and Love, they were "insiders." More importantly, of course, the onslaught of the actual crisis made further infighting an intolerable luxury. The Federal Energy Office was underway.

Simon swung into action. His strategy was Rooseveltian: act, show leadership, restore confidence. He launched his campaign to overcome the energy crisis with a press briefing in the White House Press Room. He was tough and graphic. For those who couldn't grasp what a barrel of crude petroleum was, Simon had a barrel painted different colors, each indicating a different petroleum derivative. The clanking and banging that inevitably accompanied moving an empty oil drum through a room full of reporters was not easily or quickly forgotten.

Simon's role was a simple one—he convinced the American people that something was being done. In fact, as he knew, what was being done was minimal in relation to the overall problem, because there was very little that could be done overnight. A chief accomplishment was in the area of energy conservation. Electricity consumption dropped sharply. Gasoline usage went down as speed limits were reduced across the country. The federal government itself set an example with lower thermostat settings (except in Simon's office, where the mercury hung at a defiant eighty-two degrees through the winter), fewer light bulbs connected, fewer elevators running, and car pooling encouraged.

But there is an irreducible minimum beyond which consumption cannot go without severe and damaging impact. Something had to be done on the supply side of the problem, and there was very little that could be.

Much of the time at the energy office was actually spent trying to spread the shortages around through a jerry-built allocation program. The Congress, reacting to intense public pressure, only gave the agency four weeks to draw up a national allocation plan, and as one agency analyst said, it was "like trying to fix a flat on a car going fifty miles an hour." The agency itself wasn't helped by the fact that, for much of the time, its staff was scattered at nine different addresses across Washington, and Simon and Sawhill were continually called to testify before forty different congressional committees.

What prevented disaster were factors beyond the control of the Federal Energy Office. Chief among them were an unusually warm winter and the willingness of OPEC oil producers, including the Arab bloc, to "leak"—that is, to find ways of selling their oil to the Western world in spite of their embargo. Naturally, they sold at highly inflated prices. When the embargo was lifted, the prices remained high. And the American people adjusted their budgets accordingly. The U.S. economy suffered badly, but the immediate crisis was over.

The Federal Energy Office was not finished, however. It had only begun. Under Simon, the organization had grown from 12 to 1800 people. It soon took on a new name: the Federal Energy Administration (FEA), and John Sawhill was named Administrator. The group moved to the Post Office Building on 12th and Pennsylvania, which had previously housed the entire postal bureaucracy. There the number grew to some 3400 people with a budget of $142 million.

As the FEA became a permanent installation on the federal scene, many began to wonder whether it had long outlived its usefulness. By April of 1976, Simon would tell an audience in Houston that, "speaking from personal experience, I know all too well how an originally small, temporary bureaucracy can take on a life of its own and is still a large and growing part of the Washington scene—a striking example of the cancer of big government."

In truth, three years after its founding, the agency (now consolidated into the new Department of Energy) has almost no legitimate function. It continues to be sustained by high energy costs and spends millions of dollars to encourage conservation measures which have already been effected. It has evolved various regulatory tasks. A typical one is the entitlements program, which, in a nutshell, penalizes the large domestic energy companies for owning domestic oil by making them subsidize smaller companies that rely on foreign crude. One of the subsidized companies took advantage of the program to the tune of $228 million, collecting all that money for doing absolutely nothing.[1]

In the area of developing new energy sources, the Federal Energy Agency has only a small residual role, for this task has been delegated to another new bureaucracy, the Energy Research and Development Administration.

In 1976, President Ford appointed a task force to investigate the performance of various regulatory groups within the government, and in early 1977 the task force, headed by Yale Professor Paul MacAvoy, published their conclusions on FEA in a report printed by the American Enterprise Institute. Among other points, the task force underscored the fact that FEA had already generated over 600,000 federal forms to regulate the energy industry at a cost of over $500 million. Moreover, much of the regulatory structure was already obsolete or ineffective. Concluded the study group:

> FEA regulations as they now exist confer few, if any, benefits on the public. . . . In return for this lack of benefits . . . the American businessman, the taxpayer, and the petroleum consumer must incur higher costs that might otherwise be the case. Indeed, continuation of the present regulatory mechanism will result in long-run inefficiencies for the American economy.[2]

In spite of everything, the Federal Energy Administration still exists. It came into existence because of a lack of foresight, and it continues to exist because of political expediency. It exists in no small measure by inertia, and it exists, above all, because of bad management of the energy problem for more than twenty years. It is not unique. The Federal Energy Administration shares much in common with all branches of the bureaucracy, which is why I have chosen it as an example; its birth and development provide a cogent, contemporary, and almost clinical study of the way failure to manage government leads to unnecessary growth, complexity, confusion, and enormous waste of money. Immediately following are brief reviews of these management failures. (Succeeding chapters will address each problem and its solution in greater depth.)

Failing To Manage at the Level of Top Leadership

In the case of the Federal Energy Administration, President Nixon, faced with the increasing problems of Watergate, withdrew from the controversy and allowed his aides to fight over the spoils. The President's time is at best limited and cannot be squandered on any one issue. But on so major an issue as the energy shortage, the President should have maintained a strong leadership position in the development of efforts to meet the problem. Without attempting to second-guess presidential judgment, it is worth noting that President Nixon's response to the energy problem was submerged in a much larger effort to resolve the entire Middle East conflict. In June of 1974 he toured four Arab nations and Israel for this purpose. Typically, greater concern was directed to solving the effects of the problem than its real causes. The causes were internal: U.S. demand was rising more rapidly than internal production. That was the problem that should have preoccupied the President, but it didn't.

Selecting the Wrong People, or Failing To Develop Those Selected

Top cabinet and agency positions are prestigious political appointments, and the individuals appointed are most frequently chosen for the glamour, geographic or ideological balance, or other virtue they bring to the task. Talent is often a factor, but rarely is managerial talent a prerequisite. Therefore, the actual work of running an established bureaucracy falls to those who have no direct accountability for their actions. The relative lack of control over government and the so-called unresponsiveness of the bureaucracy are due more than anything else to weak leadership from top political appointees and high-level civil servants. Careful selection and complete support of top officials chosen to deal with the energy crisis might even have precluded the establishment of the Federal Energy Agency.

Bureaucracy lacks a systematic procedure for recruitment, training, and reschooling of top personnel with line authority. The Federal Energy Agency was created in a single day from such disparate sources as the Department of Interior, the Office of Management and Budget, the Justice Department, the Department of Defense, and other agencies. Significantly, those who were best qualified to deal with energy matters—members of the energy industry—were proscribed as political liabilities. Instead, as Simon often complained, the FEA was more often a dumping ground for bureaucrats that other agencies no longer wanted. Even today, unlike many other agencies, FEA has no organized programs for training personnel.

Ignoring the Need To Plan Past the Next Crisis

One of the earmarks of bad management is the absence of a long-range planning capacity. The energy crisis was certainly anticipated (experts had warned of it since the fifties), but the absence of sound long-range planning in the government failed to provide the necessary mechanisms to prevent or meet the crisis. The Federal Energy Office was finally formed in response to political pressure, with no objective consideration of its utility or long-range goals.

Failing To Set Objectives and To Follow Through on Priorities

An executive who sets meaningful objectives, articulates these to his people, and follows through to ensure that all employees are working intensively toward these objectives is apt to accomplish something meaningful and positive. His organization can manage and respond offensively, not defensively, as problems change character. In the early stages of the energy crisis no one adequately defined the objectives or the results expected from the energy organization. Instead, the development of that agency was characterized by an effort to stay one stroke ahead of the political tidal wave generated by the crisis.

Permitting Bureaucracy To Be Self-Perpetuating, and the Allocation of Resources To Be Distorted

Cabinet departments and agencies all have committees in the Congress that oversee their activities, authorize their funds, and, in the nature of the congressional seniority system, frequently develop a long, close, and proprietary relationship with the department or agency for which they share responsibility. In addition, bureaucracies are masters at self-promotion, skillfully acting under the guise of "public information"—a term that skirts a 1913 law prohibiting government agencies from the use of advertising or public relations. It is not unusual to find departments with public information offices that employ more people than other organic offices whose functions bear directly upon the department's mandate. In 1976, for instance, FEA's Public Information Office had a budget of $3.5 million and at one point employed no less than 130 people.

The "patron" relationship with Congress together with the skillful self-promotion serves to perpetuate even the most ineffective bureaucracy—as has been the case with the FEA. As all programs and agencies grow in this manner, discretionary funds are completely consumed; and nothing is left to meet emerging needs. Those discretionary funds that do exist are allocated on the basis of politics. In the FEA example, too little and then far too many resources were allocated as money was typically thrown at the problem as it became a major issue.

Being Unwilling or Unable To Fix Accountability and To Measure Performance

Objective evaluation of individuals or organizations is difficult in government and is almost never carried out effectively. Rather, superficial, more visible measures are often applied. William Simon's predecessors at the FEA developed a plausible energy program but were generally judged to have failed. The more colorful Simon on the other hand won plaudits largely due to his unique showmanship and ability to communicate convincingly. Evaluation and control over results are both made even more difficult by the concept of federalism which divides responsibilities and authorities between the federal, state, and local levels of government.

This absence of any meaningful measure of performance is one of the most distinctive differences between government and the private sector and one of the greatest problems a government manager faces.

Ignoring Basic Principles in Organizing

Again, political expediency dominates choice of organizational structure. Government is run at the top by politicians, and support is provided by short-term political appointees and career bureaucrats. Nearly all of them spend their time responding to the "crisis" of the moment, and few have a sense of organization. How else can one explain eighteen different overlapping agencies dealing with health problems and twenty-nine agencies running into one another as they handle various elements of education. The entire organization of the FEA was based more on the political needs of the moment than on any deep-rooted, substantive need.

We Americans take pride in believing that there is nothing we cannot do once we set our minds to the task. Our achievements in a relatively short history suggest that such a belief is not without foundation. But as our ambitions grow, so do the institutions and the budgets required to realize our ambitions. We launch a War on Poverty, and a galaxy of new government agencies is marshaled and armed with great sums of money. We decide to go into space, and the National Aeronautics and Space Administration is created. We proclaim a goal of energy self-sufficiency, and FEA and the Energy Research and Development Administration spring up.

All of these bureaucratic accretions function with varying degrees of effectiveness and efficiency. A number of Great Society programs were distinguished by misappropriation and misuse of funds at local levels. Fiscal management was poor. The moon landings were a great technological feat; whether they were worth the money is still being debated. The goal was set in a moment of strong nationalistic fervor, and few thought to question whether it was worth pursuing. The question was really one of how best to allocate our national resources; it should have been a management decision, but instead it was predicated on politics.

The energy crisis was predicted in the 1950s. The United States did nothing until "five minutes before midnight"— in 1973. We then blamed our problems on the OPEC nations, declared that we would lay the groundwork for energy independence, and launched a Rube Goldberg program for that purpose. The institutions already in place and responsible for dealing with energy matters were raided to create two new institutions. That these steps were necessary is not self-evident. The decisions involved were politically motivated and had nothing to do with effective government.

Management is, at bottom, a systematic means to an end. It is a process, not an end in itself. Yet the most cursory examination of government today, at every level, convinces one that this process of management has indeed become central to correcting the crisis of government in our country. In an economy of scarcity, no nation can indefinitely enjoy the luxury of poor management and remain a nation that can accomplish whatever goals it chooses.

The principal management arm of the federal government

is the executive branch. While it cannot solve all the problems of government in America—indeed, it now tries to solve more than it ought—it can at least put its own house in order, and in this manner set an example for government at the state and local levels. To do so must involve a conscious choice from the top of the executive branch. If government is to be managed properly, the job must begin with the President.

Chapter Two

The Chief Executive
as Manager

On March 20, 1976, President Ford addressed the North Carolina chapter of the Future Homemakers of America; the following Tuesday, he lost his first primary battle to Ronald Reagan—in North Carolina. That defeat marked the beginning of the end of Ford's hopes to be President in his own right. In the inevitable post mortem on the North Carolina primary, both the press and some White House advisers openly speculated as to whether the President's speech and his defeat were connected. The *Washington Post* said the remarks were "widely regarded as one of the worst speeches ever given by President Ford," and went on to observe: "That speech—which was ridiculed even by White House and Ford campaign circles—coupled with what was described as absolute junk that the speech writers initially produced for Mr. Ford's trip to California yesterday—has renewed concern among Presidential circles over the speech-writing operation." [1] It was clear in the minds of the press, if not in Ford's, that his poor performance at the podium was related to his trouble at the polls.

Wars are rarely lost for want of a nail, and one is always well advised to avoid single-cause explanations. Nevertheless, Ford's failure to win the presidency can easily be traced to his failure to present a presidential image or to project an inspiring vision of the future. And at least part of this failure stemmed directly from a continuing inability of either the President or his speech writers to craft material that had punch or lift.

Unknown to much of the public, Presidents rely heavily on speech writers for even the most casual public utterances, upon press secretaries (and an often merciful press) to cover up or correct many errors that might make the President appear foolish or uninformed, and upon advance men and quick-witted aides to guard against being photographed in unflattering poses. The effect is to present an image of an individual who is never flustered, never dribbles soup on his tie, never scratches himself, never fights with his wife. While students of government quarrel with the cosmetic presidency, the lack of attention to these details by Ford staffers and the President himself often opened him to a ridicule that unquestionably diminished the public's perception of him as the nation's leader.

Ford's problem was that he never took decisive action to create an effective, well-disciplined speech-writing staff. President Ford was sufficiently aware of the weakness of this staff that at one point he went outside the White House to request the assistance of a former Nixon staffer and worked with him in virtual secrecy on an upcoming speech, while his own writers labored along on a parallel draft, unaware that it would never be used.[2] While the action was a measure of the President's concern about his speeches, it was also a measure of his reluctance to rehabilitate his staff.

Old habits die hard, and Ford's personnel policies were simply another manifestation of his disposition to fall back upon the ways of the House of Representatives—avoiding confrontation or conflict, conciliating where possible, and retiring to the company of old and trusted retainers or friends when challenged or threatened. Mr. Ford himself, a thoroughly human and generous man, frankly acknowledged this shortcoming regarding people: "I probably don't come down hard enough on people. I don't reprimand. I don't fire people. . . . That's probably one of my admitted errors. I can't be a toughy when it comes to friends." [3] From the outset, then, Mr. Ford failed in three of the basic requirements of the government manager: (1) selecting strong, competent people for key functions; (2) evaluating the results on a continuing basis; and (3) taking decisive action to correct weaknesses in his organization. In this case the managerial failures resulted in Ford's presenting a mediocre image to the public and was a key contributing factor to his loss of the presidency.

FAILURE AT THE TOP

Successful management of any organization—from a small company to the United States government—makes the same demands on its leadership: establishing goals and choosing priorities for the organization; selecting people whose dedication and skills are compatible to achieving the goals; developing objectives and plans to reach these goals; allocating resources rationally; establishing an organizational structure and working relationships conducive to carrying out these plans; motivating and leading people to put forth their best efforts; and evaluating results, ensuring that planned progress is proceeding, and taking corrective actions where necessary.

While the general demands upon a manager in the private sector are the same as in the public sector, there are also enormous differences between the two. Some of these differences will be explored in the next chapter. One that is particularly pertinent as we focus here on the chief executive is that the presidency is preeminently a political job, and the qualities of successful politicians unfortunately seem antithetical to those of a good manager. Where a superior manager must be bold and take large risks, the politician is schooled to be cautious and wary, watching the small points so as to avoid mistakes that can be used against him in the next election. Where the manager must be decisive, the politician learns to smooth out differences and gain compromise. Where the manager generally cannot succeed without being objective in evaluating people and replacing substandard performers, the politician is more concerned with keeping friends and avoiding the enemies that can be created by firings. Where the manager must look to the long-term future, the politician is held accountable only for what he achieves before the next election. Finally, the politician is concerned with making policy and enacting laws, seldom with how well these laws are implemented.

Historians record American Presidents' former professions as teacher, tailor, soldier, and (overwhelmingly) lawyer; but few have acceded to the presidency with any substantial training in the managerial arts. In addition to the poor administrative preparation of most politicians for the job of chief executive, there is little political incentive to focus on sound management once in the job. It is almost impossible for most of the public or the press to evaluate with any accuracy how well the government is being run. Then too, there is little incentive to report on this aspect of government when the public interest is so much more easily titillated by controversy, mishaps, or major policy developments that may affect them directly in the near future. Without the incentive of a report card that has impact on the voters, most chief executives are encouraged to follow the natural direction of their training and ignore the managerial functions that determine the effectiveness with which government is being run. Thus, it is not surprising that few presidents have proved to be effective managers.

Today, the changing nature of the presidency has made this shortcoming in managerial skills increasingly detrimental to the national interest. In recent years, interest in government has focused on two disturbing trends. One is the growing role of the federal government in our national life;

the other is the expanded role of the President himself in the governing process. As these trends converge, the effectiveness with which the President conducts his office has an unprecedented impact on the well-being of the nation. A President cannot discharge his duties adequately by attention only to traditional macrocosmic concerns: foreign policy, the economy, domestic welfare. He must also keep a firm hand on the tiller of the ship of state. He doesn't have to rig the sail, pump the bilges, load cargo, or cook for the crew—he doesn't have to involve himself in operational details. But he does have to manage those who man the ship: he does have to manage his government. The country may have recognized this in 1976 when they elected a President whose appeal was based at least in part on his experience as an executive and his avowed interest in improving management of government. Based on President Carter's first year in office, the country's hopes were not well-founded. In evaluating the President's role as manager, however, it is instructive to examine the contrasting approaches taken by President Nixon and President Ford.

Breakthrough Initiatives

Richard Nixon came to the presidency with the conviction that his job was to determine policy and establish direction on matters of major consequence. He wanted to be judged on a few major thrusts that would change world history. Consistent with this view, he further believed that the time of his cabinet members and top staff should be spent on so-called breakthrough initiatives, steps that would radically alter and improve the course of government, and not on mundane matters providing little or no opportunity for discretionary action. He was convinced that progress in dealing with established concerns such as wheat subsidies or tariff rates counted for little because whatever he might do in these areas would be significantly altered by the heavily Democratic Congress and would be undone or reversed by succeeding administrations regardless of his own actions or wishes.

Nixon's experience in government had also convinced him—correctly, in my view—that the greater part of what most political appointees spend their time on would ultimately be determined by the career bureaucracy whether or not the appointees became involved. Therefore, it was better to let the bureaucracy continue to handle the routine administration while he and his appointees searched for and initiated major improvements. In short, it made more sense to invest time and effort in those undertakings that only a President and those acting with presidential authority could accomplish.

One of the principal tasks of his chief of staff, H. R. Haldeman, was to manage the daily schedule in such a way as to provide Nixon with uninterrupted time, and Haldeman usually succeeded. While it conflicts with the public perception of the presidential day as a twenty-four hour whirlwind of activity (which idea White House flacks usually try to promulgate), Richard Nixon had an amazingly uncluttered schedule. Many days were left almost completely free of formal meetings, and most days had at least one three-hour stretch without interruption. If Nixon wanted to spend half a day studying Chinese history or philosophy to help plan his approach to Red China or its leaders, he had the time available. He spent much of his time in study, contemplation, and discussion of world affairs.

This careful study and planning laid the groundwork for negotiating breakthroughs with the Soviet Union, a major opening in U.S. relations with China, and a qualitative alteration in the United States's posture vis-à-vis both its allies and its adversaries (the Nixon Doctrine) aimed at preventing future variations of the Vietnam experience. Domestically, the New Federalism, and particularly the revenue-sharing component of the New Federalism, brought about a discernible restoration of fiscal decision-making authority to state and local governments. While one may quarrel with the content of the policies, it is clear that Nixon was successful in his quest for major breakthrough initiatives, especially in foreign policy.

This style of management, however, frequently insulated the President from a number of problems and points of view. In spite of his interest in some specific domestic initiatives, such as revenue sharing and welfare reform, he was generally not concerned with most elements of domestic policy. Nixon himself readily admitted his preoccupation with national security matters to the detriment of domestic affairs when he told author Theodore White: "I've always thought this country could run itself domestically without a President . . . . All you need is a competent Cabinet to run the country at home. You need a President for foreign policy . . . the President makes foreign policy." [4] This view was brought forcefully to mind when I served as Deputy Director of the Office of Management and Budget and was asked to condense billion-dollar domestic policy decisions to one page or, in some cases, one paragraph, for the President to review and decide on.

During most of the Nixon years, management of domestic affairs was left principally to John Ehrlichman, an attorney whose specialty had been zoning law in Seattle. Ehrlichman had many positive talents, but he lacked the training or experience that would prepare him to mastermind a creative reorganization of national priorities in the post-Vietnam era. Ehrlichman was also allowed to use the Domestic Council for political fire fighting rather than for forging grand strategy and to appoint a number of young staffers who preempted even cabinet officers in many policy decisions.

Nixon held the view that government was poorly managed and that the bureaucracy was largely out of control. He felt strongly that his administration should improve government management. Legislatively, his efforts to reduce existing shortcomings took the form of sweeping proposals to reorganize the bureaucracy and a more successful effort to strengthen the workings of the Executive Office of the President by creating the Domestic Council and converting the Bureau of the Budget to the Office of Management and Budget. Administratively, within the Executive Office, the President's approach was to bring in strong managers, impart to them a sense of urgency in their mission, give them the authority to act, and support them when they needed support.

President Nixon did not, however, choose to manage or to get involved with management himself. When he selected Roy Ash and me to run the Office of Management and Budget (OMB) in November 1972, he impressed on us at length his desire to reform government and assured us of his full support. Over the next six weeks, Ash and I traveled to Camp David at least twice a week for meetings to refine our plans for second-term organization and our approach to managing government by objective. In January we spent just one hour discussing our final plans with the President. He approved them, instructed us to implement them, told us to involve his name and desires freely in pressing our points, and to come back to him only when we absolutely needed presidential support or involvement. The problem, however, was that one of the main ingredients of effectively directing a large organization with the management-by-objective approach is persistent involvement by the chief executive. In essence, President Nixon wanted sound management but did not wish to devote his time to its attainment. Thus, Nixon the manager like Nixon the man was something of a paradox—he acted with singular excellence in developing strategy on the large scale and in pushing bold initiatives but left much to be desired in his direction of the whole domestic side of government.

The Habits of the Legislator

Gerald Ford provides a striking contrast with his predecessor. Mr. Ford served for twenty-five years as a member of the House of Representatives—a collegial group whose decisions are usually reached through endless discussion, debate, negotiation, and compromise. Mr. Ford brought this style to the White House with the result that the President's door was opened to many more people and points of view than was the case under Richard Nixon.

Genuinely interested in the mechanics of government and familiar with the intricacies of the budget, he spent countless hours immersing himself in a welter of issues and decisions. Where Richard Nixon spent less than ten hours with Ash and me in discussing the 1974 budget, Gerald Ford spent as much as fifty hours with the OMB staff on the 1976 budget. One of the high points of the Ford presidency, in fact, was his unusual decision to make a personal presentation of his 1976 budget to the Washington press. It had not been done since the days of Harry Truman, and was far more complicated because the 1976 budget was more than four times as large as Truman's budgets a quarter of a century earlier. Uncomfortable with "ringing phrases" and unskilled at handling alliteration, inversions, parallelisms, tricolonic progressions, and other speech-writing devices, Ford was at home with his budget. His performance brought accolades from the press. It was one of the few times a verbal presentation by Ford was called "masterful"—and in this case Ford truly deserved the credit.

Aside from the amount of time expended in the decision-making process, there was a fundamental difference in the way Ford and Nixon reached decisions. On those major issues in which he chose to become involved, Mr. Nixon would inject himself deeply into its substance, gain a thorough understanding of all pertinent factors, retire to study and contemplate the issue in relative solitude, and come to a conclusion based upon his own beliefs and experience. Mr. Ford, on the other hand, was disposed to fall back upon the habits of the legislator. While he too would dig deeply into the substance of an issue, he was generally apt to reach his decisions not so much on the basis of personal insight tempered by fact and circumstances, but by judiciously weighing the views of others and leaning in the direction of a consensus.

Ford's easy, open process of managing and shaping policy has definite advantages over Mr. Nixon's tightly controlled method of operation. It also has serious pitfalls. One is that presidential authority is diluted when decisions are based on the number of advisers who agree on any given point, rather than on the informed judgment of the President. Another is that if the President tends to listen to the last person through the door, as did Ford on occasion, he can easily stumble into serious trouble. The classic example of these pitfalls in the Ford presidency occurred on the common-situs picketing bill when, long before the legislation had been reviewed by all concerned within the administration, Labor Secretary John Dunlop privately lobbied the President and obtained his promise to sign the legislation if it was enacted. Dunlop then used that promise to obtain congressional enactment of the bill. Ford, on the other hand, was suddenly faced with almost unanimous cabinet opposition to the bill as well as a right-wing revolt from the Reaganites. After much agony, Ford vetoed the bill; Dunlop resigned over the issue; and organized labor, feeling betrayed, worked hard for Ford's defeat in the November election. Another danger of indiscriminately "opening" the office of the President is that the number of decisions the President is called upon to make increases, and their importance decreases. It was not unknown for President Ford to participate even in minor personnel decisions, including such matters as increasing the pay of individual White House secretaries.

It is virtually impossible to allow oneself to be submerged in administrative details of this nature and still maintain the vision and breadth of understanding needed to shape and guide a government. In May 1976, columnist David Broder, writing on the anomaly of a popular incumbent trailing in the race for nomination, stated that Ford's basic shortcoming was "his inability to define the goals, the vision and the purposes of his presidency in a way that gives coherence to this administration and to his campaign." [5] During this same period, a high Republican official said of Mr. Ford's incumbency, "He comes across as a blob of good intentions, but there's no pattern to it."

Looked at as a whole, the record of Gerald Ford's presidency must be favorably judged, for he was undoubtedly the right man for a very difficult period in our history. But the points raised by Mr. Broder and others are well taken. In attempting to "open up" the office of the presidency, Gerald Ford did in fact participate in more decisions, but radically reduced the impact of the presidential decision-making process. In so doing, he slighted a critical task of the chief executive—to think creatively and exert bold leadership on issues of major importance.

Which style is right, Nixon's or Ford's? Historians normally fold this sort of question into the determination whether an individual was a "good" or "bad" president, criteria that are themselves determined in a highly subjective manner. The real question is whether either President was effective in directing his administration toward nationally acceptable and productive goals in domestic and international affairs. Against this objective, the inescapable conclusion is that both Presidents demonstrated strengths and weaknesses, but neither was a totally effective manager.

Perhaps we can expect a new breed of politician to evolve to meet the need for greater managerial expertise. Occasionally, a President will come to office with greater preparation for managing government, as President Carter does with his experience as manager of a small business and as chief executive of a state government. As of this writing, Carter, like Ford, seems to want to become immersed in every issue. It will be instructive to see how much difference Carter's experience will make in his ability to make government work effectively and whether he will be able to step back from the detail and formulate sound, coherent goals and strategies.

For the most part, however, we should realistically assume that any President and indeed most other high officials elected and appointed will not be "good managers." Rather than expecting voters to begin electing good managers, or politicians to develop managerial expertise, we should look fully at the role of the chief executive and identify those management tasks that the traditional politician can and should perform, even with a limited understanding of management.

THE JOB OF THE CHIEF EXECUTIVE

While my own government experience has been chiefly with Presidents and cabinet-level personnel, most of the job elements and considerations discussed in these sections will apply equally well to mayors, governors, and other governmental leaders.

The duties of the chief executive fall into five broad categories: ceremony, communication, politics, policy development, and management. His ceremonial roles lend the prestige of the presidency to a reaffirmation of the legitimacy of certain national icons. These include having his picture taken with the 4-H Club member of the year or the March of Dimes poster child, issuing appropriate proclamations on Thanksgiving, Veterans Day, and National Doughnut Week, lighting the national Christmas tree, and a range of similar functions. President Nixon set aside time most days from about 11:30 A.M. to 12:30 P.M. to attend to such responsibilities in five- to ten-minute segments. The White House staff was constantly looking out for events that would, by association, contribute to the President's popularity. In one case, a survey revealed the most popular (read "best-attended") national sport was stock-car racing, and plans were initiated by the White House staff to put the President in the pits at a major stock-car race. The plan was never implemented, though many drivers did come to the White House to see the President.

Among other presidential roles, communication with the public is one of the most important. In fact, to some observers, it is *the* most important task. In developing a political strategy for President Carter, his pollster and adviser Patrick Caddell wrote: "Too many good people have been defeated because they tried to substitute substance for style. They forget to give the public the kind of visible signals that it needs to understand what is happening." [6] It is in this role as communicator that the President presents his broad policy outlines and specific programs and seeks approval for them. He does this through formal devices such as the State of the Union and the Budget messages, through news conferences, speeches, messages to the Congress, and private backgrounders for the media, and through other ad hoc means. Preparation for a news conference can consume as much as two full workdays; and every speech and message must be carefully reviewed to avoid a misstep when the whole country is listening. The President is also the head of his party, a role with as much importance as a President chooses to assign to it (normally not much) and as much or as little importance as the two political parties have between elections (again, normally not much). Policy formulation is one of two substantive parts of the President's job. Depending on his view of the presidency and the needs of the nation as he perceives them, this may be all-consuming and, since Roosevelt's time, has been.

The President's performance on all these activities is highly visible to the electorate and constantly subject to their assessment. The President's execution of his second substantive responsibility—management—is not nearly so visible, nor is it susceptible to popular judgment. The possibilities for mischief became evident when we consider that the President is responsible for over 100 departments and independent agencies that report directly to him, that he has to manage relationships with some 150 separate countries, and that he is charged with supervising the wise allocation of efficient spending of over $460 billion a year. Thus, despite the fact that only limited discretionary time and even less incentive is present, there is a management role of major proportions to be performed. While the authority for performing much of this function may be delegated, there are certain responsibilities that can and must be borne by the President alone.

DEFINING THE PRESIDENT'S MANAGEMENT ROLE

The word management brings visions of the corporate executive deeply involved in all aspects of operations, monitoring costs, slashing payrolls of inefficient divisions, pushing for greater efficiencies, and the like. Even if he wanted to, the President could not manage in this manner. In most instances, the combination of congressional influence, interest-group pressures, public expectations, and political realities militate against crisp managerial actions. The President's responsibilities are of a much higher order of management leadership and are characterized not by depth but by breadth.

Setting the Tone

Only the chief executive can establish an administrative environment that is conducive to effective long-term performance. The hallmark of this environment must be an insistence on high ethical standards in all dealings and on all matters in and out of government. It includes an adherence to a decision-making policy that is understood by everyone to be objectively based on facts and analyses (including political) and not on personalities or seat-of-the-pants judgments. It is of particular importance to impart a sense of urgency and develop a sense of team spirit that make it all seem worthwhile. Setting the right tone also means evaluating people on their performance—the actual results achieved—and not on personalities. An important aspect of this (recognizing that political considerations must occasionally prevail) is to award major promotions and appointments on merit and performance.

We have seen in recent years that failure to insist on high ethical standards can bring the downfall of an administration. The atmosphere in the Nixon administration was clearly one of high performance standards—more intense than in any organization I have ever seen. At the same time, it was generally understood that one did everything possible to obtain results, and failure would not be tolerated. This results-at-any-price approach, with its attendant pressures, tacitly tolerated and even encouraged some within the Nixon inner circle to operate on the fringes of the law and of moral behavior. Watergate may well be regarded as a disaster that was just waiting to happen. No one told Jeb Magruder to bug the Democratic National Committee. But due to the pressure to perform—to obtain sound intelligence on the opposition's plans—Magruder overstepped the boundaries of propriety in an effort to please his superiors. Lacking any real maturity or experience, he felt that the result justified the means. Unfortunately, it spelled the beginning of the end for Richard Nixon.

No modern President was faced with more of a need to restore a sense of moral tone and ethics than Gerald Ford. Whatever he may have lacked in managerial capacity and vision for the country he more than made up for by bringing to office precisely the temperament, character, and truthfulness that the country so badly needed at the time.

All Presidents have enjoyed great loyalty from their immediate staff and, in varying degrees, from members of their cabinet. Of modern Presidents, however, none inspired fiercer loyalty than John F. Kennedy. This was based on a combination of youthful enthusiasm, personal charisma, and a general sense of camaraderie that few Presidents have been able to instill. Lyndon Johnson demanded and gained loyalty and a sense of urgency by the forcefulness of his approach and the strength of his personality. Under Richard Nixon, most of the top staff felt an urgent sense of mission based on a deep belief in the programs and philosophies that were being pursued, as well as a deep respect for the President.

No President has completely measured up to all aspects of setting a good tone within his administration. It is even questionable whether most Presidents have clearly focused on this role and all its parameters. Historical significance aside, however, the important point is the utter necessity of the chief executive to establish and maintain the tone for his administration as the threshold requirement of management.

Selecting the People

Next to setting the proper tone, the selection of key personnel is the most important task of the chief executive, for an administration will be only as good as the people comprising it.

While most Presidents have been able to develop a cohesive staff with a sense of urgency and dedication to the President's purposes, few have shown as much discipline as they should in selecting, evaluating, and promoting people on the basis of results achieved rather than on personalities or politics. It has been my experience that when a President has tried to base a major personnel decision on competence and merit, he was well rewarded in the process. James Schlesinger, for example, was an unknown Associate Director of the Office of Management and Budget when President Nixon, in spite of his personal dislike for Schlesinger, tapped him to be Chairman of the Atomic Energy Commission. Though cold and analytical in demeanor, Dr. Schlesinger proved to be an extremely adept and popular Chairman and instilled some much-needed reforms into a very stodgy agency. Based on the strength of his performance at the AEC, Schlesinger was moved to the directorship of the Central Intelligence Agency. He barely had time to begin some long-needed reforms there when he was appointed to fill the vacancy created at the Department of Defense by Elliot Richardson's departure. Again at Defense, Schlesinger proved himself to be a master of efficient and astute policy analysis and development. His government service, of course, was abruptly, if only temporarily, ended when Gerald Ford decided he would be more comfortable without the abrasive, arrogant brilliance of Schlesinger and replaced him with a man he could work more comfortably with.

While Richard Nixon made many appointments and promotions based on merit, he, too, frequently yielded to political considerations. Shortly after the 1972 elections, President Nixon decided he wanted a cabinet reflective of the majority of Americans that had elected him. In his view, this included Irish Catholics, Americans of Italian descent, officials from the labor movement, veterans, and people from other walks of American life. His ambition was to dismantle Roosevelt's Grand Coalition, and in his second term he wanted a cabinet that reflected elements of the coalition he had won over in his reelection.

As his chief recruiter, it was my job to find these people. He was particularly annoyed when, after a period of time, we were not able to turn up a qualified Italian-American who was willing to accept a high post in the administration. Unable to solve the problem head on, he went around it by appointing John Scali, a distinguished TV correspondent and then White House assistant, to be Ambassador to the United Nations. Nixon then elevated the post to cabinet rank so that he could honestly say that he had an American of Italian descent in his cabinet. Similarly, Peter Brennan was selected to be Secretary of Labor not solely on the basis of his abilities, but also because he was Irish Catholic and was a true representative of the labor movement.

Developing an Organization

At the early stages, the chief executive must develop a decision-making system and a top-level organization that is suitable to his own style and is also able to achieve the lofty goals he has set. Similarly, he must select the right people to man this organization. There are tasks he cannot delegate, and time invested at this stage will pay rich returns later on.

The President cannot try to work with all cabinet officers and agency heads, and he must develop a staff structure to help him review options and manage the substratum of government. He hasn't the time to sit and listen to arguments on the two hundred substantive differences on a health insurance bill or the dozen major issues of energy policy. Moreover, the agencies and departments of government may or may not be organized in a manner that permits continuing personal overseeing. Further, this organization is largely fixed. While he can tamper with the organization to a minor degree, any major changes will most likely consume his entire presidency, as will be amplified on in a later chapter. The only domain in which he has real flexibility is in the Executive Office of the President itself.

The choice is not whether the White House should be organized to help run the government, but whether to organize by intention or by default. The President's span of control is so wide that he cannot possibly deal on a personal basis with the unwieldy structure of the entire government. If he does not carefully plan his own organization to manage this built-in problem, patterns of communication will develop in a haphazard manner and results will inevitably fall short of expectations.

Richard Nixon's eight-year tenure as Vice President provided him with some revealing insights into White House organization, and he, along with his chief of staff, created an organization and staffing system that was custom-tailored to Nixon's style. Gerald Ford, on the other hand, was thrust into the presidency with limited preparation and a different style of operating and reaching decisions. He had considerable difficulty molding an organization that was compatible with his own style and could also achieve results. In his first hundred days in office, President Carter also found that he was having difficulty forming a smoothly working staff operation; the problems are just much more difficult and the pressures more intense than even he realized.

Those individuals a President appoints to top coordinative positions must bring with them a rich background in their field and sufficient humility to ensure that they do not act as a barrier between the President and his agency heads. One of the worst sins of a top staff member is to misuse his position to assume greater power at the expense of others. To discourage empire building and to ensure that the major analytical work for decisions is developed in the agencies or in OMB where professional staff work can best be done, it is also essential to limit the number of aides reporting to each of the top presidential assistants in the White House.

Clearly Enunciating Goals and Objectives

Each agency head needs clear guidance as to the direction the President expects him or her to take, the general philosophical framework he is to operate within, and what precisely he is expected to accomplish. It takes a great deal of energetic thought and a certain amount of time at the start of a term to clearly set these guidelines, but without them there is no road map to shape the activities of the administration.

Early in his term, the President should require from each major agency chief a definite set of objectives—what the agency expects to achieve in the coming year over and above its ordinary work of dispensing grants or running parks. Having agreed on the framework, the President can then delegate responsibility to the agency head to fill in the pieces. To do less is abdication; to do much more or to tell people how their objectives are to be achieved is overmanagement. As former HUD Secretary Robert Wood has written: "Confusion is created when men try to do too much at the top. A curious inversion occurs. Operational matters float to the top, and policy making emerges at the bottom. At the top, minor problems squeeze out the major ones." [7]

Once the President has agreed with his agency heads on the goals and objectives they are to achieve in their agencies, the President can meet on a quarterly or semiannual basis with an agency head to discuss his progress and, in the process, provide the direction needed to do his part in properly running the government. We will return to this subject in a later chapter.

Insisting on Sound Management

As mentioned earlier, the President cannot take the time to become personally involved in the operational details of managing the government. Nor can he take a direct part in effecting the many projects aimed at improving the effectiveness of the government. He can, however, hold his agency heads and cabinet officers to high standards of managerial excellence. Richard Nixon generally did not involve himself personally in the management of the government; he did strengthen the Executive Office of the President, and he instilled a sense of urgency among all of his people that good management was something he expected, and in fact demanded, from them. With this atmosphere and his implied support, those people appointed to top positions had an almost unlimited opportunity to exercise improved management techniques throughout government.

Providing Leadership to the Career Executive

Few Presidents have really taken the time to think about the need to provide leadership and build confidence among the 2.5 million civil servants who will carry out their policies. Yet there is little else that could have as much of an impact on the effective running of government and on the achievement of a President's goals. There are several things the chief executive can do. First, he can insist that only well-qualified people are appointed to top positions of leadership in his administration. So much of the legendary lack of responsiveness on the part of the career bureaucracy is due to inexperience and inept management leadership from political appointees. For the most part, civil servants have a great deal of professional pride and a desire to accomplish worthy ends.

Properly led by good people, most of them will do every-thing in their power to achieve the goals and aspirations of a President, no matter which party he represents.

The President should do everything possible to provide opportunities to career public servants to perform in an at-mosphere where their efforts are appreciated and to give them every opportunity to develop their managerial skills. Partly because of the rapid turnover of political appointees, there has been little incentive for the political appointee to try to develop the skills of the people under him. Rather, the tendency is to deter the best people from developmental experiences so that they can continue to contribute to the appointee's programmatic goals and enhance his own reputa-tion and future.

Thus, it is imperative for the President to communicate clearly to his own appointees the need to work with and develop the career bureaucracy and to take every oppor-tunity to impart his own sense of confidence and apprecia-tion to these dedicated people.

Management will never head the priority list of any modern President. Yet there are things the President can do with a limited expenditure of time, particularly at the start of a term, that can have an enormous influence on the suc-cess or failure of his administration. As pointed out above, one of the most important early tasks is the judicious selec-tion of qualified people, a subject I treat at length in the following two chapters.

Chapter Three

The Government Executive

The departure of Walter Hickel from the Nixon administration underscored for me in a very personal way how different the demands of government management are from those in the private sector. A former Governor of Alaska who had been appointed Secretary of the Interior, Hickel had national political ambitions nurtured by years of political success. Early in his tenure at Interior, he began diminishing his involvement in the substantive duties of his office and turned instead to extensive travel and speech making. His strong advocacy of conservation, however, struck a responsive chord with many young people, and he rapidly developed a constituency among them.

During 1970, President Nixon was under strong attack by liberals and youth groups trying to force an unconditional withdrawal from Vietnam. The President was attempting to lay the groundwork for solid negotiations with the North Vietnamese. Part of the problem in this endeavor was the propensity of Hanoi to misjudge the impact that demonstrations and editorials had on the will of the President. In the midst of these difficulties four young students were shot down at Kent State University by Ohio National Guardsmen.

The aftermath of this shocking event saw a reassessment of positions and a general lowering of voices all around. Sensing the youth disaffection, however, Secretary Hickel wrote the President a letter of advice counseling that he be more receptive to the admonitions of the young. Someone on his staff then leaked the letter to the press, and the President read about the letter before it was actually delivered to him. The White House interpreted this act as an attempt by Hickel to boost his own popularity with youth groups (which he did) and to strengthen his political position, all at the expense of the President.

Unwilling to tolerate such tactics, the President saw no alternative but to fire Hickel, which he did the day before Thanksgiving. He immediately directed me to take charge of dismissing several members of Hickel's inner staff group. In a follow-up conversation, Bob Haldeman pointed out that the President wanted the resignations effective that day so that a new Secretary could get off to a running start and we could avoid having the story dragged out over a period of weeks to the embarrassment of both the administration and the people involved. Although this seemed a bit abrupt, I agreed to carry out the order.

Early that afternoon the Deputy Under Secretary of Interior and I held individual meetings with those whose resignations were sought. I thanked and complimented them for their service on behalf of the President, explained that a decision had been made requiring that Secretary Hickel's staff depart to make room for a new team, that the resignations were desired that same day, but that individuals could remain employed as consultants for as long as it took them to relocate.

Although they complied, several took their story to the press. In the meantime, Ron Ziegler, the White House Press Secretary, had directed me not to speak to the press and neglected to offer an explanation himself. Thus, with no explanation from the White House, the headline stories that evening and the next morning said that six Hickel aides had been "ordered to clean out their desks by 5:00 o'clock." What we considered an unpleasant necessity was depicted as an act of brutality. Overnight I had become Nixon's hatchet man, and while this ensured that my phone calls were always quickly returned, it gave me an image that was detrimental to future efforts to improve managerial performance in the executive branch.

This experience vividly illustrated to me the impact of the media on the government executive, and the added nuances to which the government executive must be sensitive in order to succeed. An action that seemed reasonable on its face had become a political liability to the President and to me because we failed to consider how our actions might be construed in the press. In retrospect, we should either have gone immediately to the press with a full explanation or delayed the departures for a few weeks, allowing everyone a more graceful solution.

Just as the government executive must be more sensitive to press relations than the business executive, he must also meet several other demands in the government that are absent in the business environment. The failure to recognize these demands upon the government executive is one of the major reasons why the wrong people are sometimes recruited for Washington service and why their performance is often mediocre. This chapter first describes those key differences between managing in government and in the private sector, and then describes the personal qualities that should be sought in government executives.

COMPLEXITIES OF GOVERNMENTAL MANAGEMENT

Like industriousness and inventiveness, management ability is one of those entrepreneurial virtues that not all Americans possess, but which is usually included in descriptions of our national character. In the 1950s we made of "management" a kind of secular religion, and the conviction persists at home and abroad that we are a people peculiarly adept at the business of "getting things done." While the record of U.S. business and commerce since the Great Depression has not been one of completely unqualified success, it is certainly one that justifies and sustains our pride in our managerial skills. This being the case, it is somewhat puzzling to reflect on our increasingly obvious inability to manage government.

A major reason why managerial expertise in the private sector has not been carried over to the public sector is that the qualities that provide success in one area may actually assure failure in the other. A study prepared for the Eisenhower administration concluded:

> A majority of business executives are uncomfortable and unsuccessful in the federal government's topmost political, policy-making posts as department heads and assistant secretaries. They are unaccustomed to and sometimes resentful of the interest of the legislative branch in administrative affairs. They are unfamiliar with the necessity for clearance and coordination with numerous other departments. They are irritated by public scrutiny of their actions and by the rigid controls exercised over recruitment of supplies and equipment.[1]

A decade later, a foundation-supported study rated businessmen a poor third after lawyers and educators in terms of likely effective public service.

It is not my purpose to write a how-to manual for businessmen about to undertake a stint in government. Since businessmen have more managerial training than any other profession, however, it is likely that they will continue to provide a great reservoir of talent for government service. Thus, it is important that there be a clear understanding of the differences between public and private management and of the unique qualities and skills that a successful government manager must have.

THE GLARE OF PUBLICITY

From the days of Frank Norris, Upton Sinclair, and the other self-described "muckrakers," the media have sought to lay bare real or fancied corporate misdeeds in great gasps of journalistic outrage. The effort has met with mixed success and has been hampered by everything from libel laws to public indifference. In addition, digging out hard facts about alleged corporate crimes is not easy work. Business has the right and the means to keep the media at arms length whenever it chooses. Consequently, the corporate executive acts in relative seclusion. Moreover, he acts within a shared value structure—one that shuts out those not in sympathy with it. Competition, however severe, takes place in an atmosphere of collegiality. The corporate executive is accustomed to the informed and usually sympathetic scrutiny of his colleagues, his stockholders, and, only occasionally, the public through various reports mandated by law.

The government executive, on the other hand, is subjected at every turn to the constant glare of publicity.[2] Every department and agency has a cadre of newsmen whose primary job it is to cover its activities. There is little emphasis placed on straight news—programs initiated or terminated, their budgets, their success or future prospects. Instead, there is a premium on novelty, controversy, personalities, failures, and—most especially—on any activity that smacks of indiscretion. The media will also seek to reveal programs, plans, and projects while these are still in the planning stage and not ready for public airing.

At the least, premature disclosure can be embarrassing. The government executive must be prepared to endure the discomfort of having his "discussion drafts" leaked and printed as if they were final recommendations. As long as he can follow through on his decisions, no harm is done— except perhaps to his ego or political future. But premature disclosure can also disrupt carefully developed plans. A couple of years ago a cabinet officer decided that one of his bureaus needed "shaking up" and to accomplish it he would have to replace three of its top-level managers. As he was proceeding carefully to arrange "transfers" that looked like promotions, a newspaper report disclosed the plans in a way that made his action look extremely devious. The cabinet officer chose to proceed with the transfers, but the morale problems that resulted in the bureau negated many of the positive effects of the management changes.

From my experience the best way to deal with the press is to be totally open and direct. There are times, such as in the formative stages of policy development, when premature disclosure could be harmful to the ultimate success of the initiative. In such cases, again, an honest explanation of the reasons for not disclosing the information will best serve the government executive.

PUBLIC OPINION

The manager in government soon learns that public opinion is everything. The most effective manager is one adept at sensing the mood of the public and at winning acceptance of his department's goals. Indeed, before an agency can successfully proceed with a major new initiative, it is essential to gain public support for its goals. More than one good idea in Washington has failed because it lacked public acceptance at its inception. There is no corresponding necessity for the average private-sector executive. To him, "public" support means the support of his board of directors or stockholders, and depends more on the law of supply and demand than on the whims and vagaries of the national mood.

Former Secretary of Commerce Peter Peterson, who has spent most of his career in business, once remarked: "In Washington, your ability to articulate your accomplishments in a way that is memorable and persuasive generally counts for more than the objective standards of efficiency and suc-

cess as we know them in business." The accuracy of his ob-
servation is reflected in the public career of a leading member of the Nixon and Ford administrations, Rogers Morton.
Morton served as Secretary of the Interior under President
Nixon and as Secretary of Commerce under President Ford.
Over the years, he has also served as a congressman from
Maryland, Chairman of the Republican National Committee,
and head of Ford's presidential campaign. For all of his long
years of service, it is difficult to pinpoint many major accomplishments. Yet "Rog" is a smiling, gregarious fellow
with a lot of friends among his former colleagues in the
Congress, as well as having a pleasant personality and a nice
way with words. As a result he enjoys a public reputation as
an effective and able leader.

Contrast Morton with former Office of Management and
Budget (OMB) Director Roy Ash. A founder and one-time
president of Litton Industries, Ash led the Presidential Commission on Government Organization, which resulted in the
creation of the Environmental Protection Agency, OMB, and
the Domestic Council, as well as solid legislative proposals
for much-needed government-wide reorganization. As OMB
Director during Nixon's second term, Ash was easily among
the brightest men in the top ranks of the administration, and
was largely responsible for adherence to a sound, stable
course in dealing with our energy and economic crises during a period when the President was preoccupied with
Watergate. Roy Ash was Alexander Haig's silent partner in
holding the executive branch together and governing the
nation as Watergate threatened complete paralysis. Yet Ash
did not have a particularly outgoing personality and was not
willing to spend time building relationships with the Congress and the media; he thought other, more substantive
issues deserved his full attention. As a result, his motives
were questioned, he was often portrayed as a villain by the
media, and he was suspect on Capitol Hill. Ash's record of

achievement easily eclipses that of Rogers Morton, yet the latter enjoys a public acclaim rooted in his sound sense of public relations.

The Congress constitutes an extraordinarily active and sometimes dominant board of directors for the executive branch. Its influence and discretionary power extend from budget allocations to the content and direction of programs, to number of personnel and their assignments, and even to questions of departmental organization. It is essential to devote considerable time and effort to informing, persuading, and gaining the confidence of members of Congress, particularly those who sit on the committees and those who address themselves to the constituencies affected by a department's functions.

Because corporate executives are accustomed to giving orders and having them carried out without question, the act of influencing politicians is a mystery to them. The unaccustomed necessity of cajoling and persuading a large number of strong-willed and diverse men can prove to be a time-consuming, frustrating, and humbling exercise. Most executives coming into government avoid it or do it poorly.

PARTISAN CONSTRAINTS

Paying respectful attention to congressional sensitivities is only one of two considerations the manager in government has when dealing with the legislative branch; the other concern is simple partisan politics. Any initiative that requires legislative action must run the gauntlet of partisan analysis in Congress, in the press, and among the public, no matter how nonpolitical, necessary, or high-minded it may seem to the department or agency involved. Criticism will range from the highest to the lowest levels of rhetoric and imputation, from the most philosophical and detached to the most visceral and prejudiced. Whatever the motives behind it, such criticism means that no subject or proposal can be considered solely on its own merits. For this reason, no government executive can ever have complete freedom of action in framing or implementing a program to meet a perceived need.

Complicating the problem of partisanship is a functional dichotomy. The principal role of the Congress is to legislate. The role of the executive branch is to implement laws, to "get things done." This division of purpose leads to a questioning of motives from both sides. The executive manager frequently feels that the Congress—especially when dominated by the opposition—opposes his efforts for partisan reasons, as it frequently does. In addition to partisanship, however, opposition often comes irrespective of party affiliation when one branch or the other feels its prerogatives or powers are being usurped.

The government executive, normally unskilled at partisan infighting, is concerned with doing a job. The manner in which he proposes to go about doing his job, however, may look suspiciously like poaching on the opposition party's preserve. In 1971, for example, President Nixon proposed sweeping changes in the nation's welfare system. It required then, as it does now, only the least pretense at objectivity to see that our system of welfare has become a patchwork shambles that helps to perpetuate poverty, gives the poor neither the incentive nor the opportunity to get out of the welfare jungle, and costs the taxpayer far more than the system is worth in terms of the national interest. But welfare, per se, is a "people-oriented" issue. And when Nixon set forth his proposals to a Democratic Congress, the "party of the people" was not disposed to allow the "party of big business" to co-opt a position on this issue, regardless of the need or the merit of the proposed alternative. Not surprisingly, Democratic presidential hopefuls in 1976 were saying that the welfare system was a mess and had to be reformed. In government, it seems, one of the chief criteria for an idea whose time has come is who is presenting it. The Republican administration faced similar difficulties when it sought to reorganize the federal bureaucracy patiently erected over the years on the foundation of the New Deal. What Franklin Roosevelt brought together, Richard Nixon would not be permitted to put asunder.

BUREAUCRATIC OBSTACLES

Managers in and out of government have to cope with bureaucracy, but even here there are both quantitative and qualitative distinctions that limit the value of private managerial experience in preparing for the responsibilities of a government executive.

Bureaucratic Behemoth

The sheer diversity, complexity, and dispersion of government programs is a new experience for the person entering government from the private sector. Proliferation of agencies with duplicative responsibilities radically reduces and often eliminates accountability. When everyone is responsible, no one is responsible. And when everyone has authority, the need to obtain a consensus from all affected agencies inhibits initiative and protracts the time required to accomplish even the simplest objectives.

Three different agencies deal directly with housing policy. In addition, since any housing decision is affected by monetary, fiscal, and wage-price policies and itself affects environmental conditions, residential relocation, tax losses, minority relations, as well as labor problems, the building of a consensus in this area alone involves five departments (Treasury, HEW, HUD, Labor, and Agriculture) and four agencies (IRS, OEO, EPA, and VA). At last count more than 850 interagency committees existed for coordination of matters such as the above that affect more than one agency.

Shortly after he was appointed Secretary of the Department of Housing and Urban Development, George Romney created a stir by displaying a 30-inch-high, 56-pound stack of paper that represented a single urban renewal application. A principal reason for the red tape, he decided, was the fragmentation of program administration in HUD. For example, one assistant secretary administered the public housing program while another administered the other subsidized housing programs, though the clientele overlapped. Each group had its own staff of architects, engineers, inspectors, and other specialists, as well as its own set of regulations and specifications.

Pressures of Time

The dictum "haste makes waste" must be completely set aside in assessing the role of the government executive. Whereas the executive in the private sector acts on a continuum encompassing years of growth and development within an organization or related organizations, changes in the executive branch and the higher turnover of personnel in government generally require greater effort to learn rapidly, take hold quickly, and exert forceful leadership. Still, an executive moving from the private sector to the government needs at least two years, and preferably more, to make a meaningful contribution. Except in unusual cases, a shorter tenure does not give the executive enough time to know the intricacies of his programs and to make beneficial contributions to them or through them. In spite of this, however, the average cabinet or subcabinet appointee remains in office just twenty-two months.

The corporate executive is accustomed to fast and purposeful action once a problem has been isolated and the solution agreed to. But the government executive must accept the fact that after he has done his homework and planning and gained the necessary support in Congress and in the nation, he still faces the long lead time needed for project completion.

Detailing of a budget justification, obtaining legislative authorization, and securing an appropriation can be a frustratingly lengthy operation. For example, almost ten years will have elapsed between the discovery of oil on the North Slope of Alaska and the arrival of the first drop of oil in the United States. In the Department of the Army, full implementation of a new directive at the level of troops in the field usually takes from two to five years. In the Bureau of Reclamation, ten years may pass betwen conception of a project and the start of construction. Completion of it can take another fifty years.

Management Competence

While lack of accountability and the pressures of time are frustrating impediments to the government executive, they are impediments to which he can become acclimatized and which he can override to some extent by sheer hard work. One problem that he will find almost entirely beyond his control, however, is the lack of management expertise among many career officials in top-level positions and the disinclination of some of them to accept new leadership willingly. This problem is partly the result of an institutional inability to set precise goals. More important, however, is the predominant tendency to select the heads of major divisions or bureaus on the basis of technical expertise rather than managerial ability. A study made a few years ago by the Committee for Economic Development showed that almost 70 percent of those in supergrade positions (GS-16 and above) in the federal government had spent their entire careers—an average of more than twenty years—in no more than two bureaus. This career pattern neither encourages nor nurtures the development of competent managers with broad-based skills.

Lack of managerial competence among top officials is often compounded by a lack of commitment and divided loyalty. In business, penalties and rewards are meted out by an employee's superior, and the employee's major means of advancement is within the company. In government it is quite different for both the senior career official and the political appointee. The career official looks to Congress and outside interest groups for funding of programs, recognition, and postgovernment employment. Therefore, the tendency is to direct loyalties to these outside entities rather than to give total support to the administration. Some political appointees, concerned with outside job prospects, also seek their rewards outside the structure by emphasizing relationships with key industrial figures or by focusing on image-building public relations. They in effect "go into business for themselves," often at the expense of substantive accomplishments and the chief executive's program.

In recent years this divided loyalty at the career level has been vividly illustrated by young employees in social action programs and agencies who have shown no reticence about going to the media with stories of their heroic struggles against what they conceive to be an unsympathetic or unresponsive establishment. While this can serve a useful purpose, it sometimes serves only to undermine effectiveness.

After Vietnam, the single greatest problem facing the Nixon administration was to repair the economic damage done in the late sixties when the Johnson administration insisted the country could enjoy both guns and butter at the same time. Dampening the destructive fires of the Great Society became almost as difficult as quenching the flames of Vietnam. One of the agencies targeted for extinction was the Office of Economic Opportunity (OEO). To enhance coordination of related programs, those functions of the OEO worth preserving were parceled out to the cabinet departments that would normally have been responsible for them. Most of the remains were left to be closed down by OEO Director Howard Phillips.

The effort to dismantle OEO generated anguish in a number of quarters. OEO staffers remaining from the Great Society days quickly began sending distress signals to the liberal establishment, with predictable results. There were court suits, vituperative editorials, threats of every imaginable kind, congressional inquiries, demonstrations—all of which served to obscure the central issue, which was whether the Office of Economic Opportunity provided economic opportunities sufficient to justify its cost. Phillips himself contributed to the problem on several levels. He was an ideologue, not a manager, and he went about tearing apart his agency with unconcealed glee. Of course, defiling one of the frayed edges of a liberal dream drove former staffers to new heights of inventiveness in trying to save the agency. Yet even without the heavy-handedness of a combative administrator like Phillips, the easy availability of a sensation-seeking press combined with a group of employees loyal to their own peculiar views of the objects of government insured that OEO would not die the quiet death ordained by managerial logic and fiscal common sense. The OEO experience provides yet another example of a deep-rooted institutional problem—divided loyalties—that militates against effective management.

Avoiding Mistakes

Private business has always been well served by a set of well-defined, internalized sanctions. The discipline of the balance sheet provides its own sanctions for mistakes in business judgment, and mistakes of sufficient magnitude can

be accompanied by such sanctions as termination of employment. Few executives have ever progressed very far in business without the opportunity to make mistakes and learn
from them. This opportunity is largely nonexistent in government.

The "business" of government has few sanctions, and the
few that do exist are vague in description, uncertain in application, and indeterminate in impact. Where a mistake in
judgment in the business world is commonly assessed against
an individual's professional capacities, a mistake in judgment in government may be construed as a lack of ability
or may be attributed to personal ambition, political motives,
vindictiveness, or a host of other causes, depending on who
is conveying the information. So long as the mistake remains
known only within the government, however, it rarely leads
to corrective action.

Thus, the press does have an important watchdog role to
perform. The trouble is that the press too often gets only
part of the story. The ever-present threat of having one's
executive actions misunderstood, misconstrued, and mis-
represented by the press has a deleterious effect on the management of government. It commonly results in one of two
courses of action. The manager in government may fall back
on the principle that he can't be blamed for what he does if
he does nothing. In this situation, epidemic in the federal
bureaucracy, we find no inclination at all to be innovative,
to take risks, and to make real decisions. The other alternative is hypersecretiveness, overclassifying every memorandum or other communication, overreacting to the media's
natural and legitimate right to learn what government is
doing, and adopting an us-and-them attitude toward the
everyday relationships with the press.

The process of accommodating to the shifts in public sen-
timent is the underlying political reason for government's
inability to establish and adhere to long-range goals. The
"party of big spending" (in office) is countered by the "party

of fiscal responsibility" (out of office). In the next round, the "party of the tight wallet and the closed heart," is countered by the "party of the people," and so forth. Programs are expanded, stunted, or distorted for political expediency. The end result is that government concerns itself with how programs are perceived to work and not how they do work. The problem is further compounded by the need to create a perception that has the broadest possible appeal, and in practice this means that goals and objectives are stated so that the average person can read in the statement of objective whatever most appeals to him. From the executive's standpoint, this produces a rubber yardstick, elastic guidelines, and, ultimately, managerial mush.

To cite a few examples of elastic goals, the Demonstration Cities and Metropolitan Development Act of 1966 calls on HUD "to improve the quality of urban life" through a combination of public and private efforts. The law that created the Inter-American Social Development Institute in 1969 stated as its purpose

> to provide support for developmental activities designed to achieve conditions in the Western Hemisphere under which the dignity and the worth of each person will be respected and under which all men will be afforded the opportunity to develop their potential, to seek through gainful and productive work the fullfillment of their aspirations for a better life, and to live in justice and peace.

Such verbiage is altogether typical, and its most important consequence is to raise expectations far above the level of potential achievement. Bitter frustrations inevitably follow.

WHAT IT TAKES

Just as the problems of managing government radically differ from those of managing in the private sector, so the qualities a government executive must bring to his work differ from those preferred by the private sector. Indeed, the government executive must cultivate some qualities that are virtually opposed to those often found to succeed in the private sector. In an atmosphere where self-confidence may be construed as arrogance, single-mindedness as ruthlessness, persistence as pushiness, candor as naiveté, and a reluctance to suffer fools as plain bad manners, the government executive must adopt behavior patterns that will set him apart from his fellows in the world of private enterprise. Certainly, he must be a good manager, because all the traditional management tools are required in government. But beyond these, he needs certain personal characteristics and resources to meet the complex demands of the more highly convoluted framework of government and the more public-oriented and politically determined atmosphere of government service.

Ability To Communicate

George Romney, with distinguished careers in both business and government, once observed to me that "success in government depends upon the attitude of the people you deal with—the bureaucracy, the Congress, the media, the public. To shape this attitude there is a much greater need for the ability to communicate than exists in any business I can think of, including advertising."

Former Commerce Secretary Peterson put it even more strongly: "In business, a man's ability to communicate, while important, is hardly the dominant consideration. If confronted with the choice between someone with a great track record or great ability to articulate, the businessman would take the track record. But in government, the choice might be different."

An excellent example of the force that the power to communicate can produce, especially when linked with the power to operate, is the record of John Connally. Connally swirled into the Department of Treasury on the heels of the taciturn David Kennedy and turned it into a major power center not merely within Washington, but internationally as well. Connally's success was due in large measure to his ability to communicate and to the force of his charismatic personality. The terrific impact of the news media on the operation of government has turned "charisma" into a household word. At the highest levels it has probably become a sine qua non for notable service. Inspirational leadership is in fact a form of communication that can earn essential congressional or public support for departmental programs and initiatives. It serves as a catalyst. mobilizing the force of a vast and unwielding bureaucracy and moving it toward the administration's goals.

Sensitivity and Empathy

A high degree of awareness is essential to sense and understand the real—often different from the apparent—motives, desires, and reactions of the public, the media, the Congress, the bureaucracy, and the special-interest groups with which the government executive must deal. Most people who have worked in conventional surroundings for a few years come into government lacking the required political instinct, savvy, or intuition. However, anyone who possesses sensitivity and empathy for human situations can develop this astuteness quite naturally, once exposed to the demands of the government. Increasingly, he will be able to judge in advance how people react to various actions and will incorporate this factor into his planning and decision making. The executive who lacks sensitivity may be a competent manager, but he will never gain the support needed to function effectively in government. And he can easily be carved up in the politically charged atmosphere of Washington.

Mental Toughness

Even the most charismatic, articulate, and hard-charging business executive in government must steel himself to meet and cope with the sheer inertia of government. Dealing with the vagaries of the Congress, the slow movement of the bureaucracy, and the erratic turns of public concern, he must have the persistence and resilience to bounce back and pursue a target despite repeated diversions. This requires a determination to reach the goal by a variety of means and a grasp of how much one must accommodate to circumstances.

The Nixon administration's efforts in the early seventies to translate "black capitalism" into a workable and productive program provide a good example. Recognizing that he could not win immediate approval for a full program, the Secretary of Commerce settled for a small budget that included only salaries and expenses. Then he directed Office of Minority Business Enterprise personnel to concentrate on cajoling other departments and agencies into using their program funds to support minority businesses. After a year of operating in this manner, the Secretary felt that he had sufficient grounds to request that OMBE be allowed to control its own program funds and thus provide grants directly to minority businesses. His initial proposals were rejected, but the Secretary persisted. He finally received the funding in late 1971—two and a half years after receiving the responsibility.

Flexibility and Humility

These are difficult qualities to obtain for some businessmen whose success, public esteem, and even self-esteem are based on their ability to drive hard toward the solution they have decided is right and to resist compromise along the way. But in government a rigid approach to problems only courts failure and leads to frustration. Here, the executive must be willing to adopt or modify programs or shift direction to meet the changing needs of other agencies, the public, Congress, or different interest groups. He must realize that some progress is better than none and that he must at times move obliquely rather than straight ahead.

Above all, he must be willing to compromise. He must understand that few of his ideas will survive to completion in their original form, and that plans are seldom implemented without major adjustments somewhere along the line. He must realize from the outset that the process of compromise and trade-off is as integral a part of the administrative process as it is of the legislative process.

Managerial Ability Plus

Too few businessmen succeed or reach their fullest potential in government service. Some never perceive the importance of external forces—the Congress, the public, the media —and thus commit the error they would never commit in business: they misunderstand their market and do not orient their actions and organization to meet the market's needs.

As former Secretary of Labor James Hodgson, himself a former businessman, once put it:

The most general of the reasons for the failure of successful businessmen in government is lack of breadth—an inability to conceptualize rather than merely achieve, an inability to understand and be effective in the relations element of a governmental role, and an inability to deal with problems indirectly rather than through authoritarian line control.

The corporate executive turned government executive must be able to sense and accommodate to the peculiar nuances of government and avoid the pitfalls of pride I have discussed. He must be endowed with sensitivity and empathy to human motives and problems and have a flexibility of mind, a high tolerance for frustration and even abuse, and a good deal of humility. A sense of humor is no detriment either.

A major challenge to any President or administration is to find and attract men and women who possess these extra dimensions, a topic we turn to in the following chapters. The degree to which they succeed will have a powerful influence on the effectiveness of government, and, consequently, on the quality of life in the United States.

Chapter Four

Attracting the Finest

Finding and selecting exactly the right person for a top position in government can be a painstaking and laborious process. Even when it is done with great professionalism, it can have unforeseen consequences, as I learned in the early seventies.

The 1970 congressional elections resulted in significant gains for the Democratic party. At the White House, this was seen as a bad omen for the 1972 presidential elections and caused great concern. Lacking broad personal appeal among the voters and remembering his narrow win in 1968, the President needed to broaden his constituency in order to be reelected in 1972.

White House political strategists perceived a fundamental shift taking place in the attitudes of millions of American voters, away from the liberal beliefs of the leading Democratic contenders and more toward the moderate to conservative values that Richard Nixon espoused. By highlighting the right social issues and social groups, it was thought, this "new majority" could be lured away from the Democrats into the Republican column in 1972. Therefore, labor, Southerners, veterans, and Americans of Irish, Italian, Eastern European, and Mexican descent were targeted for attention. The wisdom and success of this strategy was a major reason for Mr. Nixon's substantial reelection margin.

One important element in this strategy was to place more

minorities and women within the administration. Raised in Southern California, the President felt warmly toward Mexican-Americans and recognized their circumstances as a long-neglected minority. In early 1971 the President directed me to undertake a concerted drive to bring Mexican-Americans into high positions in his administration.

When the Treasurer of the United States died in the spring of 1971, the President asked me to find a Mexican-American woman as a replacement. So there could be no public doubt about what and who she was, she had to have a Mexican surname and be a Catholic. She was also to be poised, attractive, articulate, a Californian, and involved in the Mexican-American community. She was to have a record for accomplishment that qualified her for a high post. And I was to recruit her within thirty days.

One of our top recruiters immediately began a comprehensive search, outlining the job specifications to dozens of leaders in the Mexican-American community and a range of financial and civic leaders across the country. Two weeks later, after a series of reference checks and interviews to narrow the selection, our recruiter introduced me to Mrs. Ramona Banuelos of Los Angeles. She was president of a $5 million food company, a bank director, a civic leader, Catholic, an attractive wife and mother, and a Mexican-American. After Mrs. Banuelos agreed to accept the position, the normal FBI security investigation was completed, the appointment was cleared with all relevant offices, and the President announced the appointment.

Then in succeeding weeks, before Senate confirmation, the Immigration and Naturalization Service (INS) raided a food plant operated by Mrs. Banuelos in Los Angeles and discovered that the plant employed a number of Mexicans who had not entered the United States legally. The incident with its attendant publicity was a distinct embarrassment to the White House. Nevertheless, recognizing that the employment of illegal aliens was quite common and that there was no way an employer could detect their illegal entry, the Senate quickly confirmed Mrs. Banuelos.

The Banuelos case underscores several points. Her recruitment is a good example of how qualified people with a very tight set of specifications can be located and attracted to government through a systematic, professional, and thorough nationwide search process, using professional recruiters and established sources. Clearly, what the President demanded was tantamount to the proverbial "finding a needle in a haystack," and could not have been accomplished without a highly competent recruiting organization. Beyond that, the INS episode illustrates the difficulties in avoiding unpleasant surprises no matter how careful the preappointment screening may be. Finally, her appointment is an excellent example of how pragmatic politics determines key appointments.

Of the nearly three million civilian employees of the federal government, the President or his designees have the authority to appoint some 2600 to full-time posts. The President himself has the power to appoint some 650 of these (e.g., cabinet, assistant secretaries), and the remainder are appointed by the cabinet and other agency heads. Besides the White House staff, these 2600 appointees include the top fifteen to twenty officials for each of the eleven cabinet departments (e.g., State, Justice, Labor, Agriculture) and each of ten major agencies (e.g., Veterans Administration, Federal Energy Administration, Environmental Protection Administration), heads of lesser agencies, and members of regulatory agencies. These are the so-called policy officials who participate with the President in development of policy for his administration, and who have the major responsibility for running the government.

While public attention during an election year tends to focus only on the two major presidential candidates, the selection of top people surrounding a chief executive can be just as important as the President himself. In today's government, the cabinet and White House staff exert powerful influence on the direction of an administration, and most decisions that are credited to a President are actually made at the staff level with only pro forma approval from the President. The people around the chief executive are the ones who actually run the agencies, sift through the issues, identify the problems, and present analyses and recommendations for the chief's decision. It is they who give shape to the administration's governing strategy and transform vague party platforms to hard policies and legislative proposals. This does not mean that the President is only an automation, but one should never underestimate the power of those around him.

Consequently, the key to establishing some measure of managerial control over the executive branch and having any hope of making government work better is to select the right people for the many positions. Despite its obvious importance, however, the personnel selection process in government is usually conducted in a haphazard fashion and the results are generally mediocre.

In the last chapter, the qualities required for effective government leadership were identified. But this is only the first and perhaps the easiest part of building a strong team. This chapter focuses on how to locate and attract men and women of exceptional abilities to government service. The best people, of course, are often the most difficult to recruit and once located are not easy to attract or retain.

PITFALLS AND FAILURES OF GOVERNMENT RECRUITING

Unfortunately, the most traditional means of recruiting in American politics is the colleague approach, which some have labeled the BUGAT (bunch of guys around the table) system. It amounts to trusted advisers compiling long lists of people whom they personally know who may or may not have the necessary credentials to serve effectively. This is the premise of the political axiom that holds that "you don't get the best people, you get the people you know."

The strong point of this approach is the speed with which appointees can be selected. The weak point is that it automatically excludes 99 percent of potential candidates, and narrowing the size of the universe in this manner severely limits the chances of finding the very best people. Moreover, the people selected are often veterans of the campaign and may have qualities more suited to campaigning than to governing. As Stephen Hess has pointed out, "Choosing presidential assistants from the campaign organization has a certain superficial logic. . . . Once in the White House, however, these aides became drawn into governance . . . . The free-wheeling mind-set useful on the campaign trail can be dangerous when transplanted to the seat of power." [1]

President Kennedy, backed by his "Irish Mafia," used the old-boy network or BUGAT system to a high degree. Not long after President Johnson took office, there was a marked entrance of Texans (Jack Valenti, Bill Moyers, Postmaster General Marvin Watson, to name a few). President Johnson, however, recognized the limitations of such an approach, and he eventually directed the Chairman of the Civil Service, John Macy, to develop a recruiting team that could find the best people in the country.

In selecting his top staff and cabinet members, President Nixon in his first year relied heavily on people already known to him. Following traditions of the past, most of Mr. Nixon's cabinet then recruited key subcabinet officials from those they knew in their home states. Secretary Romney brought a large cadre of top officials from Michigan to the Department of Housing and Urban Development, Secretary Volpe stocked the Transportation Department with people from

Massachusetts, Secretary Finch relied heavily on Californians, and so on.

President Ford appointed several long-time associates from Grand Rapids to top posts and also recruited a large number of his former colleagues from the Congress and the congressional staffs. In the Carter administration, eight out of nine top White House staff appointments have been native Georgians with long associations with the President. Cabinet officers and agency heads have in turn tended to hire their friends or the friends of their friends. In an analysis of Carter recruiting methods, a *Wall Street Journal* article commented, "Without solid connections on the inside, it's almost impossible to get a job in Jimmy Carter's Washington."[2]

Another approach to recruiting that has been tried from time to time by state and local governments, and which was unsuccessfully attempted during the early days of the Nixon administration, is the "shotgun" approach. The centerpiece of this approach is to seek recommendations and applications from the broadest possible range of people. One of the first acts of Nixon's personnel assistant in 1969 was to send a letter to every person listed in *Who's Who in America*, asking for names of prospective appointees. The process was a notable failure, resulting in a flood of résumés and recommendations, a lot of injured feelings, and very few people who had the qualifications required. Eventually it was dismissed as a publicity gimmick. President Carter used a variation on this approach with similar results. After Mr. Carter described his Talent Inventory Program (TIP) on national television, the White House was flooded with some 34,000 applications. Most of these were quickly packed away in crates and filing cabinets, and few of the applicants were given serious consideration.[3] The shotgun system for the most part does not attract the best applicants but rather those who are dissatisfied with their jobs or for other reasons are seeking something new and different. Generally, the most competent people are so involved in their professional responsibilities that they are not considering anything else. They are not likely to respond to a blanket invitation and must be sought out on a selective basis.

Regardless of the method used, one can be sure that each new administration must start from scratch to develop its own recruiting methods, contacts, control files, candidate sources, candidate information, and the like. There simply is no institutional mechanism for recruiting political appointees at any level of government.

For a newly elected chief executive the problem is compounded by the fact that there is such a short time in which to act, and there are so many other "crises" to solve during the crucial early days of a new administration. In theory, a newly elected President has ten weeks before inauguration to make his key personnel decisions. In practice, however, the President-elect is under intense pressure to move more quickly so that new appointees have time to wind up their private-sector responsibilities and prepare for their new posts. President Eisenhower, for example, selected his cabinet by December 1, President Kennedy by December 17, and President Nixon by December 11. As Harold Laski has noted:

> A President elect has to choose, not merely his Cabinet colleagues, but a vast horde of minor officials in an atmosphere that is not seldom akin to pandemonium. . . . Every action of his, every thought almost, is surrounded by a fierce light of publicity which makes the calm appropriate to thought almost impossible.[4]

In this kind of atmosphere it is not particularly surprising that most politicians and even agency heads resort to the BUGAT or shotgun approach for most positions rather than taking the time to establish a more systematic, comprehensive approach. Once settled into office, most administrations develop a more organized method for personnel recruitment, but in the initial stages a great deal of the taxpayer's money is spent needlessly in reinventing the wheel, and even more is wasted as unqualified people take office.

Beyond the problems of hasty and ineffective approaches, political considerations exercise a constant and generally troublesome influence on appointments. The need to achieve true managerial coordination and effectiveness is of secondary importance or ignored altogether in the selection process. The predominant tradition is for a new chief executive to name a balanced team, choosing men and women who represent the geographic regions, political persuasions, and ethnic backgrounds that the chief feels are necessary to strengthen his political base and heal political wounds. The appointments normally contribute to the feelings of a honeymoon, but lasting political harmony is seldom achieved. As in any marriage, hostile feelings can spring up if a President and members of his cabinet discover afterward—and not beforehand—that their personalities or philosophies are incompatible. This can easily lead to a costly dismissal or resignation, as occurred when Republican conservatives could no longer live with the Secretary of Labor whom President Eisenhower had selected to appease the labor movement.

The cabinet appointments of the Ford administration look almost as if they followed a textbook sequence in terms of political balance, and it is a credit to President Ford that he was able to combine this balance for the most part with people of ability. President Ford first appointed a Southerner, David Mathews, as Secretary of Health, Education, and Welfare; then a black, William Coleman, as Secretary of Transportation; followed by a Jew, Edward Levi, as Attorney General; and then a woman, Carla Hills, as Secretary of Housing and Urban Development. Each of these people was highly competent in his or her own right. There can be no denying, however, that in each case the President's recruiters had one eye cocked on the constituency that each candidate represented.

Unfortunately, there is no constituency or special-interest group that lobbies for better managerial talent in the government, and, as a result, this aspect of a candidate's background is often overlooked. No major corporation anywhere in the world would ever dream of placing someone in charge of five thousand employees despite a total lack of managerial ability, but in government we do it all the time. The public has little recourse against such practices, and members of Congress, who are often pushing favorite candidates for political reasons of their own, are only too eager to share in the spoils. During my tenure as the President's principal assistant for personnel, an average of five hundred letters per month were received from members of Congress urging the appointment of one or another of their favorites. Few of them were qualified, but due to political necessities more than a few were appointed. This practice of rewarding the party loyalists and ensuring at least token representation from various political factions and geographic areas is so well established that no one else, the media included, really gives serious question to the practice.

Some political figures are ideally suited for cabinet or sub-cabinet-level responsibility, but the net effect of such traditions is that most administrations are typically a mixture of the competent, the semiqualified, and the politically faithful. As might be expected, the end result is performance that is far from the optimum. But the political leaders are satisfied, the party leadership is happy, the Congress is mollified, and the party workers are ecstatic. Only the taxpayer loses.

A final contributing factor to the weaknesses of government personnel practices is the short tenure of political appointees. Most are not in their jobs long enough to learn them well, and many leave before they can really accomplish anything. The average tenure of presidential appointees in the federal government is twenty-two months. Over a recent eight-year period, the Securities and Exchange Commission and the Federal Trade Commission had six new chairmen each. Too many people come to government only to develop a credential or to become publicly known and then flee back to the private sector, their newly acquired pedigree highlighted in their résumés. According to an unpublished survey by government consultant Thomas Cody, 70 percent of appointed executives attributed high turnover to the tendency of appointees to use government positions for career enhancement. No modern business could work effectively with this kind of turnstile management, and neither can the federal government.

STAFFING A NATIONAL ADMINISTRATION

My experiences in developing a recruiting system for President Nixon and assisting in the recruitment and selection of people for cabinet and subcabinet positions serve to illustrate the problems that can develop as well as some of the measures that can be taken to improve the quality of the personnel selection process.

The Purpose

In late 1970, President Nixon realized that he lacked the means to identify and recruit top talent on a continuing basis for his administration. There were simply no effective recruiting mechanisms for filling top positions at the White House and in the agencies. Most top government executives had to conduct their own recruiting. Lacking the time and expertise, their efforts were haphazard and mediocre, especially in comparison to the more advanced methods of private industry.

As the newly appointed principal assistant to the President for personnel, my highest priority was to develop a new personnel system that would be able to identify and recruit the best available talent to key positions. I decided that the heart of the personnel organization should be four professional recruiters who could focus their energies on recruiting only for high-level presidential appointees, as opposed to other positions in the White House and departments. Most of these recruiters were obtained by canvassing the best executives search firms in the country, identifying their top performers, and appealing to the individuals and their firms to join the team on either a permanent or a short-term basis. Our White House recruiting team, for example, included at one time or another, Frank Rocco from Arthur Young & Co., Pendleton James from Heidrick & Struggles, Robert Martin and John Clarke from Booz Allen & Hamilton, Richard Ferry of Korn-Ferry International, William Marumoto, from Peat, Marwick, and Mitchell, William Zook from Boyden Associates, and Barbara Franklin from First National City Bank of New York.

While the recruiting staff was centrally run from the White House, the largest number of presidential appointments were not to White House slots but to posts in the subcabinet. Naturally, each cabinet officer or other agency head had to be deeply involved in the process and had to retain the right of final selection because he or she was held directly accountable to the President for the performance of his or her organization and had to deal with the new appointees on a day-to-day basis. Consequently, our White House recruiting staff treated the agency heads as clients, consulting at every step and providing service, much as a successful corporate staff might work with the line divisions of the company. In addition, we encouraged each agency to develop a professional recruiting capacity to handle the many positions below the assistant secretary level.

The Approach

The approach we developed was similar to that used in industry and consisted of the following five steps:

1. The first and generally the most important step is to carefully determine the criteria for the position in question and from that a precise profile of the type of person required. No search can be successful unless you know exactly what to look for, and this is generally not very obvious on the surface. For example, in filling the positions of Assistant Secretary for Education and Commissioner of Education in HEW, we might suppose that two distinguished educators were needed. In fact, the two jobs require distinctly different talents. The Commissioner must manage an agency of over three thousand people, work in close concert with state and local school districts, and wisely disperse billions of dollars of grant funds in an even-handed fashion. Above all else, therefore, the Commissioner must be a talented manager. The Assistant Secretary, on the other hand, has more of a coordinative function, has a staff of less than one hundred, and is primarily concerned with developing and analyzing policy matters. Thus, the primary requirements for this post are analytic ability and substantive depth on the issues rather than managerial talent.

Another important but easily overlooked consideration was the specific accomplishment expected of the appointee. That task can change from time to time for the same job, as noted by the current HEW Secretary Joseph Califano. In 1964, Califano said, "When the bulk of . . . controversial and far-reaching health and education proposals was working its way through Congress" the primary need as HEW head was a person "who knew how to lobby . . . ." After legislation was enacted, the requirements changed to a Secretary "who could add a special prestige to service in the department and who could attract . . . brilliant and imaginative talent." [5]

2. Having established the composite profile of qualifications for a job, the next task was to sound out a network of established and newly developed sources of talent. The development and cultivation of these sources was more im-

portant and pursued more aggressively than the search for candidates themselves. If the right sources were persuaded to cooperate, they would lead to the right candidates and help apply their expertise to the evaluation of other candidates. These sources included leaders in the professional field in question, community and civic leaders across the country, business leaders, and certain interest groups. From them emerged the names of a majority of candidates who were actually chosen for jobs. Only a bare handful of really qualified candidates were found among the raft of unsolicited applications.

3. Our talent search usually generated more than fifty candidates for every open position. The next step was to screen and evaluate the candidates by comparing their experiences with the criteria established, sounding out still more sources, and by evaluating the success and progress of a candidate compared to others in his career field and age group. In regard to this latter factor, we customarily used a rough ratio of age to achievement to compare accomplishments and abilities of various prospects. When recruiting an Assistant Secretary of Labor for Administration, for example, it was obvious that the final selection, Frank Zarb, had unusual talents and was well ahead of most of his peers, having advanced to the executive vice presidency of a major investment banking firm by age thirty-five.[6] This screening process would narrow the field to ten to fifteen candidates.

4. Our semifinalists were then sounded out for willingness to serve, and those who were willing were subjected to a careful reference process and personal interviews with the White House recruiter assigned to work with the agency in question. This process normally narrowed the field to four or five. At that point. it was imperative to capture the candidate's interest by selling the challenges of the post in question, the broad responsibilities, the opportunity to grow, the President's possible need of his services, and the like.

5. The final candidates were then subjected to intensive

interviews at the White House and with the appropriate cabinet officer and his staff. Further reference checks, FBI security clearances, and conflict-of-interest checks were all conducted concurrently with the interview process. Consultations with appropriate members of Congress and state political leaders would also take place at this time—though the latter was intended only to avoid any local political embarrassments, not to give the local party leaders ultimate vetoes over the decision. After all of these steps had been completed, the names of three candidates would be submitted to the President with one name bearing the recommendation of the cabinet officer as well as myself. Generally, any differences between a cabinet officer and White House staff would be worked out before submittal to the President. In keeping with the cabinet officer's responsibility for his agency, it was our practice to support his preferred candidate among the three finalists so long as that candidate met the minimum requirements.

Applying the Process

In 1971, President Nixon was determined to mount a major fight against cancer. The focal point of this effort was to be a vastly enlarged National Cancer Institute within HEW. To assist the institute, the President also wanted to create a "Cancer Panel," comprised of three eminent part-time advisers with the authority to bypass the chain of command and appeal directly to the President on key issues. The President directed that an exhaustive search in and out of government would be conducted to find the best candidate in the country for the panel and for the position of Director of the Cancer Institute. The starting point for defining the requirements of the positions was a "Report by the Senate Panel of Consultants on the Conquest of Cancer." Our views were refined by consulting with eight organizations, including the American Cancer Society, the American Medical Association, the National Academy of Sciences, and the Federation of American Societies for Experimental Biology. Final touches were put on our job definitions in discussions with the White House Office of Science and Technology, staff members of the Domestic Council, and key HEW officials. During this process, it was determined that the people sought both for the Director's post and for membership in the panel needed a knowledge of medicine, but as opposed to expertise in cancer research per se, they should have great managerial talents, preferably with a strong background in managing complex research-oriented organizations. The ideal candidate was probably an M.D. who was president of a technically oriented company or the director of a large research institute in the public or private sector.

The same sources who had been consulted on the job specifications were then asked for recommendations, and 160 names were submitted. A large number of other sources in research and industry were also contacted, and they provided another thirty candidates. The list was narrowed by removing all scientists who had had no opportunity to display managerial skills, and these names were held for possible research jobs in the new cancer agency. Others were eliminated for lack of other requirements. Eighty candidates survived this process.

A review panel was then established, consisting of key members of the associations mentioned above as well as selected administration officials. The panel was asked to evaluate and rank the eighty remaining candidates according to how well they met the criteria for the jobs. From this evaluation, twenty people were selected as the leading candidates and submitted to further intensive evaluation by the review panel and careful reference checks. This resulted in the selection of six outstanding finalists, all of whom had the desired background and qualities. A selection panel comprised of five top officials at the White House and HEW interviewed the finalists, and their recommendations were forwarded to the President for selection. From these names, the President selected a distinguished Cancer Panel, and for the Director's post a highly talented medical researcher with considerable research management experience, Dr. Frank Rauscher, who served with distinction for the next five years. Not only was a fine team assembled, but they proceeded with the full confidence and support of the medical and scientific communities.

Developing a New Team

The recruiting process moved into highest gear in preparation for the President's second term. Toward the end of his first term, President Nixon concluded that improved performance was essential should he be reelected. Some officials wished to leave government, while some simply did not measure up to expected levels of performance and were not equipped to cope with the problems of directing huge organizations.

In order to ensure that we had combed the country to find the best possible people for the second term, we began our talent search in April of 1972, seven months before the election. Our goal was to find two hundred to three hundred highly qualified individuals by election day with the substantive skills and the motivation to serve in the administration. Our top recruiter was assigned full-time to this project from April through November. Because in many instances we were not certain who would be leaving or replaced and in other cases did not want to embarrass incumbents, we did not search for candidates to fill specific positions. Rather, we tried to identify people who met the general criteria of excellence in fields such as business, law, health care, education, science, and state and local government.

To ensure the effectiveness of the program, we expanded

our network of sources to over two hundred geographically dispersed people, covering a wide range of professions. These sources in most cases were leaders in their fields and were sufficiently knowledgeable and well connected to provide high-caliber candidate recommendations. During the time that John Mitchell was campaign director, he insisted that contact also be made with the state chairmen of the presidential campaign to discuss recruiting plans in their states and to obtain their recommendations. In this case, the political contacts did not result in much modification since these people were for the most part too involved in the campaign to contribute much, and we, in fact, did not pursue them seriously.

All sources combined contributed résumés of well over two thousand recommended candidates. These résumés were screened and evaluated, and from them some five hundred people were selected for personal contact and evaluation. Many others were eliminated because they simply did not have a sufficient record of success for their years of effort. Through this screening process as well as further research and personal interviews with over four hundred candidates, we gradually pared the list to the roughly two hundred candidates we desired. Each of these prospects was interviewed by several people at the White House before completing the list. Appendix A contains a copy of the plan submitted to and approved by the President for this extensive recruiting project.

As November neared, most of the attention in the White House was focused on the reelection effort, but the recruiting project moved ahead at a rapid pace, as several reviews were held with the President to survey our progress and the available candidates. By early October the President knew which members of the cabinet were planning to depart, and he had decided on several others he would transfer to other posts.

By late October the President had already begun to zero

in on choices for key positions in the new administration. By October 27, a discussion paper had been drafted and sent to the President making initial recommendations on composition and compatibility of the new cabinet. Although a number of revisions were subsequently made in these recommendations, several useful points can be drawn from this paper. The most significant is the way that we found it necessary to look beyond pure competence to other considerations in making up a new cabinet. For example, John Connally was emerging in the President's mind as the best choice to succeed him in the Oval Office in 1976. This fact, along with Connally's superior abilities, suggested that he would be a natural choice for Secretary of State because he could serve there with distinction and could remain in the public eye. However, it was obvious that two strong personalities such as Connally and Henry Kissinger could not coexist in such close proximity, and the appointment of Connally would be tantamount to forcing Dr. Kissinger's resignation as the President's Assistant for National Security. In the final analysis, Mr. Nixon decided against creating this inevitable conflict and eventually decided to end the competition between the State Department and Dr. Kissinger's National Security Council staff by naming Dr. Kissinger Secretary of State.

The process also demonstrated the wide difference in presidential involvement in the selection of appointees for key posts. In the case of the State and Defense Departments, the President was deeply involved in developing criteria and evaluating candidates, and he made the ultimate selections himself in a highly personal way. In the case of the Commerce and Transportation Departments, on the other hand, he engaged in the most limited scrutiny, reflecting the level of presidential interest. The President in fact had not heard of the final selections for these posts until we recommended them to him, and he had never met them until they traveled to Camp David where he personally offered them their jobs.

It was significant in the search process that a number of people already in the administration were favored for appointment to the cabinet. Someone who has proven himself in the Washington environment and has demonstrated the leadership qualities described in Chapter 3 is a better bet for the top job than an untested newcomer, regardless of his past credentials.

Further papers were drafted and tentative decisions were also made about the end of October on subcabinet appointments. Thus, by the time of the election, significant progress had been made toward staffing the cabinet and developing a small but strong talent bank from which to select the subcabinet. We had been scientific and thorough, had canvassed the entire country, and had uncovered and gained tentative commitments from a group of exceptionally talented people.

After such painstaking effort, it was a shock to all of us when the election itself caused the President to order a complete change in direction. Apparently he had never been certain that he would win by a landslide; but when he did, he decided that there really was a "new majority" forming in the United States. Further, he became determined that his administration would be representative of this new coalition. Therefore, he quickly directed us to find new candidates for the cabinet and subcabinet who would be more representative of the various voting groups who had voted heavily for him. This meant a renewed emphasis on appointing people of various ethnic backgrounds as discussed earlier. It was also deemed essential to recruit more older Americans, veterans, and people representing the young voters. We were to ensure more appointments from what were considered under-represented geographic areas such as the South.

There was far too little time to locate top-quality candidates with "new majority" backgrounds, and this development threw the entire recruiting process out of kilter and resulted in tremendous delays in appointing people to key positions. In some cases it also resulted in tremendous compromises in the suitability of people appointed. For example, the President was determined to have representatives from the labor movement in his new administration. As a result, he selected a number of union officials, some of whom lacked the substantive qualifications required for a number of the top positions in the Labor Department.

Similarly, the President demanded that we find at least one cabinet officer from the South. After much searching and several turndowns, he finally selected the head of a medium-size firm in South Carolina, Frederick Dent, as Secretary of Commerce. The same consideration was also important in the later appointment of a Georgia native, Howard "Bo" Calloway, as Secretary of the Army. Amusingly, one of the prime reasons Claude Brinegar (a highly capable man in his own right) was selected as Secretary of Transportation was faulty work by my staff, which incorrectly identified him as Irish Catholic rather than German Protestant.

The end result was mixed, hardly surprising in view of the political factors that came into play. While a number of outstanding people were recruited to the new team and a certain political balance was achieved, there were also a number of substandard appointments. The quality of some of the appointments, plus the delay in filling positions, resulted in a slower start in the second term and a less effective government than had been expected.

A decision made during this preelection period that proved to be a tremendous blunder was to require every appointee to tender his or her resignation immediately after election. There were a number of people who planned to leave anyhow after four years of Washington life. More importantly, there were many appointees who, in our view, simply had not performed well during the first term and whose replacement was in the public interest. At the staff level, we agreed that these forced changes should be made quickly and decisively so the President could absorb all the criticism at once, replacements could be rapidly appointed, and we could get on with the business of making government work better. To facilitate this, I recommended and the President agreed that all resignations be tendered automatically, just as in a change of administration from one party to the other. We would then quickly accept the resignations from those who genuinely wanted to depart as well as from those who we thought should depart. Those who were to remain in their posts would be quickly reappointed, showing how much confidence the President had in them.

Unfortunately, we had not thought through the consequences of this action as well as we should have. On the human side, men and women who had worked their hearts out for the President's reelection were thanked by a demeaning request-for-a-resignation letter. Also, there was no way of separating those who were leaving voluntarily from those being asked to resign, and the result was acute embarrassment for all departing officials. Due to the inordinate delays in selecting replacements, as discussed above, a number of people were kept in a state of uncertainty for as long as two to three months. The net result of the whole episode was to breed a good deal of justifiable resentment toward the White House from many of our appointees and to communicate a heartless portrait to the public.

SOLVING THE PERSONNEL PROBLEM

The major problems discussed in this chapter can be summarized as follows:

1. Most administrations resort to highly ineffective and subjective means of recruiting talent to the highest government posts, confining themselves to an unnecessarily small universe from which to select their team.

2. Every administration seems to start from scratch in devising a system for finding talent. Under pressure to appoint quickly, they succumb to expediency and substandard appointments.
3. Political considerations often govern selections, resulting in mediocre choices.
4. People who are selected do not serve long enough to master their jobs, let alone make a meaningful contribution.

These problems can be disabling and certainly mitigate strongly against serious attempts to make government work. While there are actions that can be initiated outside of government to solve these problems, the primary responsibility for overcoming them must reside with the chief executive and with the members of his cabinet.

Finding the Best People

Any local, state, or national chief executive has the opportunity to gain the attention of the most capable people in his city, state, or country. Moreover, there are a surprising number of good people who will serve in government if only asked. The problem is that few of these people are known by the chief executive and his staff, and few are approached in a convincing or compelling manner.

The answer to this problem is not, as was done in the early days of the Nixon administration, to issue a blanket invitation to serve to all who are interested. As already noted, the best people are generally too involved in what they are doing to answer such a call and, if not, still do not want to subject themselves to a mass process in which their talents may not be properly evaluated. Many people with a latent desire to serve will not submit to this type of process because they fear embarrassment if their interest is publicized or becomes known to present employers, or they fear rejection from inexperienced political aides who are unable to evaluate their qualifications. The kind of embarrassment that can result from inexperienced aides or a disorderly process was seen in the fall of 1976 when Arthur Schlesinger, Jr., a distinguished historian and veteran of the Kennedy years, wrote a letter to Jimmy Carter volunteering his services to Carter during the campaign. To his amazement and chagrin, Schlesinger received a form postcard from the Carter campaign turning him down. Even though the card must have come from a political innocent in the Carter camp, the incident reflected badly on the candidate when it hit the press, and it planted seeds of doubt in the minds of some of his supporters.

The solution for a chief executive is to broaden his universe and systematically locate and attract the most competent people that can be found. This can be accomplished only with a professional approach to executive recruiting. While there are variations of this approach that might be equally successful, the systematic approach illustrated earlier shows that it is possible to find and recruit hundreds of talented people to government. Our own talent search, conducted with professional "head hunters" resulted in the recruitment of over five hundred people to government, including half a dozen cabinet officers; the chairmen of the Atomic Energy Commission, the Securities and Exchange Commission, and the Federal Communications Commission; two heads of the Federal Energy Administration; three Federal Reserve Board governors; ten under secretaries; and countless assistant secretaries, assistant administrators, and the like. To be sure, mistakes were made along the way, but, all in all, such a thorough approach showed that it was possible to raise the quality of appointees. It might be noted that not one of the people recruited in this manner was ever indicted or otherwise drawn into the Watergate affair or resigned under anything less than favorable circumstances.

An important precondition for success is that recruiting

for top positions must begin from the office of the chief executive with the agencies themselves recruiting for lesser positions. The White House should not make all personnel selections, but the office of the chief executive (the White House, the State House, or City Hall) has the prestige needed to open doors and gain the attention of the top candidates. Thus, the chief executive should take the lead in coordinating the recruiting effort, with selections made with the review and approval of appropriate members of his cabinet and other agency heads. In short, any elected chief executive should assume leadership in developing an executive search organization and a professional approach to recruiting to attract the very best qualified people to his administration.

Harnessing the Political Forces

It is neither desirable nor probable that political considerations will ever be completely removed from the choice of top appointees. Most likely, political leaders will always base their selections more on political than on substantive qualifications. To the degree that such choices allow a chief executive to solidify his support and thereby govern more effectively, some of these political appointments arguably serve the public interest.

There are certain steps, however, that can and should be taken to limit the damage from unqualified appointments without giving up entirely the pursuit of political support and party unity. The most effective is to ensure that the qualified and appealing candidates are discovered and presented as alternatives for all important positions. It is much more difficult for a chief executive to justify a truly substandard appointment to himself or his team when the quality differential with the alternate is vividly apparent. A sound, professional approach to recruiting is most likely to result in such undeniable alternatives.

In many instances it is desirable to make a special effort to appoint women and minorities to top posts in order to encourage diverse points of view as well as to gain political support. The professional executive search approach can accomplish this while enhancing the administration's substantive strengths by searching out and identifying talented people who might not otherwise have been considered.

Finally, to ensure that the recruiting operation itself is not subsumed or overly influenced by the ongoing patronage process, the two functions should be separated. This separation was accomplished in my White House experience by establishing a separate patronage office to handle the five hundred politically sponsored job seekers and the several thousand unsolicited job requests that were received each month. The function of the patronage office was to handle all cases courteously but to provide support only for the few candidates identified as having truly important political value. Where valuable candidates were brought to light, they were referred to the recruiters for evaluation. Candidates who have high political urgency but lack any real qualifications should be guided away from more sensitive posts toward lesser noncareer posts.

In the long run a chief executive is more likely to receive political credit and reelection from the public appreciation of good government than from the superficial and short-lived value of politically representative, cosmetic appointments—unless, of course, the political appointees also have the qualities to serve effectively.

Institutional Assistance

While a professional recruiting team can be assembled by any chief executive, it takes time to develop. Further, prior to an election, most prospective chief executives (other than comfortable incumbents) and their staffs concentrate only on the election battle. The new administration then has only a short time to make its personnel selections and to resolve many other issues that come with incumbency, and it does not have the benefit of prior experience to aid in personnel decisions. Under pressure to get under way, and without the time to develop a systematic approach to recruiting, the only recourse is to resort to ineffective and less organized approaches. Once the wrong cabinet is appointed, the rest of the governing task becomes nearly impossible.

There is also a tendency to select a cabinet first, and then give them responsibility for staffing the subcabinet. However, the cabinet appointees can encounter even more difficult problems than the chief executive. Many of them receive little advance notice of their appointments, they are busy wrapping up their responsibilities in the private sector, and they must do their homework on the issues of their departments prior to confirmation hearings. Consequently, they, too, generally resort to ineffective means of recruiting and do not find the best available talent.

To help overcome these problems, a small but permanent professional recruiting arm in the office of the chief executive should be established to assist the new team. Taking the case of the President, this could be part of the Office of Management and Budget or could be a small, independent office in the Executive Office of the President. The office should be headed by a person named by the President, and additional people of the President's choice could be added as desired. The office would also have a small, permanent career staff who would be expected to follow the direction of every President impartially and professionally, much as the six hundred personnel in the Office of Management and Budget currently serve Presidents. An important distinction could be that this office would come under the purview of the President-elect immediately after the election rather than after his inauguration ten weeks later. It would not be realistic to assume that a President would immediately trust an unknown staff to handle his most sensitive political appointments. Consequently, it would be expected that the President and the men and women he chooses to head his talent search would further mold the office to fit the President's needs. The important ingredient, however, is the institutionalizing of a professional executive search team.

As envisioned, this office would address itself only to serving the President by recruiting talented people for presidential appointments (roughly 650 top posts), thus eliminating the need for each new administration to "reinvent the wheel." If staffed with competent executive search professionals, it would improve the chances that the best people in the country are systematically sought out and considered for top positions.

A secondary but important function of this institutionalized personnel office could be to develop and conduct orientation/education programs for new presidential appointees in conjunction with the Civil Service Commission. At present, it is a hit-or-miss affair as most appointees enter government with only limited understanding of the complexities of government policymaking, the interaction with Congress, the role of the media, and the other differences between the government and the private sector pointed out in the previous chapter. The result of such orientation programs would be a faster start-up and improved understanding and performance for most government executives.

Using Panels

A further element of institutional assistance, which would also help to limit undue political influence on appointments, is the wider use of expert panels to guide presidential personnel decisions. At present this system is used effectively within organizations such as the National Institutes of Health, where distinguished peer groups counsel the director on appointments to advisory panels, which have so much influence on health research priorities in this country. As noted earlier, this same approach was indispensable in developing new leadership for the nation's fight against cancer. It is also used to an extent in judicial appointments, where all prospective appointees to federal judgeships are first subjected to a professional appraisal from the American Bar Association. Without question, the ABA procedure has prevented Presidents from nominating many unqualified political allies to the judiciary, and in some cases has prevented the confirmation of others such as Judge Harold Carswell. Attorney General Griffin Bell has announced his intention to create judicial nominating commissions to recommend circuit judges, and President Carter has formed a distinguished new advisory board on ambassadorial appointments, though there is some question whether the ambassadorial board has served its purpose.

The use of panels should be broadened in the personnel area. For example, it might be useful to establish panels of state and local officials, together with other substantive experts, to evaluate candidates for top domestic posts prior to appointment. Likewise, political scientists and other experts could be used in the foreign policy field; and top economists and business and labor leaders might form panels to evaluate appointments to economic policymaking positions.

These panels should be appointed by the chief executive, should advise only him and his staff, and should not have the power of selection or veto. Otherwise their function would be resisted or ignored by a chief executive not wanting to relinquish his power, or they would be stocked with his intimates whose only function would be to put a respectable stamp of approval on his selections.

Less than fifteen panels would be sufficient to cover all spheres of the federal government, and they could be administered with relative ease, particularly if the institutional office discussed above were established. Far fewer panels would be needed at the state or local level. No chief executive or his staff is omniscient, and they need all the help they can get. There is little question that the judicious use of selection panels would make a real improvement in the quality of selections.

Term Commitments

Even if an administration successfully establishes a system for professional recruiting, expert evaluations, and sound selections, there remains the problem of rapid turnover of appointees. If we are to seriously attack personnel leadership deficiencies in government, the twenty-two month average tour must be extended so the people selected can make a real contribution and not just learn a new field at the taxpayer's expense.

Typically, when top people are recruited to government, they serve at the pleasure of the President and have no guarantee of job stability. Likewise, with a few exceptions at the cabinet level, such people generally are not asked to commit themselves for any fixed period. One of my principal recommendations to the incoming Carter administration was to insist on a moral commitment of at least four years from each appointee. President Carter has done exactly that.

Any chief executive would be well advised to insist on a moral commitment of at least four years from each of his appointees, with the further understanding that earlier resignations would be requested if performance did not measure up. This would not necessarily restrict each executive to one position during the four-year period, as changing assignments at the two-year mark is often a good way of maintaining vitality and freshness while taking advantage of prior government experience. Admittedly, a four-year commitment would be a deterrent to entering government for some people; however, it is worth the price to build some stability into government leadership, limit the wasteful start-up periods for new appointees, and ensure knowledgeable management from sincere people dedicated to making government work.

Franklin Roosevelt, the first modern President to attempt major reform of his office, said in 1937, "How is it humanly possible to know fully the affairs and problems of over one hundred separate major agencies, to say nothing of being responsible for their general direction and coordination?" At the time there were thirty-seven employees in the White House and 109,000 in the federal government. By comparison, there are today more than five hundred staff members in the White House and almost three million civilian employees of the federal government.

Personnel selections have become one of the most important tasks and earliest challenges to a chief executive, and the recommendations in this chapter are designed to help him meet this challenge. Only by mastering the issue of personnel selection can an administration turn to the even more complex job of improving the management of the career bureaucracy.

Chapter Five

Making the Bureaucracy Work

Down through the years, bureaucrats around the world have always been caught in a direct line of fire—with the public shooting at them from the front and the generals from behind. In Russia, the classic comment on bureaucracy came from the czar Nicholas I: "I do not rule Russia, ten thousand clerks do." In France, Balzac wrote a novel on the subject, acidly observing that "bureaucracy is a giant mechanism operated by pgymies." In nineteenth-century America, one of the most acute writers of the time, Henry Adams, said that "the work of internal government has become the task of controlling the thousands of fifth-rate men." Almost a hundred years later, after Eisenhower was first elected, Harry Truman told a friend, "He'll sit right here and he'll say, 'Do this, do that,' and nothing will happen. Poor Ike! It won't be a bit like the Army. He'll find it very frustrating."

Here in the United States today, it's not hard to discover why so many Americans share deep misgivings about government workers. The public knows that government has become the biggest single employer in the country. One out of every six members of the work force is now employed by the government at some level. While most of the recent increase has occurred at the state and local levels, many of these "street bureaucrats" seem to be taking orders from Washington and are thus interchangeable with the federal bureaucracy. The public also knows that government workers have been increasing their pay more rapidly than private workers. In 1962, an employee in private industry earned on the average about $116 more a year than a federal employee; by 1972, the federal average was $1,783 ahead of the private. The outskirts of Washington, D.C., chock-full of federal workers, are now the richest suburbs in the country. Yet for all the growth in government and the growth in government pay, services delivered to the taxpayer seem to show little, if any, improvement. To the average citizen, dealing with the government can mean long lines, incomprehensible forms, frustrating delays, and a constant wonderment whether they are obeying every rule and regulation written in Washington.

Because our society is complex and we have come to depend upon government to help us reach so many important national goals, we will always have a sizable army of government workers and we will always encounter a degree of confusion. But it is possible that government can be made more responsive and sensitive to the needs of our people and the bureaucracy can contribute more to making government work better.

My first encounter in trying to cope with the bureaucracy came at the Department of Health, Education and Welfare, a vast conglomeration of programs and concerns. Senator Abraham Ribicoff, an early HEW secretary, once said it was the department of dirty water, dirty air, and dirty looks. Since then, water and air have been moved to other agencies, but the dirty looks remain. HEW administers some three hundred federal assistance programs—more than any other department. Excluding Social Security payments, those programs account for about 90 percent of HEW's budget, and they cover a wide range of activities such as education assistance, vocational rehabilitation, and Medicaid. Most of the assistance programs are in the form of grants to state and local governments, colleges and universities, private voluntary groups, hospitals, and the like.

When the Great Society brought a proliferation of programs in the sixties, incredible amounts of paperwork and administrative procedures evolved to the point that they interfered with program purposes. In some cases, the cost of processing individual grant applications actually began to exceed the grant itself. As Deputy Under Secretary of HEW, one of my highest priorities was to spearhead a department-wide effort to cut red tape. Forty outstanding, experienced people were selected from within the department to serve full-time on a task force to accomplish this goal. Each careerist was assigned to analyze programs in agencies other than his own, thus ensuring objectivity and minimizing the "vested interests" that would arise if an individual were asked to examine his own program.

The career executives applied themselves with great diligence, and after eight months we could boast of significant results: fifty programs had been reviewed, 90 percent of the steps required for grant approval had been eliminated, the time required for processing grants had been cut by 50 percent, and millions of tax dollars had been saved. That experience convinced me that career government employees, if given the proper opportunity and incentives, can become part of the solution in government—not just part of the problem.

Our efforts were not entirely welcome within the department. A special problem arose, for instance, in the program that provides money to local mental health centers so that they can hire qualified psychiatrists and other professionals to help low-income citizens. Several thousand community mental health centers across the country participate in the program. To receive a grant, a local center had to run a gauntlet of three different approving bodies, climaxed by the review of an advisory committee—a team of outside psychiatrists and lay experts who would meet in Washington every few months.

Our task force thought the approval process was cumbersome, and we questioned the wisdom of a panel of experts in Washington trying to decide which community mental health centers in a city as large as Los Angeles ought to receive grants. Upon our recommendation, Secretary Robert Finch approved a plan to define the guidelines or criteria for grant selections more precisely and to delegate authority for awarding the grants to the top health official in each of the ten federal regional offices around the country. Decisions would thus be made by those closest to and most able to evaluate local needs, while the time required to obtain a grant would be cut from five months to a few weeks so that funds would be more timely and, presumably, more useful.

When implementation directives were issued to the National Institute of Mental Health (NIMH), however, severe resistance was encountered. The Director of the NIMH was responsible for administering the program. He was also a distinguished psychiatrist who had spent most of his career in NIMH and felt strongly that the program still ought to be administered out of his preserve. Instead of appealing to the Secretary, he resorted to an old bureaucratic dodge in Washington: a back-door, covert appeal to the congressional subcommittee that appropriated funds for NIMH. The subcommittee, in turn, wrote into the coming year's appropriation a requirement that all staffing grants receive advisory committee approval in Washington. While the director of NIMH was a careerist and could not be fired, Secretary Finch soon transferred him—correctly, in my opinion—to a lesser, nonsupervisory role where he could not obstruct departmental policy. Nonetheless, he had turned the tide on this issue: the new requirement passed by the Congress effectively blocked our chances of streamlining the program that year.

In retrospect, it is apparent that our difficulties in restructuring the community mental health program flowed at least in part from inadequate leadership and communication from the top presidential policymakers within HEW—including the Secretary, the Assistant Secretary for Health, and me.

Inadequate leadership at the top is at the core of many problems within the bureaucracy. In this particular case, we should have spent far more time working with the Director of NIMH and others on the advisory committee to convince them of the value of our approach. At the same time, the incident well illustrated how difficult it can be to cope with the entrenched bureaucracy. The director had reached the top rung of the career ladder through a succession of specialty assignments and without benefit of any significant management training or exposure to other, more broadening experiences. In addition, his close professional associations tied his personal future very clearly to an external constituency in the mental health field. No matter how rational the administration's policies might be, he would not willingly side with the political appointees—all transients—against the wishes of his professional constituency. Instead, he instinctively viewed the problem from a narrow perspective, refused to accept the Secretary's larger vision, and tried hard to preserve his own personal fief.

His resistance typifies the problems encountered at all levels of government in trying to bend the bureaucracy to the will of the people's elected representatives. There can be no question that public management is the toughest job in the country. The stakes are so high, the demands so constant, that public purposes can be achieved only if our governments are managed by the most able, the best prepared, and the most totally committed people. Yet few elected chief executives have harnessed the power of their career bureaucracies, and this is an important reason why government doesn't work as it should. Stephen Hess, a scholar long familiar with the problems of the presidency, summed it up succinctly: "Blaming the bureaucracy is an easy way to gloss over the failures of government, yet running a government without the support of the bureaucracy is like running a train without an engine." [1]

It has been my experience that career government employees are as intelligent, talented, and dedicated as any group of people in any private organization in the country. There is no acceptable reason why they should convey an image of unmotivated people interested only in their own job security and spending more than their share of the tax-payers' dollars. To repeat: the core of the problem is the typical failure of substandard political appointees to rise to the demanding challenge of providing genuine leadership to the careerists. Appointees conveniently set aside their own inadequacies while placing the onus on the relatively de-fenseless career people. One obvious answer is to recruit better political appointees, as I have suggested earlier. But this alone will not get the job done, for there are many other problems inherent in the bureaucratic system.

A comprehensive discussion of civil service reform is be-yond the scope of this work. Nonetheless, there are five gen-eral problem areas that should be addressed here because they are basic to the inefficiency of government, because their effects are pervasive, and because they can be solved. They are (1) adversary relations between the political lead-ership and the career bureaucracy; (2) resistance to change and innovation within the career civil service; (3) inade-quate training and development of career professionals; (4) narrow career patterns; and (5) poor pay practices.

ADVERSARY RELATIONSHIPS

Distrust of the bureaucracy has been a headache that has plagued political leaders of both major political parties for many years. As a reporter for the *New York Times* once wrote, Robert Kennedy "was baffled, beaten and ultimately reduced to helpless anger by the refusal of bureaucrats in the Department of Agriculture to cut red tape and deliver free food to the starving children in Mississippi." [2] At the same time, Senator Strom Thurmond, light-years away from

Kennedy in political orientation, found that despite the soothing assurances of a succession of HEW secretaries, the Office of Civil Rights in HEW continued to send enforcement agents to South Carolina. As Thurmond said, "The trouble around here is that what goes in at the top doesn't come out at the bottom."

After their victory in 1968, Richard Nixon and other prominent members of his team approached Washington with an understandable chariness. Nixon was the first President in more than a hundred years to arrive in Washington with the Congress firmly in the hands of the opposition party. Moreover, a long period of Democratic rule within the executive branch—they had held the White House for twenty-eight out of the preceding thirty-six years—had left a huge reservoir of Democrats in senior positions within the career civil service. A study of top-level career officials undertaken in 1970 by two university scholars showed that only 17 percent of the top careerists were affiliated with the Republican party—well below the national average at the time. After 125 interviews, the researchers concluded: "Our findings document a . . . social service bureaucracy dominated by administrators ideologically hostile to many of the directions pursued by the Nixon Administration in the realm of social policy . . . . We know enough about . . . the tendency of bureaucrats in any Administration to protect their programs to infer that the Nixon Administration's suspicions about them were not wholly groundless." They concluded that in this instance there was some truth to the quip, "Even paranoids may have real enemies." [3]

At the outset, Nixon tried to create smooth working relationships with the bureaucracy by making a personal visit to each of the major departments. It didn't take long, however, before a mutual sense of distrust began to develop between the administration leadership and the civil service they inherited. As the President began putting his own team into place, as it become evident that he wished to scrap many symbolic programs such as OEO, and as he showed that he had little real empathy for career civil servants (Nixon's own experience in the Office of Price Administration during the 1940s had permanently soured him on the bureaucracy), the gulf widened between the top and the bottom of the government.

Thereafter, little effort was made to communicate the administration's aims and goals to the men and women supposed to carry out the policies—better, it seemed, that they did not know so they would not oppose them. Information was held back, leaving top career executives without a clear understanding of the rationale for many key decisions. There was probably no clearer example than in foreign affairs: diplomacy was run increasingly out of the Oval Office and foreign service officers manning the area desks at the State Department sometimes learned of new policies through the newspapers. At the same time, the administration was reluctant to consult and work with many career experts. The careerists were used only sparingly in developing policy initiatives or analyzing key decisions. The deepening of mutual distrust seemed to fulfill the original hypothesis of the administration and led in many cases to unproductive clashes. More commonly, there was simply a failure to employ the best manpower resources in reaching and carrying out decisions.

My two years as the President's principal adviser for recruiting appointees and handling patronage requests caused many career officials to question my own commitment to working with the career service. A few months after I left this position, a draft manual was revealed that described how to operate a political personnel system and in the process openly suggested subversion of the Civil Service merit system. Despite the fact that it was prepared after my departure and I had never seen it or authorized its preparation, it was highly publicized as the "Malek Manual."

While tension between the Nixon administration and the

career civil service is not at all unique, particularly for new administrations, there is no reason why a wall of hostility should be built. The degree of loyalty and responsiveness of career employees is in most cases directly related to the quality of leadership they receive. Most careerists are service oriented and take enormous pride in contributing to the "greater good" of the country; frequently, that was the motivation that persuaded them to enter government service in the first place. But if a new political appointee is remote or uncommunicative, the careerists become discouraged and restless. They seek fulfillment in other ways. Careerists want direction and are willing to follow, but they must be led by someone who inspires confidence and respect. A leader who sets meaningful goals, articulates them clearly to career workers, and ensures that all employees—from top to bottom —are working intensively toward them will seldom have serious problems of disloyalty, unresponsiveness, or protest. Subordinates will be too involved and committed to achievement to have the inclination or time for protest.

My earliest experiences at HEW put me in contact with many career executives of extraordinary ability, such as Social Security Commissioner Robert Ball. Those exposures convinced me that the best career executives are able to lay aside their party identifications and their ideological preferences in order to carry out clearly stated objectives of an incoming administration. They were ready, willing, and able to join the new team, so long as they could have confidence in the new political appointees and sufficient communication to gain a firm sense of direction.

There are several tactics that political appointees can adopt to ensure healthier relationships with career employees:

Avoid middlemen or assistants as much as possible, particularly when assigning or reviewing work and reaching decisions. Deal directly with the bureau chief or responsible career officials so their own communications can be clearer down the line.

Ensure that the person who performs the work receives due recognition. Insist, for example, that an analysis prepared by a career civil servant bear his or her name, not just the name of the bureau chief who is forwarding the work. Include such people in key meetings. There is nothing more frustrating or demoralizing for a professional than to have someone up the line claim exclusive credit for a classy product. On the other hand, a just sense of recognition will quickly reverberate through an organization and make it apparent that the appointee cares.

Pull career people into key projects, especially those that have real bite. Not only are they capable, but they will appreciate the demonstrated confidence. Early in his tenure as Secretary of Labor, George Shultz began relying on this technique to plan and carry out a complicated, controversial reorganization of the Manpower Administration. The project went forward without a hitch, and Shultz went on to become one of the great pillars of strength in the administration, serving in three different cabinet posts. Everyone understands that the political appointees are supposed to set policy and the career executives are supposed to carry it out, but it helps immensely to have the career professionals "present at the creation."

Finally, it is imperative to recognize outstanding career performances on a regular basis. Every department has an awards program, and it is an excellent vehicle for ensuring that the best career people receive due recognition.

Beyond these measures, the most important and productive approach for any administration is simply to enter into the relationship with government civil servants with a sense of openness and trust and then to invest considerable amounts of time in communicating the goals of the administration and understanding the problems of the permanent staff. Elliot Richardson demonstrated the success of this approach in 1970 as Secretary of HEW. When he entered the position, there was unrest not only on campus but also within HEW toward administration policies on civil rights, Vietnam, and other issues. Confronted by a hostile bureaucracy, Mr. Richardson devoted enormous quantities of time to learning and understanding HEW's problems, holding in-depth discussions with career executives, bringing top career people into all key meetings, and ensuring that their point of view was fully aired and considered. Every month he met with the staffs of every agency within HEW to review their objectives and progress. He also went out of his way to praise the best HEW careerists—both in public and in private.

The Richardson approach paid off. He developed consid-erable loyalty from the bureaucracy and persuaded key people to move in desired directions. Even the most disaf-fected employees seemed to feel that their views were being fairly considered, and they no longer felt it necessary to go outside the system to the Congress or the media to gain their ends.

RESISTANCE TO CHANGE

Government workers are like workers in private industry. In addition to challenge and job satisfaction, they want com-fortable compensation, proper working conditions, and per-sonal security. The idea of reform and innovation can be threatening to them because it may risk their security. Their instinctive reaction in many cases is to perpetuate or enlarge their own areas of responsibility and to oppose any changes that might diminish their jobs or status. "As you go down, grade by grade," one top level HEW manager has said, "people tend to think a little less in idealistic terms. They're more concerned with maintaining their function and income. Enthusiasm is a luxury." [4]

At the federal level, this resistance to change is reinforced by the fact that most officials have spent their entire careers in a single program, bureau, or agency. They come to identify with the program in which they have invested so many years of their lives. They tend to believe sincerely in the program's goals, and they spend enormous psychic energy in advocating it, running it, and protecting it from change. Loyalty to program can come before loyalty to newly appointed superiors, simply because the career executives deeply believe in what they are doing and how they are doing it.

There is also a great fear of risk taking within the bureaucracy, passed on in some instances from their political superiors. A series of articles printed by the *Washington Post* caught the spirit of it: "How does a competent bureaucrat—a man who is thinking of getting through an administration—react? He rides the waves, tries to avoid being caught up in a career-slowing storm." [5]

Unfortunately, dedication to the status quo is reinforced by the government's personnel practices. Most individuals in the government enjoy almost total job security regardless of performance. The security of civil service status along with many years of familiarity with an individual agency, its constituencies, and its decisions of the past ultimately leads many a civil servant, no matter how competent, down the road toward staleness.

Resistance to change is also attributable in part to the limited flexibility of government leadership in mobilizing, leading, or changing the habits of career employees. There may be fifteen thousand employees in an agency, but the director may be entitled to fill no more than six positions with people of his own choice. The other employees have career status, which means they cannot be easily fired, reassigned, or given different pay. The sound executive in business will not, of course, frequently use his power to fire people, but at least there is a tacit understanding that the power exists. Employees who will not respond to normal, positive motivation will sometimes react more quickly if there is a "club in the closet." In government, however, the agency head can be a toothless tiger. While employees will rarely refuse to act or follow, they can and will passively resist, slow down, or impede the efforts of an unpopular leader.

Some agency heads faced with unresponsive bureaucracies simply suffer along and make the best of it. This is generally the most expensive answer because agency effectiveness suffers so much. Another tactic more commonly employed by appointees is the costly and personally demeaning practice of assigning work around the unwanted career executives. The old executive is given busywork and becomes essentially a burden on the taxpayer, while a new executive is brought in at the same salary to perform the required work. This practice is unfair to both employees and taxpayers. It also can lead to another malignancy in government —the creation of new special assistants for various functions, young men and women whose main assignment is to undercut and take over the duties of the shelved careerist. Bureaucracy piles upon bureaucracy, waste upon waste.

At the federal level, flexibility and effective personnel management are further weakened by the presence of over a dozen different personnel systems, each with its prescriptive and restrictive requirements, administrative work loads, and lack of interchangeability. Most government workers belong to the regular civil service and are paid on a general schedule. But there are many others in both professional and blue-collar jobs whose skills are similar but are employed under different systems. In HEW, I found it was almost impossible to transfer trained health officials from one of the major health agencies (part of the Public Health Service personnel system) to the largest and most poorly managed health program, Medicaid, because Medicaid is governed by the civil service personnel system.

The solution to problems of rigidity and resistance to change in the government is *not* to increase the number of appointive positions at the top, as so many politicians are

wont to do. In the federal government, an incoming administration already has the opportunity to appoint some 2500
people, including assistant secretaries and in most instances
deputy assistant secretaries and bureau chiefs. As pointed
out earlier, this task is difficult for an administration and is
seldom done effectively. Layering the civil service with even
more political appointees would only serve to widen the
gulf between the chiefs and the Indians, robbing the career
executives of an opportunity to carry out many of the more
demanding jobs in the government, weakening the attraction
of civil service, and reducing the incentive of the best career
people to remain in government. Instead, agency heads
should seek to make better use of the experience that the
career executives do have and should recognize that some
continuity of performance can be an invaluable tool for
effective management.

Surely there is an optimum balance between the number
of career and noncareer appointments in every government
organization. At the federal level, that balance should be
struck in favor of fewer political appointees, not more. In
many cases, the effectiveness of an agency would be improved and political appointments would be reduced by
roughly 25 percent if line positions beneath the assistant
secretary level were reserved for career officials.

Another way for the government manager to remove
some of the rigidity from the bureaucracy is to take a totally
open, straightforward approach to permanent personnel.
Despite an inability to remove or shift career executives, the
agency head can often achieve results by just informing an
official that he would prefer someone else in his post. So
long as his own personal security is not directly threatened,
a career executive will usually choose to move on to another
post that offers a different challenge, more satisfaction, and
a better opportunity for recognition. Like everyone else,
career workers in the government want to be appreciated.

Perhaps the most difficult problem to attack is the bureau-

crats' propensity to avoid risks and to shy away from innovation. Somehow we need to encourage people to be
willing to accept an occasional failure—to stick their necks
out with controversial, unique solutions, knowing full well
that a number of such measures will fail. Several approaches
can be taken. First, top political appointees must be willing
to accept the mistakes and public criticisms that will inevitably arise from a failure, recognizing this as a cost of more
effective, more innovative government. In addition, flattened
organizational structures should be encouraged, so that
layers of fat can be removed and managers can have direct
reporting relationships not just with two or three people or
bureaus but with five or six. This flattening would force top
managers to delegate more authority, it would discourage
overmanaging and overcontrolling, and it would create more
centers where innovation is likely to take place. More extensive use of task forces and ad hoc groups, cutting across
agency lines, also tends to broaden people's horizons and
increases their exposure to new ideas. Finally, increased job
rotation of the upward-bound government executive would
stimulate greater thinking and creativity, a point to which I
shall return.

Within the federal personnel systems, definite adjustments
are needed to diminish staleness and afford flexibility in
setting pay and assigning personnel. In 1972, President Nixon
submitted to the Congress a Federal Executive Service System, which would do much to accomplish these objectives.
The proposal was passed by the Senate but not by the
House, and it ought to be considered once again. This proposal would replace the many overlapping and competing
personnel systems with a single executive personnel system
governing the nine thousand top-level or "supergrade" employees in the federal government. Initial appointment to the
new executive personnel system would be made on the basis
of merit according to qualifications determined by the Civil
Service Commission. Classifications such as GS-16, 17, and

18—the current "supergrades"—would be eliminated, and, within certain limits, each agency could then set a person's pay based upon his performance. The agency manager would thus have more flexibility in making assignments and establishing pay standards, while the individual in the new system would retain his job security (he could not be removed from the system except for extraordinary reasons such as criminal malfeasance) and would have the added incentive to produce so that he could earn higher pay and greater responsibility.

INADEQUATE DEVELOPMENT OF EXECUTIVES

The problems arising from poor leadership among political appointees are often compounded by the lack of managerial skills among top career people. Throughout the top levels of the federal executive branch can be found career executives —department officials, agency heads, and program chiefs— who have shown a technical proficiency but have no training or background in management.[6] The shortage of managerial training is particularly acute among program chiefs, who are often chosen with an eye only on their professional credentials in the fields of medicine, education, etc. It's simply a variation of the "Peter Principle": a man is continually promoted up the ladder until he reaches a rung where he is no longer called upon to apply his original skills, but different skills for which he has precious little preparation. The promotion of these unprepared people to positions of major managerial scope is one of the most serious shortcomings in government.

A prime reason for the failure to train career executives for managerial responsibilities in goverment must again be placed at the doorstep of the political appointees. Because of their short-term perspective and their tendency to milk career executives for short-term results, appointees are inclined to ignore the vital investment that must be made in preparing organizations for the future. I know from personal experience how easy it is to fall into this trap. In 1973, as Deputy Director of the Office of Management and Budget, I consistently espoused the need for executive development throughout the government and insisted that agencies add new funds to their budget toward that end. But when it was our turn in our own agency to select a promising young executive for an extensive civil service training program, I weighed the immediate needs of the agency against our long-range needs for more executive training and decided that OMB executives already received enough training on the job. In retrospect, that was a small but significant mistake.

By any standard, government invests too little in the training of its future elite. Large private companies invest from six to eight times as much as the average agency in career training. In the military services, it has often been true that for every three officers in the field, one other officer is in the classroom. While there are no quantitative measures on how much time and attention are spent on grooming replacements, the good business executive takes replacement very seriously. He knowns that human investment is every bit as important as capital investment. Unfortunately, that wisdom has rarely prevailed in federal agencies.

Building strong institutions capable of meeting tomorrow's demands should be considered just as important to the political executive as achieving today's programmatic goals. In the private sector, failure to provide for the future frequently results in a loss of market position and eventually threatens survival. In the government, the consequences may not be immediately apparent to political appointees. By the time organizational rot sets in, they have gone on to other pastures and do not have to live with the consequences of their neglect. The bureaucracies that are left behind are used-up hulks, not self-renewing organizations with a drive to serve the public.

Not only have political appointees fallen down in this area, but there has also been a sad lack of aggressiveness among career executives in insisting upon their own training. Few top-level career federal executives seek new educational or training experiences. Many career executives either fear an absence from their jobs for training purposes or just do not appreciate the value of managerial training. In the OMB incident described above, one of the reasons I decided not to send anyone into training was the fact that no one showed the least bit of interest in participating.

The key to improving executive development is to create a strong set of incentives for aspiring careerists. So long as their superiors treat managerial skills as irrelevant to advancement, most career people will naturally treat them the same way. What is needed is a change in the criteria for promotion so that every candidate must present evidence of managerial experience and training before advancing to the highest positions. Technical competence should, of course, remain a factor in filling executive positions, but a demonstrated managerial capability should also be required. This does not mean that engineers or accountants will lose touch with their disciplines. It simply means that in order to lead other engineers and accountants, they must learn another discipline—management.

Only modest amounts of funds would be needed to accomplish this goal, and the funds could be focused mainly on two targets. First, money should be employed to improve the quality of people before they enter public service. Specifically, I recommend that a federal loan program be set up for graduate education in management or public administration with the loan being forgiven if graduates spend at least four years in public service. While the funds would be federal, graduates should be permitted to fulfill their obligations by working at the state and local levels as well, since the need for better management is even more acute there. To have a significant impact, the program should be open to some two to three thousand people a year, comparable to the annual number of entries into the national service academies. Such a program would cost about $15 million a year, a reasonable investment considering the hundreds of billions of dollars that these future executives will help to manage. Students would compete for the program under standards set by the Civil Service Commission, and selection should be accorded the same honor and respect as selection for the service academies. In addition to providing better training for future executives, such a program would enhance the prestige of government service, raise the caliber of people seeking government careers, and give graduate schools a badly needed shot in the arm in the field of public management.

A second target of funding for better executive development should be the careerists who have already reached middle and top level in the civil service. Specifically, I recommend that a federally funded fellowship program be established whereby some one thousand federal, state, and local managers could be annually selected for one year of graduate-level management education. That would be five to ten times the current number being sent to school now and would still fall short of practices in the military and in the private sector. Such a program would cost in the range of $10 million, but again it is an investment that should pay handsome dividends.

There are a number of other development initiatives that should be launched or expanded for mid-career, advancing executives including increased federal grants to states and cities for training purposes; expansion of the government's in-house training facilities (the Federal Executive Institute in Virginia); expansion of the personnel interchange program (an effort that permits business and government executives to trade positions for a year or two); and individual counseling and training for those careerists who demonstrate the greatest leadership potential. While each of these steps would be worthwhile, major long-term breakthroughs are more likely to come from the more fundamental training suggested above as well as broader career experiences.

NARROW CAREER PATHS

The inadequate preparation of future executives is only aggravated by their normal career patterns. As noted earlier, almost 70 percent of senior federal executives spend their entire careers in no more than two bureaus. Instead of seeking broadening experiences—as the best executives in the private sector try to do—executives in government tend to become technical specialists. As they march along their career paths, they burrow more and more deeply into program specialties. Too often, technical expertise is the only skill that is rewarded by the political appointees. But the long-range consequences are again sad: management skills and executive sensitivities simply cannot be developed by acquiring an encyclopedic knowledge of one law or one program.

The situation is different in private industry. Top and middle-level officials in industry nearly always are selected because of managerial and broad leadership skills as opposed to technical expertise. Specialists are used to support top and middle-level managers where their technical competence is required: the specialist, as the cliché goes, should be on tap, not on top. Specialists in industry do, of course, rise to the top, but rarely without acquiring general managerial skills.

The narrow career pattern in government also discourages innovation and reinforces the tendency to resist change. The career employee who spends his entire career in a single bureau almost inevitably becomes a blind devotee of the program and its way of doing things.

As an executive progresses in government, divided loyalties are encouraged by increased involvement with constituency groups and congressional committees that have a vested interest in the program. In fact, the constituency groups often determine the specialist's standing and prestige in his field, serve as his major source of employment opportunity after he leaves the government, and display greater longevity than the political leadership of the executive branch. In short, outside constituency groups can become compelling competitors for the loyalty of the careerist, generally at the expense of his loyalty to the administration in power.

One means of broadening the career patterns of rising government executives would be the creation of the federal executive service, as mentioned earlier in this chapter. This would encourage broader career experiences by facilitating mobility between agencies. The government could also encourage greater mobility by recognizing service in more than one agency as one way of fulfilling managerial experience requirements for promotion.

To achieve a major breakthrough, however, something far bolder is required. Specifically, I recommend that the government experiment with periodic rotations to other agencies of selected executives at the GS-15 level and above who aspire to managerial responsibilities. Rotations would occur roughly every four years. Further, promotion criteria would be revised so that such rotation, or the equivalent in executive training, would be required for promotion to the supergrade level. Such a change would, of course, require a new way of thinking about career planning: managerial skills would no longer receive mere lip service but genuine commitment.

The rotation concept seems quite basic, but it would be complex to administer. Some classes of employees would have to be exempted, and special arrangements would be needed for others. Quotas for transfer would be difficult to establish and perhaps even more difficult to control. There might also be a tendency for agencies to transfer only their weakest people. These obstacles, however, should not be a reason for timidity. A planned program of job rotation would clearly enhance the creativity, responsiveness, and managerial capacity of career executives.

INADEQUATE PAY PRACTICES

The financial plight of Dr. Frank Rauscher, Director of the National Cancer Institute (NCI), vividly illustrates the inadequacies of government pay practices at the highest levels. In 1976 Dr. Rauscher was responsible for leading the nation's fight against cancer, managing annual expenditures of $700 million. Dr. Rauscher was uniquely qualified for his post, and under his leadership over a four-year period considerable progress had been made in research to identify causes and treatments for cancer.

Under one federal law, officials at Dr. Rauscher's level were entitled to $48,654 a year, but under another law—the law that was enforced—Dr. Rauscher's pay was held at the $37,800 civil service salary ceiling, so as not to exceed the executive-level pay scale. With three children in college and two more heading in that direction, he soon found himself financially strapped and unable to fully meet his family responsibilities.

At the same time some seventy-three other people in the same National Cancer Institute—people who worked under him—were receiving precisely the same salary as Dr. Rauscher. Moreover, directors of similar institutes that were part of the same National Institute of Health were receiving more money than Dr. Rauscher even though most of them had less responsibility. They were better paid because they were compensated under separate pay systems of the Commissioned Corps of the U.S. Public Health Service rather than under the civil service. For example, the Director of the Institute of Aging with a $26 million budget received $46,000; the Director of Environmental Health Services was paid $49,000 for administrating a $46 million budget; and the Director of the Neurology Institute drew a $50,000 salary.

Recognizing the ridiculous inequities in such a system, and anxious to keep Dr. Rauscher in his post, the Congress attempted to enact legislation—"the Rauscher bill"—to raise his salary to $52,000. The first obstacle was that this would have placed Dr. Rauscher's pay about $6,000 above his superior and the top health official in government, the Assistant Secretary for Health. So the legislation was rewritten to include the Assistant Secretary (who would then earn more than the Under Secretary of HEW), the Director of the National Institute of Health (NIH), and ten other institute directors within NIH. However, it was then discovered that three health institutes are not part of NIH, and their directors would not be included in the raise. In the end, Congress could not sort through the confusion, and the legislation was discarded. Dr. Rauscher left government soon thereafter.

The key spot in the country in guiding education policy and programs is the U.S. Commissioner of Education, with responsibility for an annual budget of more than $4 billion. One of the most able men to hold this post was Dr. Ted Bell. He, too, was at the $37,800 level and was starting to feel pinched. After seeing Congress once again pass over executive-level salary increases Dr. Bell resigned in early 1976 to accept a higher-paying post. It is ironic that this financially motivated move was his appointment as Superintendant of Schools for the state of Utah, a position encompassing a budget one-hundreth the size and with considerably less impact than the one he left, but with a salary $10,000 higher.

Syndicated columnist George Will summarized the problem quite well: "The hemorrhaging of the government's lifeblood of talent is making the government dumber, not leaner. But the problem of inadequate pay is a nettle that neither conservatives nor liberals will seize." [7]

The major shortcoming of the government pay system is

that the structure is quite flat, with little difference in pay between the middle and top grades. Thus, a GS-13 program specialist who develops and evaluates plans for a single grant program might earn $25,000 per year, while the Commissioner of Education with his $4 billion responsibility earned $37,800 up until 1977 and $54,410 thereafter. The end result is that there are thousands of mid-level employees who are paid more than they would be in the private sector while the top officials are grossly undercompensated.

A second major problem that became particularly acute in the early seventies and led to the resignation of Drs. Rauscher and Bell is that top-level salaries are frozen for years at a time due to conflicting legislation. Under the Pay Comparability Act, the salaries of general schedule (GS) employees are adjusted annually, supposedly to make them comparable with private enterprise for the same levels of work. However, another statute provides that officials in the general schedule cannot be paid higher salaries than the lowest grade, level V, of the executive schedule (used to compensate cabinet officers, assistant secretaries, and a handful of top career positions). This linkage resulted in an eight-year freeze in top salaries, and until 1977 employees in the top GS grades (GS-16, 17, and 18), some nine thousand in all, were paid the same salary for widely varying levels of responsibility.

The freeze was in turn attributable to congressional politics. By an unfortunate amendment to the law, senators and congressmen are also compensated under the executive system at Executive Level II. That means that congressional pay and top executive branch pay—as well as top civil servant pay—are all tied together: they go up together or they stay frozen together. Recommendations for pay increases in the executive levels are provided to the President every four years, and he can send them on to Congress; the Congress also has authority to enact interim increases in executive level pay should it choose. Members of Congress, however, habitually vote against public pay increases for themselves, preferring instead to increase their emoluments by hiking up their lecture fees or by resorting to other, less visible methods. In this way, they can convey a more Spartan image to the voters back home and capitalize on their "resounding vote for economy in government." In truth, by staying in the same boat with the executive and judicial branches, the Congress can have it both ways. Whenever pressures for higher executive and judicial pay become unbearable—as they always do—the Congress can rise on the same tide of higher salaries. Representative Morris Udall has pointed out still another reason for the absurd way in which pay is determined: "It would demean the House," he said, "to give more pay to judges and some third assistant to the President . . . than to the legislators themselves."

Whatever the reasoning, the fact is that for years at a time pay levels at the top of the executive branch are frozen, and huge personnel problems are created as a result. The combination of inequity and lack of increased salary potential mitigates against any incentive to advance or even to remain in government service. Moreover, there are no provisions for bonuses for exceptional performance, thus further reducing incentive.

A further debilitating factor in keeping top-flight civil servants on the job in recent years has been the generous retirement system that includes an annual cost-of-living escalator. For example, a supergrade-level civil servant who retired in 1971 at age fifty-five with thirty years' service would have had an initial retirement income of roughly $20,000, but by 1976 it would have grown to about $32,000 as a result of the annual escalator. If he had waited until 1976 to retire, his retirement income would be only $22,400, since retirement benefits increase only 2 percent of salary for every year of service, and the top salaries on which the percentages are based remained frozen. In these circumstances it is not surprising that many of the best and most experienced people are taking leave from government.

The problems of pay at the federal level are only magnified at the state and local levels. A $37,800 salary ceiling would seem like a godsend to many city mayors, strapped as they are for adequate budgeting resources and adequate manpower.

Temporary relief was provided to the executive pay freeze and pay compression problem in the federal government early in 1977 when President Ford recommended to the Congress that it raise the pay of the executives of the incoming administration. Mr. Ford showed considerable courage in this recommendation. The Senate shortly thereafter firmly approved the measure, but the House of Representatives avoided the issue, letting the raise go into effect without a formal vote. In any event, the raise is now in effect so that top government officials are now receiving much higher salaries (the appointee in Dr. Rauscher's job receives not $37,800 a year but $54,410).

It must be stressed, however, that the 1977 increase is only a temporary solution. The underlying conditions that caused these problems are still there, waiting to cause trouble again. Finding permanent solutions for pay inadequacy will require a level of political courage on the part of the President and the Congress that has heretofore been lacking. Several bold actions are called for to provide pay rates adequate for recruiting, retaining, and motivating a high-quality cadre of government executives:

It is essential to take executive and judicial pay out of politics by separating it from consideration of congressional pay. The Congress can accomplish this task at will, simply by amending the law and considering the issues at separate times.

To blunt public misunderstanding of large increases and to further minimize political influence, the current practice of addressing executive pay every four years should be changed. Rather, the commission studies should be conducted every second year, with the results presented in the nonelection odd years, and increases should be in annual installments rather than all at once. An acceptable alternative would be to consider executive and GS-level salaries as one, providing increases each year based on surveys of comparable industry jobs. Again, Congress could accomplish this with relative ease.

A vastly expanded incentive awards program should be initiated to recognize and reward exceptional performance. Legislative authorities already exist to carry out an expansion, but they are used only sparingly. Substantial financial bonuses have traditionally provided great incentive and improved performance in industry. Awards in government at the upper grade levels, based on achievement of predetermined objectives, can only improve performance and lead to greater accomplishment. Further, they will result in greater pay equity within the civil service and help to close the gap with higher-paying private-sector jobs.

Government managers should be permitted great flexibility in setting pay at the supergrade levels, as suggested earlier.

A faster promotion system should be developed so that the most talented and promising individuals can move up the ladder more quickly to greater responsibility and higher pay.

The President and the Congress should ensure that programs providing grants to states and cities carry with them more generous funding for better managerial talent at these levels. Further, as the revenue-sharing concept takes hold, people as well as money should be encouraged to work at local and state levels. Legislation should be enacted to provide complete transferability of pension rights and other benefits between levels of government. This will encourage the free transfer of personnel and remove a serious existing impediment to such movement.

The bureaucracy does work. But it doesn't work as well as it should because the able, dedicated people in its ranks must spend an inordinate amount of time and energy overcoming management debilities that flow from the dysfunctional aspects of the system described in this chapter. Only with more astute political leadership and with sweeping reform will the bureacracy and the government begin to fulfill its original purposes.

But before government can truly succeed, it must do a more credible job of identifying its goals and setting its direction. These concerns are addressed in the following chapter.

Chapter Six

Long-Range Planning: Shaping Our Destiny

Longtime residents of Washington are fond of telling stories about Oliver Wendell Holmes. When he was already in his sixties, Holmes was appointed to the Supreme Court by Theodore Roosevelt, and he continued serving for some thirty years, into the heyday of Franklin Roosevelt. One day late in his life, it is said, Holmes was riding on a train when the conductor came by for his ticket. Several moments of confusion followed as Holmes fumbled in his vest. Finally the conductor said: "That's alright, Mr. Holmes, I recognize you. You can just give me the ticket when you return." "That's very kind of you, young man," the Justice replied. "But the problem is not just to find my ticket. The problem is to find out where I'm going."

In a very real sense, the problem in the United States today is that we know we are on a great journey into the future but are not really certain where we are going. And, as Alvin Toffler has pointed out in *Future Shock*, the future is bearing down upon us at an ever more accelerating rate—so fast, in fact, that many people are ridden by anxiety and apprehension.

The need for mastering the future is particularly acute in the highest reaches of government because it is there that strategies are supposedly developed and policies are formed that could shape the lives of many generations to come. But as anyone who has served in government can attest, the people in Washington are no smarter than people elsewhere; they do not possess any secret fund of knowledge; and more importantly, government leaders generally have no long-range view of where the country should be twenty-five years from now. As a recent presidential advisory committee concluded in its 1976 report, "Federal policy-making suffers particularly from two deficiencies: (1) a lack of coordinated policy . . . and (2) a lack of foresight, causing our nation to react to problems after they become acute, instead of averting them or initiating them." [1]

It is both surprising and alarming that for the most part government does not engage in meaningful long-range planning. This failure not only weakens government performance today but also ensures that it will not deliver expected results in the future.

Long-range planning is the first and most important phase in a continuum that should comprise the planning process. This chapter focuses on the problems associated with long-term planning and on actions that would improve the process. Succeeding chapters deal with other elements in the planning continuum—choosing short-term objectives that are consistent with long-range needs, developing specific plans for achieving these objectives, allocating financial resources to meet the objectives, and evaluating progress on a systematic basis.

Planning means different things to different people and often stirs strong emotions, particularly where government planning threatens interference with the private sector in matters of economic choice. In my view, the market system remains our most effective economic planning mechanism. Thus, government planning should state goals, problems, and solutions but should not have a mandate to reach these goals through techniques that dictate to the private sector. Rather, the government long-range planning discussed in this chapter involves the following:

Defining the likely characteristics of the country and the world twenty-five to fifty years into the future. What resources will be available and what demand will there be for these resources? What will the size, age, breakout, and other demographic features of our population be, and what new or greater needs will be generated by these changing population patterns?

With the help of the above analyses, bringing the issues of the future into focus by identifying the priority problems that are likely to emerge, and developing alternative means of dealing with these problems.

Ensuring that policies and programs developed in response to current problems are consistent also with the long-term needs of the country.

Too often the government now fails on almost all three counts outlined above. For example, U.S. welfare policy over the past several decades has treated the symptoms of poverty by providing cash benefits, housing, or free medical treatment for the poor. However, upon entering HEW in 1969, I was shocked to learn that the government had no real concept of how to treat the causes and break the vicious welfare cycle over a period of years. There was no internal game plan, just a series of ad hoc plays called in from the bench. The government should have been determining the number of people who were likely to be welfare dependents ten to twenty years into the future, determining the root causes of this dependency, and devising programs to deal with these fundamentals. This would have been the planned approach to the problem, but, typically, it was not the approach the government elected to take.

Planning is applicable, in fact, to all aspects of government, including social issues, natural resources, economic matters, and national security. As stated earlier, government planning need not require government implementation in every area; the initiative should in most instances remain with the private sector. But the government should exercise its responsibilities for better defining the problems, needs, and possible solutions for the nation over the next twenty-five to fifty years. In other words, we do not need a larger or more powerful government—just a smarter government.

WHY THE GOVERNMENT FAILS TO PLAN

The idea that government should establish formal planning structures has been popular in Washington for forty years, but for one reason or another very few of the attempts at planning have survived.

In 1939, President Roosevelt established the National Resources Planning Board as part of the executive office of the President. It was supposed to be the "intellectual spearhead" of the government, but Roosevelt soon found that its long-range ideas were not as engrossing, nor seemingly as urgent, as the short-term problems that came across his desk every day, and he began losing interest. Then when war broke out he turned his attention entirely to other matters. In 1943 the Congress abolished the board and, fearful that such planning might interfere with their own prerogatives, stipulated that the board's functions could not be transferred to any other agency.

The next major attempt at planning was made by President Eisenhower when he established the National Security Council (NSC) for planning and coordination of overall diplomatic, defense, and intelligence matters. The NSC has perhaps been the most successful innovation the nation has had for government planning purposes. Yet even in the NSC there has also been a strong temptation to play an active role in the day-to-day conduct of American foreign policy. Under Henry Kissinger, for instance, the NSC began with a heavy orientation toward future planning but soon drew in the reins over many areas of day-to-day policymaking. It was not enough for Kissinger to sit academically on the side of the international chess board figuring how to checkmate the Russians ten moves away; he wanted to move the players himself.

While Kissinger was inserting the NSC into day-to-day diplomacy, his mentor Richard Nixon was trying to strengthen strategic planning in the domestic scene. In 1969, with considerable fanfare, Nixon created a National Goals Research Staff, directed it to draw up a goals study for the future, suggested that it might become a permanent part of the government, and asked it to make annual reports. A year later, the goals staff turned out a well-done report that contained several controversial recommendations. Some of these recommendations failed to serve the short-term needs of the administration, while others—such as a national growth policy and population planning—proved to be anathema to many conservatives. As a consequence, nearly all of the recommendations were left to wither on the White House vine, and the staff was eventually disbanded.

In 1970, Mr. Nixon also set up a Domestic Council, which was assigned specific functions such as clarification of long-term goals and development of alternatives. The council was to work in tandem with the Office of Management and Budget (OMB): the council was to set policies and OMB was to ensure that they were carried out within the executive branch. At first it appeared that the Domestic Council might be the domestic counterpart to the NSC. Unfortunately, it was constantly distracted from its original purposes, evolving instead into a coordinator of daily, short-term policy issues and a front-line fighter against the latest political fires. The development of long-range plans became less and less central to the activities of the council and soon disappeared entirely. The redirection of the council staff toward day-to-day management partly reflected the President's own inclination. It was also attributable to the kinds of people employed: many of them were excellent lawyers or managers but few were deep, conceptual thinkers who had any experience in formulating long-range social plans and forecasts.

In the early months of his administration, President Carter disbanded the Domestic Council for all intents and purposes, and his attention seems to have been diverted from strategic, long-term considerations. Four months into the Carter administration, a well-positioned observer close to the Carter team commented: "Things are being forced on him so much faster than he expected. No one has time to think about the long-range direction and the overall pattern. They're all so busy coping with the crisis of the moment." [2]

Traditionally, the departments and agencies in areas more subject to scientific measurement and quantification—Defense and NASA, for instance—have proven to be more adept at planning. Secretary McNamara's "whiz kids" at Defense engaged in strategic analyses of various weapons systems, and their influence was felt long after many of them left government. Even at Defense, however, former Secretary Elliot Richardson has noted that the planning "does not yet really embrace the national defense system as a whole; at best, it assembles bits and pieces of systematic analysis into a façade of comprehensive planning." [3]

In recent years there has also been a greater effort to foresee the future in other areas that lend themselves to quantification, such as the economy and the budget. Under congressional mandate, both the Council of Economic Advisers and the OMB now annually publish their projections for the gross national product, unemployment, inflation, and other leading indicators, as well as government spending and revenues for the coming five years. These projections have become an invaluable tool for assessing future trends in the economy and in developing the fiscal and monetary policies of the government.

Overall, then, some steps have been taken to strengthen planning in national security and economic affairs, but progress so far has been quite limited. And whatever progress has been made is more than offset by an almost total lack of planning in the more traditional domestic areas. Looking back over the government's experiments with long-range planning, it appears that there are several reasons why it has so often failed to live up to expectations.

The fundamental problem is the short-term focus of the entire political process. Elected political leaders and their appointees are evaluated by the voters on the basis of their current policies and their handling of immediate crises. They are rarely held accountable for the long-term consequences of their policies. To this day, for instance, neither the public nor the press has criticized Presidents Eisenhower, Kennedy, or Johnson for failing to look ahead and take actions to prevent an energy crisis. Even when the crisis was upon us, there was scant recognition that the problem had been building for years. It was more a matter of academic than public interest.

Further, there are usually sufficient problems, crises, and initiatives of immediate urgency to absorb the full attention of the President, his top appointees, and the Congress. The urgency of these issues very easily crowds out a more strategic or long-range approach to planning, even where a natural inclination toward planning exists. As Henry Kissinger stated in a critique of foreign policy: "The analysis of where one is overwhelms the consideration of where one should be going. Serving the machine becomes a more absorbing occupation than defining the purpose." [4]

With such a profusion of immediate issues and with the inherent difficulties of piercing the veil of the future, people at the top of the political system have a pronounced short-term focus. Consequently, when sporadic efforts at long-term planning are made, they are usually doomed to failure almost from inception.

This inclination to focus on the short-term within the executive branch of government is reinforced by the personnel generally recruited to government. Most of the men and women chosen for top jobs are lawyers and business people who tend to have highly developed managerial styles or have made their mark as problem solvers. Few have any real sense of vision or are inclined to think much about the long-term future. When broad, conceptual thinkers are brought into government, they are often discouraged or elbowed aside by the problem solvers. Daniel P. Moynihan is a prime example. Appointed by Nixon as Counsellor for Domestic Affairs early in 1969, after a distinguished career at Harvard and in previous Democratic administrations, Mr. Moynihan demonstrated a clear vision of the nation's long-term problems and what needed to be done about them. For a short period of time he brought a sense of strategic planning to the social area and functioned as an effective counterpart to Henry Kissinger in national security. Within a year, however, he was supplanted as chief domestic adviser by John Ehrlichman, a Seattle native whose chief credentials were his abilities as a real estate attorney and an advance man. On paper, Ehrlichman wasn't in the same league with Moynihan, but President Nixon found that when it came to solving daily crises, it was more profitable to give instructions to Ehrlichman than to philosophize with Moynihan.

Strategic planning has also been hampered by lack of an institutionalized organization to spearhead the planning process. As pointed out earlier, most such groups in the past have either been abandoned (e.g., the National Resources Planning Board) or have turned their attention to short-term problems (e.g., the Domestic Council).

Beyond these fundamental barriers, there are a number of other reasons why government planning in domestic or social issues has been embarrassingly weak.

For one thing, unlike many areas of defense and foreign policy, domestic programs do not pose immediate, life-or-death dangers. As a result, politicians tend to approach many areas of our domestic life somewhat nonchalantly until they, too, suddenly become crises. That accounts in part for our habit as a nation of jumping from one crisis to the next— from civil rights in the early sixties to poverty in the mid-sixties to environmental concerns in the late sixties—when, in fact, every one of these problems had been growing over the years and only aroused serious national attention when they erupted.

A second problem is that policymakers in the government have great difficulty coming to grips with the great diversity of functions on the domestic front, ranging from water resource programs to welfare reform to egg inspection. A further impediment to domestic planning is the fragmentation of authority over domestic programs among federal, state, and local officials. The greater the fragmentation, the harder it is to frame a coherent plan.

Planning is also inhibited by the fragmentation of authority within the federal government itself, since the President's policies must vie with those of 535 members of Congress. As one powerful chairman after another has been toppled from power on Capitol Hill, the Congress itself has also become highly fragmented.

Finally, the problems we face are also more complex than in the past. Many areas of our national life have become heavily entwined with the fortunes of other nations—as in the economy—so that it has become increasingly difficult for any single country such as the United States to plan its future independent of others.

In sum, the problems of planning in the government are rather imposing, and, as a result, there is a staggering shortage of sound, long-range thinking. There is no organization in the government today that can successfully deal with long-term problems—especially domestic ones. Conceptual, long-range thinkers who are now attracted to government service too often find their talents underutilized, and they are frequently ignored, replaced, or shunted aside by more politically oriented lawyers or managers. As presidential scholar Stephen Hess has stated, "Government leaves too much to chance . . . . This will continue to be the case until long-range planning is built into the regular process of running the Federal government." [5]

THE CASE FOR PLANNING

Over two decades ago, experts in the field of petroleum began to warn that our demand for oil was rapidly rising while our supplies faced an uncertain future. Some experts correctly foresaw that in the 1970s the United States would be so heavily dependent on foreign sources of oil that we could be vulnerable to blackmail. Yet the government paid little heed to these forecasts. Only when the crises struck in 1973 did the government begin seriously calling for a long-range plan to help bring our supply and demand into a better balance. Within thirty years or so all known oil resources in the United States will be substantially depleted, and the end of the "oil age" will be approaching. New sources of energy will certainly be required. Yet even in 1977, after four years of wrangling in Washington, the country still lacked a comprehensive plan for developing its fossil-fuel resources and bringing alternative energy resources into use.

There are numerous other areas where the nation would have benefited from better planning. For example, when the U.S. birthrate rose from 18 per 1,000 to 27 per 1,000 after World War II and did not fall again until the early 1960s, it was clear that a "baby boom" would ripple through our society for many years to come. But the government failed to plan. Instead, we permitted ourselves to endure a series of short-term crises and scrambled at the last minute to devise makeshift, short-term solutions. In the 1950s, for instance, we experienced a shortage of elementary schools and teachers, and in the 1960s there were similar shortages in secondary schools and colleges. Only after the fact did government begin to support intensive teacher education and construction programs; and then it overreacted, so that today, after the boom is passed, we find ourselves with an excess of teachers. Moreover, the excess of teachers has contributed to the problem of unemployment, a problem that also could have been anticipated and ameliorated, given the known fact that the baby boom would also dramatically increase the number of people entering the work force.

Another example of the government's failure to look ahead occurred in the interstate highway program. In that case, the engineers who mapped out the 40,000-mile system executed their plans almost perfectly, but no one else was adequately consulted to determine the side effects: the resulting pollution, the urban sprawl, the dissection of central cities, etc. Each of these has been addressed after the fact—and has caused far more hardship and cost many more billions of dollars that it should have.

Government has consistently failed to foresee the broader, long-term consequences of its narrowly focused programs. For instance, in the late 1960s, pushed forward by the environmental movement, the government enacted a series of air and water standards and launched a rigid program of enforcement. The theory was that our national economy was large enough to absorb the extra costs. What was overlooked was the fact that the new standards imposed unusual hardships upon particular industries within the economy. Very little cost-benefit analysis was done in advance of the programs, and, as a result, U.S. products became noncompetitive in world markets or were even priced out of their own domestic markets, contributing to unemployment and economic "stagflation."

In another case, government once set very ambitious goals for public housing in the United States and poured billions of dollars into public housing projects—only to discover a few years later that it had not anticipated the social consequences of isolating so many poor people in sterile, high-rise environments.

The photograph of government authorities dynamiting the Pruitt-Igoe housing project in St. Louis—the largest public housing project in the country—serves as a vivid reminder that programs originated without benefit of forward planning can easily lead to social disaster.

In short, the record suggests that the nation has paid a heavy price because government has failed to take adequate account of the future. Moreover, many of the most critical issues facing the country today are not the immediate ones but those with long-range implications. As Russell Train noted, "The day-to-day crises that seem to capture all our attention and consume all our energies are, for the most part, simply manifestations of far deeper problems that we never seem to get around to acknowledging, much less addressing."[6]

As a country, we can no longer afford the luxury of not looking ahead. The basic condition that has discouraged long-term strategic planning in the past—the disinterest of the White House—is no longer appropriate or politically viable. The problems of scarcity, poverty, and ignorance have become too profound, too visible, and too close to home to be ignored by the voting public. Any President who does not plan more intelligently for the long term is likely to be subjected to increasingly harsh criticism because he is playing with the lifeblood of the Republic by his ignorance, neglect, or fear of the future.

Today the tools are available. There is more than enough data on hand to develop a sense of the nation's characteristics and needs some twenty years or more into the future. Government also has the analytical capacity to put this information to constructive use. What it lacks is the will. Given government's capacity, the urgency of the issues, and the availability of information, it is scandalous for any political leader not to take the future into account in shaping programs and policies. It is even more critical to develop near-

term actions to head off the problems foreseen in the future
before they reach crisis proportion. As former Senate Majority and Minority Leaders Mike Mansfield and Hugh Scott
stated:

> The practice of waiting for the storms to strike and then,
> hurriedly, erecting shelters is not only wasteful and an ineffi-
> cient use of the resources of the nation but its cumulative effect
> may well be devastating. There is a need, it seems to us, to
> anticipate and, as far as possible, to act in an orderly fashion
> before the difficulties have descended on us.[7]

WHAT NEEDS TO BE DONE

Most of the preceding examples concerned social issues,
and indeed it is in this area that the failure to plan has been
most noticeable and has had the most damaging consequences. Accordingly, the recommendations that follow will
apply most directly to the social area but will also have application on a selective basis in natural resources, economic
matters, and national security.

What needs to be done first and foremost is for government leadership to recognize the central importance of
bringing the issues of the future into focus. Strategic long-
term planning can help to establish the ultimate direction for
government, setting the stage for all else that follows. Thus,
it is one of the most important elements in the process of
managing government and making government work more
effectively. There is already some evidence that the public
has grown more receptive to the planning idea. Voters demonstrated their concern in part in the 1976 presidential election when a popular and decent incumbent was ousted.
Political aides close to President Ford attributed the defeat
in large measure to the inability of their forces to develop
and articulate a clear vision of the future.

Once the President, the Congress, and other leaders can

agree on the need for greater planning, several concrete steps must be taken.

Involvement of Line Officials

The key prerequisite to sound, usable strategic planning is to obtain the commitment and personal involvement of line officials, especially the President, the cabinet, agency heads, and bureau chiefs. As a rule, when planning has been attempted in the past, it has been carried out by staff units with little participation by senior line executives. If line officials fail to get involved, they also fail to make decisions on the basis of staff recommendations, their minds are not attuned to thinking about the future, and staff work turns into empty paper exercises. As frustration sets in, the best people begin leaving, line officers decide to do away with seemingly unnecessary staff overhead, and another attempt at planning is finished.

To prevent such an early demise, it should be clearly understood by every top executive that long-range planning is an imperative part of his job. Unless planning is assigned a high priority and unless the chief executive holds line officials accountable for its success, the planning process will be crowded aside by the day-to-day crises.

Officials throughout an organization will tend to follow the example set by their leadership. If the President or the cabinet officer focuses on short-term crises, so will his subordinates and the staffs around him. Thus, the president should set the tone by participating directly in planning sessions and encouraging similar participation within the cabinet. He ought to meet on a regular basis with key planning executives to engage in serious thinking, consciously and collectively, about long-range objectives, goals, and strategies. Periodically—once a year at least—the chief executive should also meet for several days with his cabinet and key planning advisers for a deep examination of the country's status and outlook. This kind of session should take place away from the pressures of daily events, perhaps at Camp David or some other secluded spot. Cabinet members and other key line executives should hold similar sessions with their subordinates.

Direct involvement of the chief executive is imperative for another reason: the great resistance to change within the bureaucracy. Since planning ultimately helps to establish a framework for change, the authority and commitment of the chief executive to the planning process will be essential for successful execution.

If the President's "skull sessions" were timed near the beginning of each new year, that might also help to revive another decrepit institution, the annual State of the Union address. Typically, that message is no longer about the state of the Union at all but about the state of the President's political priorities. More often than not, it is a ritual whereby the President presents a laundry list of glittering new programs for the coming year, accompanied by bursting applause from members of his own party, quiet attention on the other side of the aisle, and blank stares by the Justices. Occasionally, it is used to articulate goals or priorities for the coming year, but seldom does it look beyond the year, and even more rarely beyond the President's term. With strategic planning, a President might employ the State of the Union address as a vehicle for talking seriously to the country about the nation's long-term needs, and steps that he would recommend to meet those needs.

Defining Specific Responsibilities

No function in the government, especially in as nebulous an area as planning, is likely to be successful unless it has a carefully prescribed mandate. In the case of planning, it would be far better to begin with modest objectives and to build a solid record than to assign an ambitious list of responsibilities that are less likely to be carried out than to alarm people as disguised forms of social engineering. One of the major principles of war, the concentration of force, is as applicable in government long-range planning as it is on any battlefield. Another way of expressing this notion is the oft-said phrase, "If we can do only a few things very well, we can let the rest go hang."

This concept of concentration indicates that long-range planning must begin by rigorously identifying those issues where the threat to national interest (domestic or otherwise) is so great that to overlook long-range planning would be sheer folly. For example, an evaluation of the long-term need for developing new oil reserves or substitutes and the development of a realistic plan to achieve self-sufficiency might well be one of the issues selected in the early stages of comprehensive planning. Another issue selected might be the means by which the growing number of older citizens will finance their retirement, considering the trend toward earlier retirement, the insufficiency of the social security trust fund, and the distinct changes in the country's age profile after the turn of the next century as the "baby boom" cohorts enter retirement.

A large number of issues simply cannot be addressed cogently at the same time, nor should they be examined until they reach a certain critical point. Rather, a fixed number of issues—say five to ten—should be selected each year for a full-scale strategic study.

The intention of planning, it should be underlined, is not to enable the government to control everyone's future but to give the country a way of anticipating the future and preparing intelligently—and freely. Thus, paralleling our earlier definition of planning, the initial missions of this planning effort might be (1) identification of emerging long-term trends and key problems; (2) formulation of alternative courses of action for dealing with the problems; (3) evaluation of these different courses, including their costs and benefits to society; and (4) analysis of the impact of short-term proposals and policy issues on the long-term needs of the country.

Establishing an Organization

To help accomplish such missions, there should be a small unit (or units) within the executive branch of the federal government with explicit responsibility for administering strategic long-range planning. This unit would not attempt to do all of the planning, but would play a lead role in selecting the five to ten issues to be subjected to intense analysis, and would serve as a catalyst for planning among the agencies. In this way, the planning office would administer the process, but the line officials—the department and agency heads and their staffs—would remain responsible for, and deeply involved in, the planning itself.

The National Security Council (NSC) already helps to serve such purposes in foreign policy, and given a more precise mandate to focus full attention on the longer-term, more strategic issues, the NSC is fully capable of fulfilling the long-range planning function in foreign policy. As pointed out earlier, the marketplace should remain the prime mechanism for planning in economic matters. The Council of Economic Advisors, with the occasional assistance of task forces to address selectively the most urgent natural resource issues, can provide the long-range planning that is needed in the economic sphere. There is no such organization dealing with social issues, where the need is most urgent.

There are two ways of establishing such a domestic planning organization. One is to set up an agency or commission reporting to the President and to assign to it statutory, formal authority for analyzing strategic issues, developing long-range plans, and the like. One problem with this approach is that, unless carefully monitored, such bodies tend to set overly ambitious goals calling for new expenditures, major new agencies, and more bureaucracy. Moreover, such an organization would tend to relieve the President and other top line officials of their planning responsibilities and would run a great risk of having its plans ignored. In taking the burden off the line officials, the organization could end up doing more harm than good.

To be effective and to generate necessary clout and interest, it would be far better if an Office of Long Range Planning reported directly to the President as a part of the Executive Office of the President. In this way the function of the office would not be to develop its own plans but to assist the President in developing his plans. It would also serve as a focal point in government for long-range planning, offering staff support and encouragement to Department and Agency Heads.

Preferably, the new office would be set up within a re-formed Domestic Council, reorienting the Council toward its original purposes. The Domestic Council has the advantages of proximity to the President and sufficient prestige to attract top minds to its service. Moreover, the Congress has already agreed to the formation of a Domestic Council for the purpose of strategic planning, so that revival of the idea should cause little controversy.

Another alternative is to establish a Council of Social Advisors, as has been advocated in the past by Vice President Mondale and Senator Javits. The council would be comparable to the Council of Economic Advisors (CEA) which, as pointed out earlier, has made significant strides toward improving government planning in the economic sphere. Like the CEA, the Council of Social Advisors would consist of three members, appointed by the President and confirmed by the Senate. This form of organization would have many of the advantages of the Domestic Council in that it would be close to the President, would be totally dedicated to his service in this crucial area, would involve the Congress more directly in planning by virtue of its confirmation powers, and would raise the public visibility of planning issues.

In either event, the new planning function should be institutionalized with an ongoing staff, and it should be led by a top-flight person or people appointed by the President and confirmed by the Senate. In addition, small counterpart offices should be established in each major department and agency, reporting directly to the agency head and maintaining a regular relationship with the presidential unit. These agency groups would bring the best thinking to bear in a range of areas without the burden of a large bureaucratic organization. They would also enhance the possibilities of attracting personnel with a diversity of backgrounds.

To the maximum degree possible, planning on domestic issues should be conducted in the sunlight in order to gain public support and bring to bear various points of view. Selection of issues by the planning staff should be based on rigorous surveillance of economic, demographic, and sociological trends and the arranging of vast numbers of conferences around the country designed to gain views on and help identify the most cogent of the emerging issues and concerns.

Personnel

One of the reasons that governments fail to plan is the failure to attract conceptual thinkers and the tendency to treat planners as fifth wheels. It is imperative that the government recruit more men and women of vision, intellect, and some working knowledge of the social needs of the country.

In addition, there should be mechanisms for ensuring that

the national planning office within the Executive Office of the President receive a steady stream of new ideas and gain the best thinking of conceptual thinkers in and out of government. One way of encouraging a steady flow of ideas and stimulating approaches to problems within the government itself is the "departmental detail"—the temporary loan by an agency or department to the planning office of its top-flight personnel. For the planning office, this would mean that it would employ a small permanent staff, but the staff would be generously supplemented by men and women from, say, the departments of HEW, HUD, Labor, and Agriculture. The detailees would rotate every year or two, thus helping to keep the central unit within a realistic framework and avoiding the ivory-tower approach that can often characterize planning units.

Formal or informal advisory commissions made up of opinion leaders outside government might also be used selectively to advise the planning office and comment on its findings. They would add further stimulus to the process and would give the public further opportunity to enter the debate on the nation's future. These advisory commissions could also be used to conduct periodic public hearings to gain additional insights as analyses proceed and conclusions begin to emerge. One of the more successful reforms undertaken by the Ford White House—and one that was little noticed by the press—was a series of discussions held every week or so, sponsored by the White House Office of Public Liaison, under the direction of William Baroody, Jr. In those discussions, representatives from various outside organizations came to the White House to share their concerns and ideas. These sessions not only give the public a greater opportunity to influence decision making in the government but also opened the White House doors to a steady flow of fresh ideas—an essential ingredient for a White House staff if it is not to become isolated from reality.

Accountability

The Congress should hold the executive branch responsible for long-range planning just as it does for all other areas. In addition to confirming the head of the President's Domestic Planning Office, the Congress might require that an annual report be submitted in conjunction with the President's annual budget. Similarly, the appropriations subcommittees of the Congress should require statements of long-range plans from departments and agencies in advance of hearings on spending authority. The Congress might even find it necessary to form a cross-governmental planning committee of its own, similar in scope and perhaps even an adjunct to the Congressional Budget Committee that includes members of both chambers. Such an effort would, of course, bring maximum visibility to planning and would tend to concentrate the attentions of the executive branch on the project.

The Limits of Planning

It is important that planning not be oversold to the public and that government planners, once in place, proceed with a sense of humility and a deep sensitivity to traditional values. Planning is not a panacea to the social problems of our society; rather, it is a tool for gaining a better understanding of them and better solutions for solving them before they become crises.

It is particularly important to recognize the traditional aversion of the conutry to social and economic planning. To many thoughtful people who are concerned with human freedoms, government planning is only a euphemism for government coercion. To calm those fears and to convince people that a planning office is not simply a camel's nose under the tent, it ought to be made clear from the start that the mandate of the office will be confined to systematic thinking about the future and options for meeting future goals—but will not include the power to compel action toward those goals. What is sought is not a planned society but a planning society.

Secondly, there ought to be some recognition that even the most successful planning process anywhere in free society—the planning employed by leading American corporations today—has not had any magical results. In some of the best examples, such as General Electric, planning has permitted the company to move several steps ahead of where it might otherwise be in anticipating the future. In many other cases, planning has become a powerful instrument for achieving better internal management and discipline. But again, corporate planning has not been a panacea; instead it has been one of several crucial tools for good management, but the most successful companies always pay close attention to their other tools as well.

Finally, it should be remembered that planning, like every form of predicting the future, is always fallible. During his tenure as Counsellor to the President, Daniel P. Moynihan fully recognized the complexity and uncertainty of the many issues. Accordingly, he was reluctant to make precise, reliable projections of the future to the President. Twice, however, he felt sure enough of the future to do so. In the first instance, he was convinced, as were a number of other leading scholars at the time, that the first five years were the most important learning years for a child. In the second instance, he developed a projection on population growth that portended serious problems in the future. Ironically, both times that Moynihan thought he was absolutely safe in predicting the future, he turned out to be dead wrong—a fact that he now acknowledges with his usual good cheer. What these examples show is that every planning system must be closely monitored, it must involve constant feedback of information, and it must be undertaken with a certain degree of modesty.

Notwithstanding some of the shortcomings of the planning process, it is still abundantly clear that the few costs we might encounter from planning are far outweighed by its possible benefits. We have already paid far too high a price as a society for our failure to look ahead. Today, the stakes are higher than they have ever been before because many of our problems are bigger than ever before. Sensible, thoughtful planning has thus become an urgent priority for government and for the nation. As President Eisenhower once said, "Neither a wise man nor a brave man lies down on the tracks of history to wait for the train of the future to run over him." [8]

Chapter Seven

Providing New Direction to Government

In the early 1970s, business and government were both suffering from the excesses of the past. After the go-go years of the 1960s, many large private companies discovered that they were overextended, that their balance sheets were out of kilter, and that they had acquired more than they could successfully manage. Several banks were tied to loans that were questionable at best. For most of these companies, it was critically necessary to begin a process of consolidation and reform, trying to put their organizations on more solid financial footing.

In the federal government, there was also an immediate and pressing need to consolidate and reform so that some added order, direction, and control could be brought to the multitude of domestic programs created in the 1960s. When President Eisenhower left office, there were about a hundred domestic grants programs on the books. By the time President Johnson left office, there were over a thousand—a tenfold increase.

During the 1960s, unprecedented attention had been given to drafting and enacting new governmental programs. This left little time for management or coordination, and, as a result, government seemed to lack a clear sense of purpose or objectivity that might give direction to its overall efforts. This failure only exacerbated the generally weak managerial system within government, a system that, as has been seen, results from inadequate political leadership and insufficient managerial skills among top officials. This chapter focuses on a means of placing government on a more solid managerial foundation by establishing clear objectives and using the objectives to provide direction and to influence the results of government.

One of the most striking examples of failure to define a clear purpose occurred during the 1960s when the Social Security Act was amended. The original act was passed in the 1930s and is probably the most significant piece of social legislation in the twentieth century. But the amendment tacked onto the act provided $75 of federal funds for every $25 put up by the states for additional "services" to welfare recipients such as counseling, job assistance, and health care.

Neither the executive branch nor the Congress recognized initially the inherent defects of the so-called social security programs. First, the services to be supported by the federal funds were not spelled out in the law, which meant that funds could be used for a wide variety of purposes unrelated to the original purpose of the legislation. Furthermore, the law placed no ceiling on the amount of money a state could receive. Thus, so long as they were willing to meet the modest matching requirements, states could make an open-ended raid on the federal kitty for anything that could loosely be construed as social services. It did not take long for officials in many states to spot these windfall loopholes and to devise a variety of ingenious "services" to obtain increased federal funds for their states.

Executives in the Department of Health, Education and Welfare who were responsible for running the program had consistently failed to develop a firm set of objectives or controls over the program. They viewed their mission as simply one of carrying out the law by awarding funds to any states that complied with the law. By the early 1970s, there had been an explosion in spending for a variety of contrived state and county services, and HEW officials were estimating that by 1973 the program would cost $18 billion a year. This unstructured, uncontrolled spending threatened to consume so great a portion of the HEW budget that it would virtually eliminate all opportunities for other social initiatives. Finally, the Congress was persuaded to place a $2.5 billion ceiling on the program, along with a more precise formula for the expenditure of funds.

This example is not unusual. It is illustrative of the problems that arise because of the government's frequent failure to set precise objectives and then to manage programs to meet those objectives. At bottom, there has long been a lack of methodology for the management of government—and beyond this, a lack of recognition that such a methodology is necessary.

An executive entering a new position in private industry will find things quite different from government service. Usually there are a number of managerial tools already available to the private executive so that he (or she) can quickly familiarize himself with all relevant details affecting his authority and can soon begin functioning with little or no dislocation within the organization. These tools include basic management information and planning systems: profit, sales, and budget plans and reports; long-range plans; and product preference and market research reports. All are prepared on a regular basis and are available to anyone who cares to use them. There is, in short, an existing system of management that one can master and through which one can exert leadership and exercise control.

As of today, there are few comparable tools in government, and those available are not widely utilized. Consequently, most government managers have no intrinsic framework within which clear objectives can be established and pursued. As a result, there is rarely any clear direction provided to the government bureaucracy and little or no real control over the activities of that bureaucracy. Yet there is no question that government can be more responsive and more effective if the chief executive and his senior appointees will adopt and consistently apply a system of management.

THE NEED FOR OBJECTIVES

No agency has achieved a reputation for mismanagement in so short a period of time as the mammoth Department of Health, Education and Welfare. It is problematical whether this reputation is fully deserved. Political considerations conspire to make HEW—the nation's largest single organization in terms of spending power—a natural whipping boy for a number of factions both inside and outside government.

In 1969, HEW Secretary Robert Finch commissioned, under my direction, a thorough review of the effectiveness with which HEW programs were managed. Our investigation found that the question of the effectiveness of management per se was not considered to be an issue in the department because the term "management" was so narrowly construed. To most people, management meant housekeeping, administration, logistics, efficiency studies, computer applications, parking places, office space, supplies, and related activities. Management was rarely, if ever, construed to involve broader tasks such as goal setting and planning. Few had ever aspired to the broader view of management as a means of running government.

Not surprisingly, the review determined that in order to make HEW "manageable," fundamental changes were needed, including the development and establishment of long-term goals and specific objectives; the assignment of responsibility and delegation of authority in a manner carefully determined to be most conducive to the achievement of those goals and objectives; the development of a system for monitoring, measuring, and evaluating progress toward the achievement of goals and objectives; and the development of a process of corrective action to modify goals or objectives as needed, to expedite their achievement, or to change methods of implemention in order to achieve results.

None of these basic functions was being performed at HEW. The various bureaus of the department had only a vague concept of the Serretary's priorities. Other than the normal budgetary process, no requests were made and no directions were issued to the bureaus that had a continuing influence on their operations. The Secretary and Assistant Secretaries received inadequate information with which to evaluate the performance of the department, nor did they have any means of overseeing the department in a comprehensive or consistent manner. In short, policymakers suffered from a lack of information, while policy managers suffered from a lack of guidance.

The study concluded that for the Secretary to fulfill his responsibilities, he must ensure that his major policy initiatives were carried out, not by injecting himself into day-to-day operating decisions, but rather by specifying to key bureau managers the results he wished to achieve and then holding these people accountable for those results. From a management standpoint, the conclusions appear simplistic. From the perspective of the HEW hierarchy and bureaucracy, they were almost revolutionary.

Unfortunately, what we found at HEW has become typical in government. Most elected chief executives and appointed cabinet heads never really gain control over their organizations. They reign but do not rule because they lack any means of providing systematic direction and evaluating results on a consistent basis. They sit atop large, complex organizations manned by career officials whose own objectives may differ radically from the objectives of the chief executive and his appointed representatives. The higher the executive's position and the larger the organization, the less time he has to devote to any one area, and the more necessary it is for him to pursue his objectives through the work of others.

Clearly, a great deal of governmental authority and responsibility must be delegated to subordinates, the President to his cabinet, the cabinet to bureau chiefs, and so on. Most chief executives do delegate authority, but often they fail to provide a clear indication of the direction the subordinates are to take and the results that are to be achieved. That is not really a delegation but an abdication of responsibility.

When decisions flow to the top for decision, they are frequently presented in a fashion that virtually eliminates true discretionary power in the chief executive. Subordinate officials cleverly design the decision they want into the presentation of the problem and recommendations for its resolution. This is the inevitable result of allowing decisions to flow up the bureaucratic pyramid rather than controlling the decision-making process with a clearly defined and communicated strategy and sense of direction.

In the absence of well-defined objectives, there is also a powerful tendency among top government officials to focus only on high-visibility problems or on major new initiatives. Commonly, it is only the top official's intense (and temporary) concern for sporadic problems and initiatives that flows through to lower levels, resulting in the concentration of almost all executive resources on a few "hot" items. This tendency is reinforced by the long time periods that are required—from two to ten years—to move forward from identification of a problem to enactment and implementation of remedial legislation. By the time this arduous, laborious process is completed, the executive and the congressional leadership have almost exhausted their interest. They are content to leave the implementation of new progrms to the bureaucracy while they turn their attention to the next problem in the headlines.

Even with the best of intentions effective managerial follow-through is an especially difficult task in the public sector. The average political appointee, whose horizon is already foreshortened by the brief period that he plans to spend in government, almost invariably finds a series of crises—some real, some apparent—that can gobble up every moment of the day. As one Assistant Secretary of Labor put it, "Government is a firehouse; you put out one fire and three more break out behind you." The energy crisis, a trucker's strike, an outbreak of hostilities abroad, an unusually bad statistic for unemployment, and similar events can easily divert management attention away from important long-range goals in order to deal with short-term exigencies.

This practice of jumping from one "hot," highly visible issue to another without regard to long-range objectives is encouraged by political necessity and the short attention span of the national media. Richard Neustadt outlines the problem by noting:

> A President's priorities are set out not by the relative importance of a task, but by the relative necessity for him to do it. He deals first with the things that are required for him next. Deadlines rule his personal agenda . . . . The net result may be a far cry from the order of priorities that would appeal to scholars or to columnists—or to the President himself.[1]

When not consumed in hot issues, many top officials have a tendency to become totally immersed in the maze of everyday business. As any government executive can attest, all one's time can be spent on "processing the flow"—dealing with correspondence, responding to congressional inquiries, returning phone calls, reading and initialing routine issue papers, being briefed by subordinates, and the like. Most, if not all, of this routine would go in exactly the same way if the executive were not there at all. Yet the time devoted to routine functions leaves no time to develop or implement key initiatives.

A final problem that hampers the ability of the top officials to plan and carry out program objectives in a consistent, effective manner is the difficulty of measuring results. Standards for measuring performance are uneven and arbitrary. It is often impossible to isolate cause and effect in public policy. For example, did the poor student do better in reading this year because his teacher's skills were improved by a government grant, or because a government-subsidized lunch program improved his nutritional situation, or because he is a year older and more ready to learn? The answers may never be clear. As a consequence, progress tends to be measured in terms of activities rather than accomplishments. The Food and Nutrition Service at HEW measured their success by the amount of dollars spent and number of families reached as opposed to the level of nutrition among the nation's poor, which should have been their primary standard of achievement. They were simply reflecting a chronic condition cited by Elliot Richardson, who has held as many cabinet posts as anyone else in history. "All too often uncertainty about objectives leads to a trap that might be called management by activity," Richardson said. "This is a euphoric state of mind which equates more with better, which suggests that, as doing good things produces good results, doing twice as many good things will quite obviously produce twice as many good results. In other words, if you don't know where you're going, run faster." [2]

A COMMON-SENSE APPROACH

If the executive branch of government is to be managed effectively, it clearly needs a system for setting priorities, pinpointing responsibility for their achievement, requiring follow-through, and generating enough feedback that programs can be monitored and evaluated from the top. The peculiarities of government demand not a complex system but a common-sense approach to managing that most people implicitly resort to in the conduct of their everyday lives.

In the early 1970s, we established such a system within the federal government, a system called "management by objectives" that I shall describe in a moment. First, let us understand the simple, common-sense notions that are at the foundation of "MBO." The approach begins with each key person deciding what is most important, in priority order, to his or her area of responsibility. The principal questions to be answered are "What are the most important objectives the organization should accomplish this year? How are they to be accomplished? Who should undertake them? How can I determine if we are succeeding or not?"

Because not everything worthwhile can be accomplished, it is necessary to set priorities. To use a simple analogy, if we are to take a sightseeing vacation across the United States, we could not see everything, but would select what we most wanted to see—let's say Philadelphia, Washington, the Grand Canyon, Yellowstone, Yosemite, and San Francisco. We assume that a finite period of time is available to us, and we assume further that an accommodation can be made with each member of the family, though the range of accommodation will be affected by external circumstances such as finances.

In managerial terms we are providing a framework that ensures, through the explicit announcement of desired accomplishments, that an organization has clearly and precisely decided where it is going and what it is going to accomplish, and that the goals have been set in a mutually agreeable fashion. Admittedly, even the establishment of this framework within an organization is not always easy to accomplish, but there is much to be gained from trying: each individual participates in setting a direction for the organization, increasing the individual's commitment and motivation toward achieving these objectives, as well as helping various members of the team work together more effectively.

Once the objectives or priorities are fixed, the next step is to develop a plan for meeting them in a timely fashion. In our trip analogy, we would use a map to chart our course across the country and would plan when to arrive at different destinations so that each major site can be reached and the trip can be completed before the holiday ends. Again, this is merely common sense and is intended to ensure that all participants maintain a sense of direction, that specific interim steps or milestones are achieved on time, and that the process results in successful completion. The plan does not have to be rigid. It is likely that some priorities will change over a period of time. But change is easier to accommodate if the goal is clear from the beginning. This makes it easier to weigh the impact of change on existing plans. Referring again to the trip analogy, we might encounter bad weather and decide to detour south to visit Carlsbad Caverns. In making this decision, however, we know we are giving up the opportunity to see Yellowstone. Along the way, of course, it is necessary to measure progress, determining whether the milestones are being met on time and taking corrective actions where needed.

In government, a major payoff from this common-sense approach is reached when executives at all levels begin setting and working toward objectives that support those of their superiors, pyramid-fashion. Ultimately, the process is not so much systemic as attitudinal. The goal is to get every party to start thinking not about the routine functioning involved in process, but about ways to bring about real improvement in his or her area—how he can find a better way to approach his job and serve the public's interests. As attitudes change and people commit themselves to specific accomplishments within a given time span, "managing for results"—or "management by objectives"—becomes a way of life. The value lies not in the structure but in the concept, which generates clear and precise thinking about plans and priorities.

It is a selective process that requires the separation of important items from those that are routine. It is based upon the adoption or development of objectives by the same manager who will ultimately be held responsible for their achievement. Since plans for achieving objectives are required, it provides the executive and his subordinates with a simple method for focusing continued attention on the highest priorities despite the distractions that may arise during the year. Finally, it enables the chief executive to delegate more responsibility with greater confidence, since he has agreed in advance on what his subordinates are to achieve and he has the means to follow their progress toward achievement.

Management authority Peter Drucker has summed up the problem and the solution in this way:

> Public service institutions are prone to the deadly disease of . . . mistaking rules, regulations, and the smooth functioning of machinery for accomplishment, and the self-interest of the agency for public service. Public service institutions, in other words, particularly need objectives and concentration of efforts on goals and results—that is management.[3]

SETTING DIRECTION: MANAGEMENT BY OBJECTIVE

Immediately following the 1972 election, President Nixon instructed Roy Ash and me, as Director and Deputy Director of the Office of Management and Budget (OMB), to develop a method of management and an organization to oversee the new system during his second term. Acting on those instructions, we were able to introduce for the first time a government-wide "management by objectives" program. While at HEW, I had successfully begun such a program, the first in a major government agency. Ash had pioneered the same techniques in building Litton Industries into a multimillion-dollar success, and he had seen them used to great advantage in a number of other companies. It was quite natural, then, that we turned to this time-proven formula to help the President manage government.

In late 1972 and early 1973 we refined the approach in a series of meetings at Camp David and received the President's enthusiastic endorsement of our proposal. He professed to see little political advantage in the new approach since he perceived management to be outside the interest of those who regularly assess the presidency. Nevertheless, he believed that the MBO approach could give his administration a stronger overview of government and that the information it provided would give him and his appointees greater ability to run the government. He further realized that, in many respects, what may appear to be routine operations in the agencies—writing regulations, approving grants, allocating budgets, etc.—actually involves a great deal of policymaking. Even though a recalcitrant Congress might block his major legislative initiatives, he thought that considerable progress could be made toward his goals by exercising greater leadership within the executive branch itself.

Ash and I began with the conviction that we had to have full agency commitment to MBO. We could not push the program through or make it work without that commitment. As one colleague put it at the time, "You can call them the President's objectives or you can call them the objectives of the Faery Queen. But if the agency doesn't take them on board, then they are dead." Initially there was a great deal of skepticism to overcome, even among some of the veterans on the OMB staff. They remembered the complicated, highly structured paper process used by the Planning, Programming and Budgeting System (PPBS) when it was initially implemented; they also remembered how PPBS was eventually cast aside by most agencies. Furthermore, our new approach was initially perceived as a threat by many seasoned agency people—a method of robbing them of their ability to function independently and forcing them to become an integral part of the total management process. They were partially right. However, we took great pains to explain the approach in detail and to persuade agency heads that it was an excellent vehicle for improving their perspectives on their own agencies. Meetings on the subject were held at the agencies rather than at the White House to avoid any appearance of intimidation. The program was presented not as a means of imposing new objectives on them from the White House or OMB, but as a management tool for the agencies themselves. OMB was to act only as a mechanic, "keeping the wheels greased" and facilitating communications between the President and the agencies.

To further ensure acceptance of the approach by key government managers, we determined that a minimum of paperwork would be required and that the program would be applied flexibly from agency to agency, taking into account their differing roles and the individual management styles of their top executives.

The purposes of the MBO initiative, as extracted from an internal paper written at the time, were simply these:

> Improve management throughout the Federal government in order to deliver more effective services to the American people.
>
> Assure that what the President wants accomplished is accomplished.
>
> Provide a program that is so relevant, so important, and so simple that department heads will play the principal role in program input and operation.
>
> Establish a method of setting priorities in order to focus the manpower and fiscal resources of the President's staff, including OMB.
>
> Open the line of communication between top OMB officials and heads of departments/agencies to discuss department and agency problems.
>
> Assure accountability for performance on the part of department heads.

Twenty-one of the government's biggest agencies, accounting for 95 percent of all federal expenditures, were chosen to participate in the program. The Office of Management and Budget was charged with responsibility for co-ordinating the review of agency objectives before they were submitted to the President. On April 18, 1973, President Nixon personally launched the initiative with a memorandum to each of the twenty-one agency heads, saying:

> I am asking each department and agency head to seek a sharper focus on the *results* which the various activities under his or her direction are aimed at achieving. . . . Your listed objectives should include new policy initiatives, major operational achievements which can be made in current programs, giving particular attention to objectives which you consider to be of Presidential-level importance.

From time to time thereafter, the President provided personal reinforcement to this direction. For example, his 1975 budget message in January 1974 stated: "These objectives will not simply be identified and then filed away and forgotten. Specific results are to be achieved by specific deadlines. These commitments will be reviewed continually and will guide day to day operations until the objectives are met."

It is instructive to note that the greatest problem of the whole approach was encountered right at the outset—in obtaining truly meaningful objectives from the agencies. An assistant secretary for management in one department stated: "You can't imagine how difficult it is for intelligent men to define what it is they're trying to accomplish. People here had assumed that what they were doing was resulting in good. MBO forces you to define what you mean by doing good."

Initially, objectives were often set forth in ideal terms, e.g., "the abolition of crime in society" or "the eradication of serious disease." Since these ideals are utopian, they could not be disputed; but since they are virtually unachievable, they could not possibly be used to hold anyone accountable for an achievement. Nor did they provide any direction to the organization and its members regarding what to do next week, next month, or next year. We also recognized that in some cases agencies resorted to vague generalities in order to avoid the risk of alienating the interest groups or congressional committees constantly watching over their shoulders.

It required a great deal of guidance and dialogue with the agencies to ensure the formulation of precise, consistent objectives that reflected sensible priorities and whose accomplishment could be reasonably measured. For example, an initial agency objective for the U.S. Maritime Administration was to "make the U.S. Merchant Marine the most competitive in the world." Through a series of discussions, this objective was modified in several stages to:

> Reduce the gap between domestic and foreign shipyard productivity and reduce subsidy rates from 39 percent by June 1973 to 35 percent by June 1975.
> Reduce or eliminate ship operating subsidies and reduce the base ship crew for bulk ships supported by subsidy to 24 by January 1975.

In a similar manner, an HEW objective was:

> Improve health care cost control and reduce medical inflation by (1) cutting the annual growth rate in hospital charges and doctor's fees to 6 percent and 2.5 percent respectively, and (2) saving $100 million in Medicare and $200 million in Medicaid through a reduction in unnecessary utilization.

Although no ceiling was placed on the number of "presidential" objectives, we encouraged the agencies to settle on between eight and twelve so that they could determine in their own minds what their highest priorities should be. As we reviewed each objective, our main concerns were its intrinsic importance and its consistency with stated presidential policies and priorities; its feasibility within budget constraints; the extent of its measurability (although many key objectives could not be measured); and above all, whether it would reflect a genuine accomplishment—something they would have to stretch themselves to reach—rather than a routine performance of duties. With regard to the last point, we asked for a brief action plan showing both intermediate milestones and projected completion dates for each objective. The program was to be dynamic: objectives could be added or dropped during the year as circumstances dictated a shifting of priorities, and emphasis was to be placed on achieving an objective or a segment of an objective within one year.

No constraints were placed on the types of objectives that could be submitted, so that the agencies proposed a wide variety, ranging from the formulation of a national transportation policy statement to the enactment of legislation permitting an Alaskan pipeline. Most objectives fell into four general categories: policy formation and program definition, legislative enactment, programmatic results, and administrative improvement.[4]

While these presidential objectives were viewed as extremely important, they were to be only the tip of the iceberg. In order to achieve the fundamental and enduring reform we desired, it was also imperative for the agencies to establish secretarial, bureau, and division objectives. Secretarial objectives, second in priority to presidential, would be monitored by the agency head and his key staff, and the agency head in turn would hold bureau chiefs responsible for their objectives, and so on. General guidance was provided to the agencies in establishing this approach to managing by objectives, but the agencies themselves were to decide on the precise means of implementation based on their own size and mission, the nature of their programs, and the management style of their leadership. The pyramidal approach to choosing objectives was well illustrated at HEW: during a single year's time, the Secretary of the department tracked seventy different objectives; HEW agency heads and regional directors tracked approximately three hundred objectives; and agency bureaus tracked about fifteen hundred.

We intentionally avoided the preparation of manuals that would tell the agencies how to prepare their objectives and establish a successful MBO program. It was thought that manuals would automatically relegate the program to a low-level staff activity. Manuals would also be used as a crutch to find cookbook solutions and ready-made systems, instead of thinking carefully about what the agency's own situation demanded and what would work for it. As a sweetener, a number of reports and other requirements that OMB had traditionally extracted from the agencies were eliminated. We thus gained favor with harassed agency officials, increased the time available to devote to the management-by-objectives approach, and underlined the importance the President ascribed to the implementation of MBO.

In place of forms, manuals, and reports, we focused on personal communications—a series of face-to-face conferences (described more fully in the next chapter) and interactions between agency personnel and a newly created team within OMB called "Management Associates." To show the seriousness that the President attached to the program, we immediately recruited some thirty highly talented men and women from the private sector or from other agencies to become management associates. They were to spend their energies on implementing the management-by-objectives approach. They provided day-to-day assistance to the department in preparing objectives and worked closely with OMB budget personnel in identifying problems, reviewing agency progress, and preparing analyses that highlighted key issues and problems for the top-level conferences.

Beginning in the fall of 1974, agencies were required to submit objectives for the coming year at the same time they submitted their budget requests. In any management process, the development of the budget should be a basic tool for implementing and reaching an agency's objectives. Moreover, we hoped that by establishing a link with a process as permanent as budget preparation, we would increase the permanence of management by objectives and encourage more explicit statements of the purposes for which money was to be spent.

At two major departments, HEW and Interior, an interesting wrinkle called the "cooperative agency management system" (CAMS) was introduced and proved effective. As noted earlier, MBO gave each of the departments latitude in the way they selected their objectives. These two departments used that discretion to establish a systematic process for determining the objectives and tied the process to the annual preparation of the budget. This process is well described in an article appearing in the January–February 1977 issue of the *Harvard Business Review* written by two men who helped to install the system, Laurence E. Lynn, Jr. and John M. Seidl.

After initial objectives were submitted by the agencies, we set up a series of management conferences, attended by the agency head and his staff members, our top OMB staff, and other selected White House officials. In these sessions, final agreements were reached on objectives so that they could then be submitted to the President. Once the President completed his review of the agency submissions, he personally communicated his thoughts to the agency head. In many instances, he noted areas of particular interest to him. In every case, he emphasized the need to be constantly on the alert for new initiatives that could be added as the year unfolded.

The problems and frustrations encountered in setting up the MBO program were substantial. In addition to the difficulty of defining objectives, the most common point of resistance came from those who did not feel their missions could be quantified or measured and who therefore saw little utility in setting objectives. We found that for many functions, such as research and diplomacy, this objection was valid. Consequently, we did not insist on quantification and precision in all cases, asking instead that the most important aims of the agency be stated for that year, regardless of whether or not they were truly measurable. Others objected that the result of MBO would be a rigid system with piles of paperwork. This criticism was met by emphasizing the need to review and modify objectives on a continuing basis and by specifically precluding written reports in favor of the face-to-face meetings. Finally, some skeptics saw this approach as a means to centralize control in the White House. However, by giving agency heads latitude in developing and implementing their objectives and by not requiring formal reports, we deflected much of this criticism.

Finally, while he supported the effort and provided periodic reinforcement, the President's Watergate problems precluded his becoming more deeply involved. He did not, for instance, personally conduct sessions with individual cabinet officers to set objectives or assess their progress. His withdrawal reduced MBO's impact and acceptance, but in large part we at OMB were able to compensate by holding regular reviews on behalf of the President.

THE VALUE OF THE OBJECTIVES APPROACH

Shortly after the MBO program was introduced, most top officials recognized its usefulness in running their operations, and many vigorously initiated the process deep in their own agencies. At an early management conference, Agriculture Secretary Earl Butz commented, "Maybe we have something here; maybe for the first time we will be able to coordinate positions and get concrete results." Shortly thereafter, he held a two-day conference at Camp David with his assistant secretaries and bureau chiefs to initiate MBO throughout the Department of Agriculture. In the months that followed,

Secretary Butz met every two weeks with his top line officers and personal staff to ensure that initial plans were properly carried out.

Among the many concrete examples of the success of
MBO, those that pleased me the most occurred at HEW
where I had helped to introduce the program in 1970. For
example, in fiscal year 1971, the first full year of MBO's
operation in that department, an objective was set by the
secretary to train and place 35,000 welfare recipients in
meaningful jobs. The objective seemed beyond hope, for
the agency that ran the program, the Social and Rehabilitation Service (SRS), had never achieved such impressive
results. SRS faced an uphill battle: it had to convince state
agencies receiving rehabilitation funds that the goal could
be achieved; and, of course, the task of rehabilitating welfare recipients has never been an easy one. Nonetheless, as
former HEW Assistant Secretary Rodney H. Brady has
pointed out, SRS actually exceeded its goal "by establishing a
results-oriented objective, carefully planning for its accomplishment, and communicating it to all levels of government."[5]
In that year, 40,000 welfare recipients were trained and
moved from welfare rolls to job payrolls. As a result of that
experience, HEW could also plan for the successful rehabilitation of 69,000 welfare recipients the following year—a
38 percent increase, or approximately double the normal
projection based only on historical trend lines. MBO thus
served as an enormously useful prod to achieve results far
above the routine operation of the department.

By June of 1974, the end of the first year of using MBO
throughout government, we submitted a report to the President on what had been accomplished. While there were
a number of instances where performance fell short of the
mark, we found that there had been significant progress toward the achievement of most objectives. For example:

Each agency had an energy utilization objective, and
the agencies as a whole achieved a reduction of 19 percent

for the year. The largest consumer of energy, the Defense Department, achieved an energy savings of approximately 25 percent.

At a time of rampant inflation, the objective of record agricultural production was realized, with farm income reaching the second highest level ever, despite substantial reductions in government support programs.

The accession objectives for the all-volunteer force were essentially met with the Air Force reaching 100 percent, the Navy 99 percent, and the Army 96 percent.

An effective state/federal effort was launched to cut back on the number of ineligible and incorrect payments made under the welfare program (Aid to Families with Dependent Children). Cooperative steps were initiated to reduce ineligible and incorrect payments from an incredible 41 percent to 8 percent by the end of fiscal year 1975.

Many agency officials credited the MBO approach with contributing a great deal to the achievements above as well as progress toward many other goals. There were also encouraging signs that the existence of objectives and action plans helped new agency heads get on top of their operations more rapidly. At the Environmental Protection Agency (EPA), for example, Russell Train was sworn in as the new Administrator on September 14, 1973, and only thirty-five days later he presided over a management conference to review progress on the agency's presidential objectives. Train played an active leadership role in the discussions and noted that his ability to do so was directly related to "the excellent management process" that made it possible for him to focus on the material within a relatively short period of time.

There was no question that the existence of specific objectives also served the interests of the President. In many cases, a high-priority objective such as national health insurance was the subject of a specific meeting between the

President and an agency head. Presidential objectives were also discussed at cabinet meetings, and other broader based sessions were scheduled with him as the need arose. In addition, agency heads and the President's representative at the Office of Management and Budget met frequently to discuss the objectives of greatest importance. In the absence of MBO, it is highly doubtful whether many of these discussions would ever have occurred. This same benefit was realized also at the agency and bureau level. As a top-level official at the National Institute of Health commented when management by objective was explained to him, "I'm not so sure of what this MBO system can accomplish in our agency, but if it gives me an hour or so each month to discuss my priorities with the Secretary [of HEW], then I'm all for it."

Finally, the technique not only proved to be just a good management tool, but also paid rich dividends in the areas of policy development and political concerns:

> Setting clear objectives often helped to enlighten the public on the President's domestic philosophy. The emphasis in the early seventies on limiting federal authority and transferring more power to cities and states was significantly enhanced by all relevant agencies working toward specific objectives related to this aim.
>
> The use of objectives tended to avoid "no win" situations. There is always room for conflict between Congress and an administration, and a hostile Congressional committee can easily rig oversight hearings to prove that the administration has failed to solve a particular problem. We were able to counter such tactics and diffuse possible criticisms by setting and meeting reasonable objectives, in many agencies, such as implementing new water-pollution control legislation at the Envinronmental Protection Agency. By setting up our own objective standards for measuring our record, we could thus head off propaganda efforts by the partisan opposition.

MBO also helped to overcome dangers inherent in new initiatives. New initiatives, and particularly new legislation, usually run into two kinds of trouble. The first is the problem of overpromising and underdelivering. The second is that even bad programs become permanent fixtures because it is impossible to prove definitively that they are worthless. Goal setting can help overcome both of these problems.

We installed the MBO program throughout government in a two-year period, 1973 and 1974. As of 1977, it remained institutionalized in departments and agencies as diverse as the Department of Defense, HEW, Commerce, the Environmental Protection Agency, and the Energy Research and Development Administration. However, as stated earlier, any approach such as this depends for its survival on continued interest and emphasis at the top. Since this emphasis has been spotty, the MBO approach has been shunted aside in a number of agencies, and it needs renewed interest from the top to be fully effective and to provide the needed system of management in the federal government. In short, despite resistance in some quarters, a number of imperfections, and a short life in some agencies, the evidence clearly supports the view that management by objectives is of significant value in making government work.

After reviewing the management-by-objective approach in 1975, Peter Drucker stated, "The introduction of MBO into public service institutions, especially into government agencies during the last few years, may thus be the first step towards making public service institutions effective.

This common-sense approach to management can and should be applied across the entire federal government and, in my view, could also be invaluable to state and local governments. The precise application will vary, of course, with the particular needs and characteristics of a governmental organization, but the fundamental principles should not differ significantly. These ten principles, extracted from the preceding paragraphs, can be stated simply as follows:

1. The top man must be committed to using the approach as a means of delegating with confidence. He must make clear that MBO has a high priority in his organization, and he must give his total support to a process whereby objectives will be set and monitored. Our experience showed that whenever the head of a department or agency failed to become personally involved, the system deteriorated badly. This involvement is mandatory for success.

2. At the outset, clear objectives must be enunciated and communicated to the organization as a whole. These objectives might be those of the chief executive or they may be developed by the lower levels of the organization and only adopted by top management. The critical point is that they be enunciated and understood throughout the organization.

3. Once the objectives are set, the system should work on a line-manager-to-subordinate basis, not on a staff-to-staff basis. That is the only way to keep the lines of authority straight and to ensure that all parties place sufficient importance on achieving objectives.

4. Every subordinate (e.g., cabinet officer, bureau chief, etc.), should be required to set priorities and establish objectives. These objectives should support those of the next higher level in the organization and, when aggregated, should ensure accomplishment of the chief executive's goals. Each of these subordinates should in turn require supportive objectives from people down the line so that managing for results becomes a way of life—a way of thinking—for all levels of management.

5. Insist that objectives are stated in terms of end results to be achieved and require simple plans or milestones with assigned responsibilities, so that the accomplishment of each

milestone in a timely manner will ultimately lead to achievement of the overall objectives.

6. Invest liberally in talented staff support. Setting objectives is the very heart of the managing process, yet it is new to most elements of government and will not come easily even with adequate support.

7. Be flexible in approach, recognizing the unique characteristics and requirements of different organizations, and keep paperwork (manuals, forms, reports, etc.) to an absolute minimum. It is especially important that an MBO program be tailored to the particular working habits of the chief executive officer.

8. Hold frequent follow-up meetings, preferably between the chief executive and his subordinates, to evaluate progress and plan corrective actions.

9. Conduct a comprehensive review at the end of the year to measure the progress that has been made and to evaluate performance based on this progress. This review provides a solid foundation for planning the objectives of the coming year.

10. Be willing to risk failure. Any system that consistently achieves 100 percent of its objectives has set its sights too low.

These principles constitute nothing more than a commonsense means of systematically attacking the problems and opportunities of government. Despite their simplicity, however, the application of these principles can have a profound impact upon the effectiveness of an organization. If faithfully followed throughout the organization, an MBO program will help to communicate clear priorities, ensuring that all members of the team are pulling in the same direction. It enables the chief to delegate with confidence since he has agreed in advance on what his subordinates will achieve and has a means of tracking their progress. Setting and following objectives forces all key executives to escape the welter of routine requirements in order to identify and act on key breakthrough opportunities, focus on actual results, and follow through important initiatives to completion rather than jumping from one hot spot to the next. This approach also provides the means by which the chief can evaluate the performance of his people and organizations—a subject that we will turn to in a later chapter. Finally, objectives provide an intelligent means of allocating scarce budget resources, the subject we will consider fully in the following chapter.

Chapter Eight

Putting Federal Money to Work

On the average, wage earners in this country spend more than four months of the year earning money that is paid in taxes to all levels of government. Many of the federal expenditures supported by these taxes defy common sense. Consider, for example, the following: $69,111 to study the long-term storage of acorns in Poland; $70,000 to study perspiration of Australian aborigines; $375,000 to study Frisbees; $15,000 for a survey of Yugoslavian lizards; $21,000 to investigate the mating calls and paratoid gland secretions of the central American toad; $5,000 to analyze violin varnish; and $19,300 to figure out why children fall off tricycles.

Finding such egregious examples of federal spending is easy; in fact, it is quickly becoming a national joke. Unfortunately, however, federal spending can no longer be a laughing matter, as its influence on society has become more and more pervasive. Any effort to improve the effectiveness of government must give serious consideration to the budget.

The Food and Nutrition Service of the Department of Agriculture provides a prime example of how the best-laid plans of the government have often gone astray. The service administers fifteen different programs aimed at improving child nutrition. These programs in turn provide subsidies for forty different types of meals, so that today there is the regular lunch, the reduced lunch, the free lunch, etc. It is no small wonder that we suffer from bureaucratic indigestion.

The programs grew out of the Depression years of the 1930s when the government was eagerly looking for ways to distribute farm surpluses. Eventually, however, the food programs became a favorite vehicle of social reform. By 1977, the federal government was spending roughly $3.4 billion a year on a hodgepodge of food programs. Over $660 million of this amount subsidized students whose family income exceeded $11,000—far above the poverty level—while investigators found that at least 700,000 children from poor families received no benefits whatever. Thus, even today, students in Fairfax County, Virginia, home of many well-paid civil servants, are receiving a 25¢ subsidy on every school lunch, while children from certain poverty areas are getting nothing. Further changes enacted by Congress threaten to result in even more government spending for nonneedy children than for those truly in need.

Because of built-in inequities and because some have obviously outlived their usefulness, these fifteen child nutrition programs will never serve the public well or deliver proper value no matter how superbly they are managed. Many government programs suffer from identical problems. Their structure and targets are faulty or out of date, and their budget levels are pushed to irrational levels by powerful interest groups allied with congressional committees and the program's bureaucracy.

Because so many programs seem indestructible and because their continued growth is almost beyond control, the federal budget is expanding at an ominous speed. From 1960 to 1976, for instance, federal spending increased over fourfold to close to $400 billion, and between 1954 and 1976, spending by government at all levels in the United States rose sixfold; today the government spends more than one out of every three dollars in our country. If government spending continues to increase at the same rate as in the 1960s and '70s, it will account for *two* out of every three dollars spent in the United States by the year 2000.

It would be difficult to overstate how destructive the relentless growth of the budget has become. Not only are tax dollars wasted and public confidence undermined, but budget pressures have added significant fuel to the fires of inflation, obliged future generations to pay off mountains of debt, and crowded out hopes for initiating new programs or expanding those that are particularly worthwhile. The central issue in this chapter is how to bring a runaway budget under control so that money can be directed to those areas where the need is greatest and where it can do the most good.

OVERRIDING BUDGET PROBLEMS

The budget process itself is relatively well managed. In fact, budgeting is probably the best-developed of all management processes in government. Over the years, it has been elevated almost to the level of a science; and thousands of professionals devote their entire careers to its mastery. While there are opportunities to strengthen management of the budget process, the bigger payoffs for making government more effective will come by setting enlightened policies, and by persuading Congress to attack the more significant problem of weeding out ineffective programs and making room for new initiatives.

Uncontrollable Expenditures

The principal deterrent to intelligent budgeting is that for the most part the budget in any given year is not determined by the executive branch or the Congress, nor is it developed in an objective, unbiased manner. Rather, the bulk of spending is determined by the laws enacted to meet a different set of needs, and that spending, once started, is generally perpetuated.

To understand why so much of the budget is literally outside the control of the administration and to a certain extent beyond the control of Congress, consider the social security program. When a President or the Congress want to tinker with social security they find that prior laws dictate what benefits people are to receive and when they are to receive them. No discretion can be used in changing these payments or controlling the number of beneficiaries unless Congress shows uncharacteristic courage in rewriting the law. Similarly, payments to individuals in other major programs such as Medicaid, public assistance, food stamps, veterans benefits, civilian and military retirement, and unemployment benefits are determined by laws enacted in earlier years—laws that contain automatic escalators and, therefore, cannot be controlled in the present. In 1967, open-ended programs such as these amounted to 36 percent of the federal budget; in 1978, they are expected to reach 58 percent of the budget. Moreover, the government must also make certain payments each year on "prior-year contracts and obligations" such as the national debt, and these too are beyond the reach of budgeting discretion. Just to pay the interest on the national debt cost over $40 billion in 1977 and amounted to the third largest item in the budget. All told, "uncontrollable" expenditures in the federal government today are thought to be 75 to 80 percent of the budget. Less than one dollar out of four is left for annual determination by the President and the Congress. At HEW, by one count, "uncontrollables" are a gigantic 94 percent of the departmental budget. The federal government is almost on automatic pilot.

These mammoth uncontrollables and their large year-to-year increases are particularly alarming because they are rising faster than the growth in the economy and faster than the government's tax receipts. Thus, in the absence of further deficit spending, they are effectively crowding out opportunities for new initiatives and new programs. For example, in the preparations for the 1975 federal budget, the administration determined that it would not be economically prudent to increase spending by more than $25 billion over 1974. That would still leave a sizable budget deficit of $10 billion and would help to increase inflationary pressures in the economy. But in considering the $25 billion extra spending available to us, I was shocked to learn that $24.7 billion would automatically be gobbled up by uncontrollable expenditures already built into the budget. That left a grand total of $300 million for expansion of other programs or for new initiatives.

Of that quarter of the budget that is popularly thought to be controllable, it is worth pointing out that a good deal of it is also beyond the power of the President or the executive branch to change from year to year. Programs such as aid to education, for example, cannot be cut by large amounts in any given year without impairing the viability of a particular school district. Similar programs exist in the areas of health, housing, vocational rehabilitation, welfare assistance, job training, and a range of other areas. Moreover, much of the defense budget—which is officially labeled "controllable"—is in fact subject to severe constraints. Certainly, not even the most radical opponent of the defense establishment would cut more than 20 percent of defense spending in a given year, nor would the most hawkish supporter of national security find useful ways of adding more than 20 percent.

Considering the relatively fixed elements of the human resource, social service, and defense components of the budget, only about 10 percent of the budget is truly subject to the executive management from year to year. Thus, government executives find they are limited if they want to use the budget as a management tool in forging new directions, launching new initiatives, or making judicious choices between alternative courses of action. There are simply not enough funds left over to do these things adequately after satisfying the huge appetite of uncontrollables.

Perpetuation of Ineffective Programs

Just as social security illustrates the inexorable growth of beneficial but uncontrollable programs, the perpetuation of Public Health Service hospitals shows how impervious even the least efficient programs can be to effective management. In 1798, the federal government created a hospital network to care for merchant seamen because there was a shortage of hospital beds, merchant seamen were poorly paid, and the seamen habitually contracted contagious and hard-to-cure diseases in their travels. But in 1977 the 272,000 merchant seamen in the United States had incomes twice the national average, their disease rate had diminished, scientific advances had quelled the chances of their diseases spreading, and the country had an excess of hospital beds of some 25 percent. Yet the Public Health Service (PHS) still had over five thousand federal employees running eight PHS hospitals and thirty-four outpatient clinics to provide free health care to these privately employed, well-compensated seamen.

The rationale for the PHS hospital system had thus disappeared, and Presidents Johnson, Nixon, and Ford all proposed phasing them out. Yet they remain. Why? Well, for one thing, the seamen have a powerful lobby, and in the states and districts where the hospitals are located the seamen exercise considerable influence at the ballot box. Congressmen pay attention to such details. Then, too, there is the little matter of the Public Health Service clinic on Fourth and "D" Streets, S.W., in Washington, D.C., that is only a few hundreds yards from the Capitol. More than one member of Congress is reported to have spent an afternoon at the local PHS clinic receiving free dental or medical care.[1]

The continuation of these PHS hospitals again illustrates the futility of good management in a bad program. No matter how well they are managed, these hospitals will not provide full value to the American people.

The "Iron Triangle"

The endurance of the PHS hospitals also reaffirms the powerful role of entrenched interests in perpetuating even the most outmoded and unnecessary programs. The hospitals are by no means an unusual example. Almost every program that is blessed by statutory enactment and receives its first appropriation creates a budgetary precedent. The fact that funds have been spent on something at least once in the past greatly increases the chances that money will be voted for it again, and probably at the same level or higher. New programs do not survive the the legislative process until they have already acquired strong constituencies working hand in hand with members of Congress. Then, as the programs develop, they further feed these same constituencies who are their beneficiaries. As a program grows, it also demands and receives dedicated service from the people responsible for administering it. These people in turn develop strong identities and loyalties to the program and then—allied with the special constituencies and the interested members of Congress—become a bulwark of support for keeping the program alive and amply funded.

The currents of power in Washington often flow in subtle and mysterious ways. Nothing can be more baffling to a fresh government executive than the link between congressional committees, special-interest groups, and program bureaucracies. So many fiscal reformers have been overwhelmed by the alliances between these three groups that they have come to be known as the "iron triangle" of government. Locked closely together by mutual self-interest and by years of close association, the members of the iron triangle are extraordinarily effective in blocking outsiders in their attempts to reduce or reform favored government programs. Year in, year out, presidents from both parties have tried to eliminate certain obsolete programs, but they have rarely overcome the resistance of these forces.

Small but highly motivated and well-organized coalitions are capable of exerting intense pressures. Politicians, of course, respond to pressure: that's the way to get reelected. Moreover, with hundreds of issues to consider, most members of Congress can take a deep interest and become expert in only a small percentage of the total. For the remainder, they tend to defer to colleagues who are more knowledgeable, or they simply vote their political interest. To succeed, therefore, special interests usually have only to persuade a small number of sympathetic congressmen to take up their cause. The much larger general public is not sufficiently knowledgeable, motivated, or organized to put up any opposition, so that interest groups prevail most of the time. Thus, the iron triangle is built.

Parochialism in the Congress

The irresponsibility of the Congress toward spending is only reinforced by the parochialism that reigns in many parts of Congress. Each member wants to have some cause to champion, something to be remembered for, something to talk to the people back home about, something that has his name and reputation linked with it. Many members are all too willing to serve as the point men for particular programs, even when the preponderance of evidence demonstrates that the program is failing. Moreover, each member must stand for reelection every two or six years and must therefore spend a substantial part of his or her energies advocating expenditures for programs that benefit the home district or state. These programs are not necessarily worthwhile, and the advocacy is based less on program value than on political benefits to the member of Congress.

This parochial advocacy is vividly illustrated by the impact aid program whereby the federal government has provided over $8 billion to local school districts because parents of children in those districts work on federal property or in federal facilities. The program was begun during the Korean War as a means of compensating school districts that were deprived of tax revenues because families lived on federal bases and payed no local property taxes. However, the program has since expanded from 2 percent to 25 percent of all school districts, enrolling half of the nation's public school children. Moreover, in 90 percent of the cases today, the parents do not live on bases but in fact live in the communities and pay the same taxes for supporting the school districts as any other citizen. As a result, some of the wealthiest counties in the nation are among the largest beneficiaries of this program. For example, Montgomery County in Maryland and Fairfax County in Virginia had an average per capita in 1973 that was 56 percent and 29 percent higher than the national average, but in that same year they received $17 million in impact aid. Nearly all of the families whose numbers are counted in computing this aid are highly paid civil servants who live in the affected jurisdictions rather than on a federal reservation. In effect, taxpayers in other, less-wealthy neighborhoods are subsidizing the schools of some of the richest parts of the country and are allowing the Montgomery Counties of America to reduce their own tax rates. In the meantime, some of the poorest school districts in the country receive almost no support from the impact aid program.

Every recent President has tried to end this program, but to no avail. Self-interest has always won the day on Capitol Hill. When President Carter tried to terminate impact aid in 1977, the House Budget Committee acknowledged that payments were made to some of the wealthiest school districts in the country and that 95 percent of the families who are counted for aid purposes actually live on taxable property and contribute to the local school revenues. Nevertheless, the committee voted 13 to 9 to restore the reductions, embracing the view of one of its members who stated: "The bottom line is that if I voted against impact aid I'd be voting either higher property taxes, lower school programs or both. I will not vote to phase it out—now or ever." [2]

In his final budget message, President Ford chided the parochial inclination of the Congress: "We need to overcome the idea that members of the Congress are elected to bring home federal projects for their district or state. . . . Members of the Congress must begin to share the burden of the President and say 'No' to the special interest groups—even those in their own districts or states."

The Concept of a Base Budget

Once money is appropriated for a program, its supporters regard that appropration as a minimum—a "base," in Washington parlance—and their efforts are directed toward obtaining higher and higher expenditures. Too often, the Congress simply joins in this assumption without asking whether the program is working properly or whether, in fact, it should be funded at all.

Only substantial departures from a previous year's budget are normally given intensive scrutiny by the Congress, and items that remain unchanged or grow slightly will probably be carried along over a period of years as a matter of course.

A study of the budgets for thirty-seven domestic agencies over a twelve-year period illustrates the point. In one-third of the cases (149 out of 444), annual increases in agency budgets were between zero and 5 percent. A little more than half the cases had budget increases or decreases in a single year of 10 percent. And less than 10 percent had increases or decreases of 50 percent or more.[3] Thus, in the overwhelming majority of cases, programs just kept rolling along like the tumbleweed, regardless of whether the winds blowing behind them were fair or foul.

WHAT CAN BE DONE

Aside from the destabilizing effects that runaway spending has on the economy—which are severe—it also has many dire implications for sound, effective government. For one thing, new initiatives are effectively curbed and the status quo maintained. For another, as Congress distributes funds in a "pork barrel" manner, policy is formed haphazardly rather than in a planned, comprehensive fashion. Further, because much legislation is enacted to reward special-interest groups, federal resources are allocated unevenly within society. The public is simply not sufficiently well informed or organized to make itself heard.

The executive branch and the president also lose out in the process because there are so few funds available to pursue new initiatives and make a mark. This lack of funds can constrain initiatives for the entire four-year term of an administration as the expanding programs use up any expected "fiscal dividend." This point is well illustrated in a 1973 publication by the Brookings Institution, forecasing that the extension of then present programs would permit a budget surplus of $13 billion in fiscal year 1977. Largely as a result of increases in uncontrollable programs and congressional actions, the predicted surplus turned into a deficit of approximately $57 billion. More often than not, fiscal dividends that are foreseen four or five years later turn out to be no more than a mirage on the highway—they recede as we approach them. That was true of the "Vietnam peace dividend" so often discussed during the war, and it will eventually be true as well of the fiscal dividend that Mr. Carter promised during the 1976 campaign.

The executive branch, of course, has every incentive to reduce or eliminate unproductive programs and agencies and to check the rise in uncontrollable spending. Unfortunately, the same incentives do not exist in Congress. There is nothing in the Constitution ordaining that uncontrollable programs must continue to grow. The same Congress that wrote the spending legislation can also rewrite it if it wishes. Yet no one in Washington holds out much hope that the Congress will prune the uncontrollables, no matter how hard the President may push. Neither does congressional behavior in the past decade augur well for reducing or eliminating ineffective and/or outmoded programs. After observing large increases in spending and the absence of any major new initiatives to account for them, scholar David Stockman concluded, "Since no major new spending programs have been adopted in the last few years, it can only be concluded that Congress abhors prospective budget surpluses, preferring to nickel and dime them into oblivion long before they appear." [4]

Nonetheless, there are tremendous targets of opportunity for sound, prudent budget cutting. Great quantities of money could be saved by eliminating spending that is now essentially wasted. In addition, the government could achieve greater efficiences by delegating to the states and cities the functions that can be more effectively carried out there and rearranging and streamling other functions so as to gain more productivity without further spending. There are no easy or pat answers to the problem of arousing the general public and influencing congressional action on ineffective programs. The ultimate answers are not at all new or radical but are common-sense approaches revolving around the common theme of developing a national will to make the taxpayer's dollars accomplish more.

Identify Ineffective Programs

The first step for any administration is to identify programs that are wasting money. There are so many examples that no one has ever found that difficult. As a general guide for selecting programs that should be cut back or eliminated, President Ford's last budget message provided several excellent criteria:

> Is this activity important to our national security or sense of social equity?
> Is this activity sufficiently important to require that we tax our people or borrow funds to pay for it?
> Must the Federal Government raise the taxes or borrow the funds or should state and local government do so?
> How has the program performed in the past? Have the benefits outweighed the costs in dollars or other burdens imposed?
> Have the benefits gone to the intended beneficiary?
> Does this activity conflict with or overlap another?

Working with Congress

Once the administration knows how it wants to reshape the budget, the Congress is the first target that should be tackled. It should be obvious that each agency should be encouraged to consult in advance with key members of its substantive and appropriations subcommittees to learn the member's needs and to discuss the administration's priorities in the upcoming budget. Yet every new administration seems to stumble over the obvious. Consultation with Congress must not come at the last minute nor can it be mere window dressing.

The executive branch should also recognize that everything cannot be done exactly as it would prefer. Rather, the executive must demonstrate a willingness to compromise to a certain extent on programs that are political or substantive pets of key members of Congress. Rigidity on the part of the executive will only make things worse. Instead, if a mutual understanding on priorities can be worked out at an early stage, there will be a much better chance of achieving at least some of the administration's reforms. For example, in the 1975 budget requests to Congress, President Nixon included $250 million for public service employment (which we did not believe was essential) in order to win congressional support for Manpower Revenue Sharing. The compromise won the favor of key congressmen, and later that year we were pleased to see the manpower bill enacted.

In addition to consideration of congressional priorities, the executive branch should approach reduction initiatives sequentially. Most programs gained support, were developed, and were built up over a period of years. This same support will not erode all at once and must be reduced the same way it was built—over a period of time. If an administration tries to take on too many programs simultaneously, it will only antagonize large numbers of congressmen, uniting them in a common front to combat all reduction efforts. This point was well illustrated when President Nixon submitted his 1974 budget, calling for reduction or termination of over one hundred popular but ineffective programs. With almost every member of Congress offended by one of these proposals, the Congress formed a solid wall of resistance and prevented most of the reductions.

A useful initiative introduced in formulaton of the fiscal year 1975 budget was a series of informal meetings between the top officials of the Office of Management and Budget and the Democratic chairman and the ranking Republican of the various substantive committees and appropriation committees in both the House and the Senate. These sessions, held several months before the budget was formally submitted by the President, familarized congressional leaders of both parties with the overall economic forecast on which the budget was predicated, the problems on uncontrollables, the need to hold down the size of the budget, and the directions the President intended to take. At the same time, congressional views were solicited on priorities in their particular areas. While no commitments were made during this time, the meetings provided a much more constructive dialogue and a better understanding of each other's aims. Furthermore, while prior consultations did not prevent congressional criticism when the budget was formally presented, they did temper this criticism and helped to create more support for the administration's budgeting aims.

Now that a Congressional Budget Committee has become a welcome addition to the committee structure of Congress, the process of prior consultation should be extended in depth to the Budget Committee and its staff. This committee shares many of the same aims as the executive branch and has already shown itself to be a natural ally in the fight to hold down expenditures.

Harnessing the Bureaucracy

Leaders of the executive branch must reinforce their efforts with Congress by aggressively seeking control over a second leg of the iron triangle, that of the bureaucracy. As pointed out earlier, senior members of the career government service know far more ways to thwart a chief executive's budgetary aims than any administration is likely to be able to counter. Therefore, it is absolutely essential at an early stage to convert them into potential allies.

Probably the surest way to gain needed support is to engage career officials in all of the planning and analysis that lead up to the final budget submission. If they are completely involved, have their day in court, and have a few victories as well as defeats in the process, they are much less likely to undercut the administration's budgetary priorities before the Congress. No administration can afford to surrender its budgetary authority to the permanent government in Washington, but a President who is willing to lose a handful of skirmishes with the bureaucracy is much more likely to gain needed support to win the overall war against the budget. As with the Congress, it is better to be realistic right from the start about the power of career officials rather than walking into an ambush later. Of course, the techniques described in Chapter 5 for dealing with the career service will also apply in helping to gain their support in the budget area.

Gaining Public Support

Public support for more responsible spending is the link that is most crucial but also most difficult to obtain. Constituent feedback is an extremely important influence on members of Congress. There is generally very little of it, however, to offset lobbying by special-interest groups. President Carter learned that lesson soon after taking office when he tried to eliminate funding for a number of dams that he considered economically unsound. The general public, which would realize the greatest benefit from his efforts, hardly said a word, but citizens and their congressmen in the affected areas rose in angry wrath. Before it was over, the Congress forced a severe compromise upon the President.

A broad-based appeal to the general public is essential to convince them of the worthiness of the administration's budget priorities and the relative ineffectiveness of some programs supported with their taxes. Persuading the public on a subject as complex, arcane, and to many as dull as the federal budget is obviously difficult. It can only be accomplished through a well-planned national campaign directed at media outlets throughout the country. Particular attention should be devoted to those groups who will benefit most from the administration's priorities so as to mobilize their support. For instance, groups like the League of Women Voters, with broad as opposed to parochial interests, should be assiduously courted since they have the power to make themselves heard and can provide an excellent counterpoint to special-interest groups.

Sunset Laws and Zero-Based Budgeting

In spite of its best efforts, no administration can fully depend on congressional cooperation in effecting spending restraint and reducing ineffective programs. Unless current practices change, we can expect that many wasteful programs will remain on the books and other, more productive, programs will never be enacted. Something more is obviously needed. The two most promising changes on the horizon today are zero-based budgeting and so-called sunset laws.

Having gained widespread interest as a favorite management tool of President Carter while he was Governor of Georgia, the zero-based budgeting technique has been widely debated. The purpose of this book is not to extend the debate or to serve as a primer on the technique, but rather to place zero-based budgeting in perspective and to advocate its selective application. Briefly stated, zero-based budgeting is a procedure that forces agencies to analyze and justify all requests for money rather than just the incremental increase over the previous spending level as is now the case. Instead of considering last year's appropriation for a program as the base for next year's funding, it pegs the base at zero and requires the agency to justify every dollar of new funding. Its basic goal is to keep government programs from surviving after they have outlived their usefulness by applying cost/benefit analysis to all items in the budget. As practiced in Georgia in the Carter years, managers prepared "decision packages" analyzing the purposes, costs, benefits, consequence of disapproval, and relative priority of every activity of each agency.

There are a number of possible advantages to this approach. Theoretically, it should resolve the problem of wasteful programs by ranking all programs and activities in order of priority so that the least useful can be spotlighted and culled out. Since each agency comes before Congress without a single dollar of appropriations guaranteed, it should be easier politically for Congress to terminate a program or at least reduce its funding. Zero-based budgeting also provides a means of reviewing broad functions such as education or energy all together rather than as parts of various agencies, thus permitting a broader and more meaningful review of policy. Finally, it forces managers to evaluate the cost-effectiveness of their operations while expanding management participation in the planning, budgeting, and decision-making process.

There are, however, two major limitations to zero-based budgeting at the federal level. First, the activities and programs of the federal government are so vast and complex that the process could generate mounds of paperwork that would so overwhelm both the executive branch and the Congress that it would not be used. In Georgia, a state where the budget is less than 1 percent the size of the federal budget, the process required some ten thousand "decision packages" every year. If there is a linear relationship between numbers of programs and activities, this would mean more than a million decision packages at the federal level. A second limitation is that there is absolutely no guarantee that the Congress would use the zero-based decision package or would allocate resources any differently than at present. Today's federal budget could be cut even with existing procedures, and no system can substitute for political will.

Despite these limitations, the advantages of zero-based budgeting are so fundamental that the techniques should be modified to fit the more complex federal budget, and then it should be thoroughly tried. The adaptation can start by recognizing that it is not necessary to evaluate every program every year. For example, once the consequence of reducing child nutrition benefits by 75 percent are analyzed, it doesn't help to ask the same question every year. Some items such as direct services (e.g. the FBI or Internal Revenue Service on the federal level) may benefit from annual analyses, but the great bulk of federal programs do not. Therefore, it would make more sense to identify the programs that seem most in need of improvement, start the approach with them, and schedule other reviews so that all programs are included over, say, a five-year cycle. This would reduce the task to more manageable proportions and ensure that the highest payoff activities are questioned right at the outset.

To repeat, the problem in the past has not been the failure of the executive branch to identify ineffective programs but rather the failure of the Congress to act on them. One way of prompting greater cooperation from Congress is to tie down the process of zero-based budgeting with legislation. The Congress has made considerable strides toward better control of the budget with its 1973 initiative creating the Congressional Budget Committee and the Congressional Budget Office, which gave it for the first time its own in-house mechanisms for evaluating the overall budget. Further legislation requiring zero-based consideration of each appropriation at least once every five years would complete the reform by ensuring that legislative and public attention are regularly focused on the value of each program. The Congress would then have no retreat from zero-based analysis, and meaningful cutbacks would be far more probable.

The state of Colorado has successfully introduced a related type of law for regulatory activities that has been copied by a number of other states and could also serve as a useful model for the federal government. It is referred to as the sunset law: let the sun set on a government agency every so many years. In 1976, the Senate Committee on Government Operations issued a report and introduced legislation to support this concept. As the report stated: "It is necessary to challenge the traditional assumption of budgeting because a program was funded last year, it deserves to be funded this year at the same or higher level. . . . If programs fail to meet the test for reauthorization, they will be terminated." [5] While the Congress has not yet voted to enact a sunset law, there has been a ground swell of interest from members of Congress. One of the sponsors of the sunset legislation, Senator Edmund Muskie stated: "The system today is so complicated that no one really knows exactly how many federal programs there are . . . or what we are buying for the billions of federal dollars we pour into them every year." [6]

Many who have tried to cut the Gordian knot of federal regulations think that a sunset law, phased in over a period of years, would be particularly appropriate for independent regulatory agencies such as the ICC, FCC, etc. The process would mean that every year, the Congress and the executive branch would systematically consider another one of the regulatory agencies and try to clean up any problems that exist in the area under regulation. As it is today, the Congress is trying to review all the agencies at once and as a result is not really succeeding in cleaning up any of them.

If Congress is to take the budgeting process seriously, it must have a reason to stand up to the interest groups and individual constituent interests. "Sunset" legislation most assuredly can help by holding Congress clearly responsible for evaluating and culling programs, providing the tools to do it, and helping furnish the public attention and support needed to stimulate action.

Sharing the Power

A fundamental problem of allocating financial resources is that the federal government tries to do too much, sliding into areas where it has little competence and emasculating state and local efforts. A major opportunity to make taxpayer dollars work more effectively is for the federal government to reduce its involvement in many activities, deferring more decision making to state and local government.

In the late 1930s, for example, the federal government began to be concerned about community development—the problems of aging cities, the need for new housing, and the like. Out of this concern grew a series of major programs, including public housing, urban renewal, model cities, water and sewer grants, and public facility grants and loans. Spending for these programs exceeded $5 billion by 1975. Federal officials were in effect deciding how the cities would allocate their resources between each of the programs, and in many instances were even deciding on specific projects within the programs.

Some curious inequities were also occurring in the distribution of the various community development program funds as some cities received over a hundred times more federal assistance than other cities with equivalent needs. "Grantsmanship" became a common practice among local city planners, and the ones who triumphed in Washington frequently were not those with greatest need but the best connections. In preparing legislation combining all community development programs into one bloc grant, a calculation was made of the funding required to prevent any community from receiving less under the new formula than it had in the past. This calculation showed that Pikeville, Kentucky, had received so much money with the multiple grant programs that a total of $80 billion would be needed in community development to ensure that Pikeville would receive as much money as before.

Beyond the inequities of many categorical grant programs, the broader and more serious question is whether the federal government should be involved at all in these detailed decisions or whether they can be better dealt with at the state and local level. The allocation of resources can be vastly improved by moving more decisions closer to the point of greatest knowledge—closer to the point of action. In community development, for example, legislation was enacted in 1974 so that bloc grants are now made to cities, and the cities decide on their own how to spend the money. While definitive proof is not yet available, the opinion of most observers in that the funds are spent far more productively under the new system. Furthermore, the bloc grant approach in community development has reduced federal grant applications from some fourteen hundred to twenty-five pages and reduced the time of processing this application from thirty-one to eight months.

The federal government needs to continue sorting out and rearranging lines of authority to ensure that the government that best understands how money should be spent—federal, state, or local—should also have responsibility for spending it. General revenue sharing and the various bloc grant programs that have been enacted (for law-enforcement assistance, mass transit assistance, manpower training, and community development) are all positive steps in this direction. The process needs to be extended to other areas where local decision making is particularly pertinent, such as education, social services, and health services. This movement would save only marginal amounts of money over present levels, but it would ensure that the money being spent has a much better chance of being effective. It would free up federal time and attention to focus more effectively on broader policy and resource decisions, and it would lead to more intelligent allocation of resources by placing decisions in the hands of those most familiar with the problems and priorities.

Streamlining Functions: The People Problem

Closely related to the issue of sharing federal power is the issue of handling people. Almost every political leader launches efficiency drives at one time or another, and the most common approach taken is to announce bold targets for reduction of people in the bureaucracy. Generally, political executives go about this with a meat ax, simply requiring every agency to reduce, say, 5 percent of their manpower. This approach neither recognizes the worthiness of the work that is being done nor does it differentiate between higher- and lower-priority programs. While it often will achieve a small manpower savings, more often than not it will act as a detriment to overall government effectiveness.

One reason personnel reductions of the meat-ax variety will not produce large budgetary savings is that excluding our military forces, personnel constitute a relatively small part of total government expenditures. For example, in the federal government, spending on civilian personnel constitutes only 14 percent of the total federal budget. The key, then, is not to reduce this 14 percent but to make the remaining 86 percent of government expenditures more effective. If this effort requires the rearrangement or even the addition of manpower, this should be undertaken so that government can meet its highest-priority tasks.

Rearranging or streamlining the procedures and people associated with grant programs can yield particularly significant savings and result in more effective government. As pointed out earlier, for example, the Department of Health, Education and Welfare administers more grant-in-aid programs than any other federal agency. The HEW grant programs are large and complicated and have grown haphazardly, with little time for real planning or systematic review. As a result, the programs have become encrusted with procedures and buried in mountains of red tape. In many cases procedures used in one program are at odds with those of another. Significant savings can be derived from streamlining these grant procedures. For example, the internal HEW study noted in Chapter 5 led to a number of significant improvements, such as the abolition of headquarters review committees and decentralization of decision making to the regional office, thus reducing the review time for short-term training grants from eight months to as little as ten days. This made it easier for the grantee to apply and, most im-

Public Health Short Term Training Grant Review Procedures

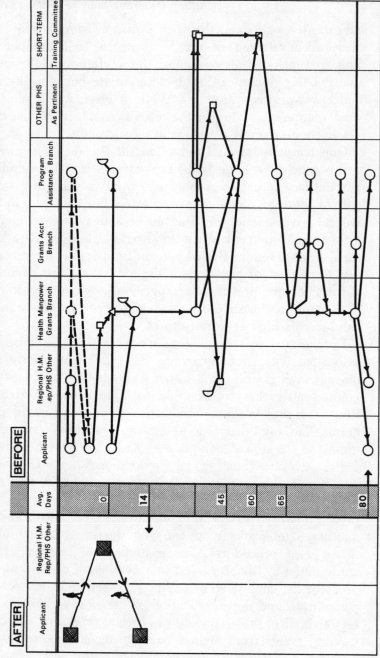

190

portantly, subjected applications to review by people familiar with local needs and resources. The accompanying chart illustrates time reductions and the simplification achieved by dramatically reducing the number of review steps and decentralizing the decision making.

The reforms called for in this chapter range from broad policy initiatives to detailed administrative changes and include (1) improved means of identifying and gaining support for the reduction of programs through congressional, public, and bureaucratic persuasion, and through a modified approach to zero-based budgeting tied to "sunset" legislation; (2) policies to delegate more budgeting decisions to state and local levels where decisions can be made on a more informed basis; and (3) restructuring and streamlining grant-in-aid procedures to reduce expenses and reassign people to more productive areas.

These reforms are not all-inclusive nor do they adequately convey the magnitude of the challenge. In the early days of his administration, as he sets his sights on a balanced budget by fiscal year 1981, President Carter has begun to realize that even with the same party controlling both the White House and the Congress, the job of bringing rationality into the federal spending process is the toughest, most thankless task of anyone occupying the Oval Office. Each of his last four predecessors took aim at the budget, especially during the Nixon-Ford era, but over the past eighteen years the nation has only managed to balance spending with revenues in a single year. Yet the challenge must be accepted, the effort must be made; for without some degree of progress in allocating resources, the government will be permanently handicapped.

As that effort goes forward, it is important that the executive branch not lose sight of the need for continuing evaluation of its people, its programs, and its organization, a subject we turn to in the next chapter.

Chapter Nine

Evaluating Results

"To get along, go along"—that old, familiar principle is alive and well in Washington today. Not long ago, a personal friend who was serving as an assistant secretary of agriculture began strenuous efforts to modernize all the finance and accounting systems in his department and to study better ways to organize the department. In short order, the Chairman of the House Appropriations Subcommittee for the department called him on the carpet, and when he persisted, the Congressman warned that the budget for the Secretary's personal office would be slashed if he continued "stirring things up." To the young, reform-minded executive, the congressional threats along with resistance inside Agriculture were just too much to overcome. "This will be the last time I go out of my way to change things," he told me. "From now on I'll accept my reward for avoiding controversy and going along. There are just no credits for being innovative."

This episode points to a principal problem in government: a lack of an objective basis for evaluating performance, coupled with a system that rewards inertia, inevitably produces mediocre leadership.

Government is the largest single human endeavor in the country that proceeds without any serious means of measuring progress and evaluating performance. Education, business, industry, science, athletics, even warfare, can be measured by standards of performance, enabling participants to make those myriad assessments that are essential to the success of the undertaking in which they are engaged. The value and necessity for such standards are self-evident. It is all the more remarkable, therefore, that an endeavor that costs more than any other, influences the lives of every single person in the nation, and is critical to the ultimate survival of the nation should have no such milestones or standards.

To be sure, the instinctive compulsion to find some means of measuring institutional progress and personal performance is not lost on government. But it only generates standards of measurement that are so fatally flawed that they are counterproductive, because they have the surface characteristics of an evaluative system with none of the implied disciplines.

Consider the food stamp program, one outgrowth of the price support and surplus removal programs described in the previous chapter. This program was originally conceived as a vehicle for making good use of excess agricultural commodities purchased by the government. Initially, needy families and institutions received "food aid" packages. The program was codified in the Food Stamp Act of 1964, which said that its goals were "to strengthen the agricultural economy; to help achieve a fuller and more effective use of food abundances; to provide for improved levels of nutrition among low-income households through a cooperative federal-state program of food assistance to be operated through normal channels of trade; and for other purposes." The act contains no provision for determing how effectively it is being implemented, it levies no reporting requirements, and it sets no procedures for determining whether (1) the agricultural economy is actually strengthened, (2) food abundances are being used more fully and effectively, or (3) nutritional levels among low-income households are being improved.

It is hardly astonishing, therefore, that the Food and Nutrition Service measured its success in administering the program by the number of dollars spent and the number of families using food stamps. More was simply defined as better. Inevitably, this approach generated higher and higher costs, duplication, large numbers of ineligible recipients, and serious overlapping with other welfare-oriented programs. Moreover, there is no clear evidence that the nutritional levels of the nation's poor have been increased. Nor is it possible to quantify the extent to which the agricultural economy has been strengthened. In short, it is not possible to determine whether the nation—including its poor—has received a benefit commensurate with the billions of dollars spent on just one government program.

The food stamp program is not an extreme example. Government programs are frequently legislated to achieve certain vague social purposes and to satisfy certain political needs—not least, the necessity for compromise. Because the purposes of programs are seldom articulated in clear, precise terms, it is difficult to measure organizational, personal, or program performance in any meaningful or consistent way. Moreover, there are few benchmarks by which to measure progress along the way, and there is rarely any effort to define how the stated purpose will be achieved or how the achievement will be measured. The absence of meaningful measurement or evaluation is a prime reason why government does not work as effectively as it should.

There are two levels of evaluation needed in government. The first should focus on the individual and the organization: are government workers meeting specific standards of performance and making satisfactory progress toward the accomplishment of their various missions? Only by asking such questions can a government executive determine who is doing the job and who is not, who should be promoted and who should be fired, what actions are needed to reach specified goals, where attention is needed to bring a program back on track, which organizations are performing and which need to be shaken up.

The second level of evaluation should be concerned with

the results of the government program itself. Regardless of the competence of the individuals and the organization running the program, is the overall effort conceived and directed in a way that produces the intended results? Only in this way can conclusions be reached as to which programs are worth the taxpayers' dollars, which should be reshaped or reoriented, and which should be terminated.

EVALUATING INDIVIDUAL PERFORMANCE

According to former HEW Secretary John Gardner, "When you figure out how to hold a middle-level bureaucrat accountable, it will be comparable to landing on the moon." [1] The frustration of setting standards for political appointees or career civil servants and then holding them to those standards causes most chief executives and agency heads to fall back upon subjective, inadequate yardsticks like personal popularity, responsiveness to agency heads, lack of controversy, ability to get along with Congress, and the like. While these benchmarks have some utility, they do not measure the ability needed to manage government nor do they inspire the hard-driving "do or die" attitude needed to bring about meaningful change. Moreover, most government executives quickly figure out how they are being evaluated and begin focusing their energies on meeting these subjective criteria as opposed to the achievement of substantive results. Recognizing that achievement, change, and reform all create controversy and often animosity, they tend to adopt a passive posture during their tour in government. This tendency is often reinforced by pressures from the Congress, as was seen earlier in the case of the agriculture assistant secretary.

Passive attitudes are communicated to and copied by the senior career officials, who quickly recognize the wisdom of "playing it safe." In this manner the status quo is preserved, reform-minded executives are frustrated, and the successful management of government is discouraged. The absence of a systematic approach to performance evaluation only serves to perpetuate this situation. Conceding that individual performance cannot be held to precise measures, it is nonetheless possible to achieve meaningful results by asking how well individuals perform in achieving specific, clearly defined goals.

Management by Objectives as a Means of Evaluating Results

Managing by objectives as described in Chapter 7 provides a framework that can be used to measure personal performance, assess progress, and suggest corrective action on a consistent basis. It can also be the prime means of evaluating the effectiveness and performance of whole organizations. This is done by evaluating the extent to which predetermined and mutually agreed-upon objectives are achieved.

The extent to which achievement can be measured or quantified differs somewhat between agencies such as Defense or NASA and social agencies with more intangible missions such as HEW or HUD. Nevertheless, in most cases even these intangible missions can be broken down into objectives that provide some degree of measurability as demonstrated by the objectives cited in the appendix to Chapter 7. The plan or milestones for accomplishing these objectives provide a further basis for measurement, both for the organization in question and the individuals serving these organizations.

The ability to measure performance through objectives in intangible areas such as diplomacy is illustrated by the State Department's 1974 objective concerning Latin America. That objective, as defined by State, was to advance friendly relations with Latin America by (1) reaching substantive agreement with OAS members in Inter-American System reform,

(2) obtaining agreement with Mexico on the Colorado River salinity problem, (3) formulating a new United States position on the Panama Canal treaty and resuming negotiations to improve political relations with Panama, and (4) reaching agreement with Chile on the settlement of investment/compensation disputes.

We recognized from the beginning that the achievement of these objectives would not depend solely upon the actions of individuals within the State Department, but would extend to other cabinet departments and government agencies and, of course, to the receptivity of other nations. The Colorado River salinity problem would engage the efforts of the U.S. Department of the Interior and the Environmental Protection Agency, among others, as well as related agencies in those states and municipalities that border on or whose activities affect the salinity of the Colorado River. The disposition of the Panama Canal is not merely a diplomatic issue, but involves U.S. defense interests and commercial interests and would engage the departments and agencies having responsibilities in these areas. The resolution of U.S. investment/compensation disputes with Chile also required actions and interactions reaching well down into the bowels of a number of U.S. government agencies.

The key point, however, is that the achievement of the overall objectives and subobjectives would be made possible by specific individuals carrying out a series of specific action steps, thus permitting an evaluation of their performance as well. It is the identification and assignment of specific objectives that allow such evaluation. Indeed, once the "habit" of managing by objectives becomes ingrained, evaluation of performance in the pursuit of those objectives becomes an almost inevitable part of the process.

The process does, of course, require leadership. At the top, the job of the chief executive and his cabinet is to ensure continued focus on key objectives, evaluate progress against milestones; and direct the actions needed to progress on plan—adding or subtracting resources, reassigning people, and providing sufficient motivation to get the job done.

In the early 1970s, having once established the management-by-objective technique in the federal government, we utilized periodic conferences as the key method to measure progress toward the objectives and through this to evaluate people's abilities. On behalf of the President, the Director of OMB and other appropriate staff members would meet with the agency head and his key people every two to three months. As described in Chapter 7, each of these conferences was preceded by considerable preparation by the OMB management associates and budget examiners. In addition to evaluating performance, the process helped to spotlight developing problems and led to a fuller consideration of major issues and opportunities. The main concerns in these periodic review sessions were:

Are the Cabinet officer and other line managers continuing to focus on the highest priorities? Are they making progress toward the desired result in keeping with the action plan?

Are there major problems that should be brought to the attention of top management for resolution?

Are there recent developments that may require the modification, deletion, or addition of new objectives?

Following a year-end conference, a report would be sent to the President on results achieved, and he would then direct a letter to each department or agency head commenting on his achievements and providing guidance for the coming year's objectives. A sampling of some of the accomplishments relating to the objectives in Appendix B and contained in these reports is as follows:

A comprehensive plan for medical health insurance was completed, and a legislative package was introduced in

February 1974. The proposed approach was in keeping with the administration's goal of ensuring equal access to private care at reasonable rates.

Trans-Alaskan pipeline legislation was signed into law in November 1973, and the permit was issued in January 1974, fulfilling a commitment by the Secretary of Interior.

The agricultural exports objective was met as exports approached $20 billion in FY 1974.

Major advances were made by the Commerce Department's Maritime Administration in improving U.S. shipping operations. As a result, new liner vessels having three to seven times the cargo-lift capability of conventional freighters were being manned with crews of 25 to 32 men, versus 40 to 50 men on older ships. Gains involving bulk and crude oil carriers were also substantial.

Efforts by the Treasury Department to terminate the Interest Equalization Tax, the Foreign Direct Investment Regulations, and the Voluntary Credit Restraint Program were successful. As a result, opportunities were increased for the full and effective use of capital resources by U.S. citizens and corporations, and the competitive position of the United States was enhanced.

Manpower Revenue Sharing was enacted, and the Department of Labor took all necessary actions to implement the program by the end of the fiscal year.

Department and agency heads also utilized the conference method for tracking objectives and also met with good results. For example, one of the important missions of the Department of Housing and Urban Development (HUD) in the early seventies was to provide rental assistance to low-income families. The stated goal was to reserve 400,000 housing units per year, which eligible families would occupy at a rent up to 25 percent of family income, with HUD subsidizing the difference between the 25 percent and the fair market value. The results for the year ending June 1975 came to only a disappointing 89,000 units. Secretary Carla Hills then established the 400,000-unit level as a secretarial priority for fiscal year 1976, and appropriate subobjectives and plans were developed. By March 31, 1975, halfway through the new fiscal year, a management conference report revealed that only 94,000 units had been reached, far less than the target for that date. In early April the Secretary called a meeting of key managers from all parts of the country to discuss the problem, identify those managers who were most responsible for the shortfall, advise all managers of certain recommendations she had approved to streamline the cumbersome processing requirements, and obtain a reaffirmation of their initial commitments. Further progress was charted each month in management conferences, and by September 31, 1976, over 480,000 units had been reserved versus the 400,000 goal; in addition, over 80,000 units had already been occupied by needy families.

In our experience at both the OMB and agency level, we found that the combination of preparatory analysis and face-to-face, top-level discussions helped to ensure a precise evaluation of progress, brought problems to the surface more effectively, and often led to general agreement on the corrective actions to be taken. These personal meetings were far superior to written documents in gaining an understanding of problems and developing actions necessary to push toward the objectives. Not surprisingly, these conferences were most effective when conducted personally by the department or agency head.

It should be apparent that not all the objectives will prove to be attainable, and others may not provide an opportunity for a clear assessment of performance. An interesting example was the Agriculture Department's effort to provide a screwworm barrier in Mexico. The screwworm fly enters the United States from Mexico and lays its eggs on open sores or cuts of cattle. The eggs hatch, and the baby screwworm flies are so voracious that they eventually kill the animal, resulting in a loss to the cattle industry of some $100 million each year. Because the screwworm was contributing to inflation through higher meat prices and was also imposing a hardship on cattle ranchers, the resolution of this seemingly obscure problem became one of Agriculture's top priorities and an objective of the President. The government's original program was to breed millions of screwworms in a plant in Texas, irradiate them to make them sterile, and then drop them by air along the U.S.-Mexican border. They would mate with fertile screwworms, but their sterility would prevent reproduction. Because the fly has a short life, the lack of reproduction would ultimately lead to its eradication.

In 1974, a new and more effective plan was developed. The objective was for the United States and Mexico jointly to construct a second breeding and sterilization plant in Mexico and drop the flies across a 100-mile isthmus in central Mexico, a far shorter distance for the barrier than the 2500-mile U.S. border. This would eventually replace the Texas facility and would also protect cattle in northern Mexico. However, because of difficuties in obtaining title to the land and delays brought about by manual construction methods in Mexico, the project was delayed over two years, while the less effective and most costly attack along the border was continued. In this case the outcome was influenced more by external, relatively uncontrollable events rather than by individual performance.

In addition to the inability to reach certain objectives, there were other shortcomings in using objectives to evaluate performance. A number of objectives were useful for setting direction, but they were not really measurable and, therefore, did not lend themselves to evaluation. For example, the Treasury Department had several objectives dealing with international economic negotiations. These goals were clearly of presidential interest, but progress toward their fulfillment was impossible to evaluate in any given year. Finally, we found that in some instances measuring objectives told us that a project was being carried out but did not tell us how well it was carried out.

Despite these shortcomings, the overall impact of the MBO approach to evaluation was thoroughly positive. By virtue of frequent management conferences, periodic reinforcement from the President, and the implied or actual use of budget and manpower incentives, it was possible to sustain interest and to ensure that most targeted results were achieved. Moreover, the program reinforced the President's confidence in many of his appointees and simultaneously identified a number of officials who were unproductive.

EVALUATING ORGANIZATIONS

The criteria used for evaluating individual performance are equally useful in evaluating the overall strength of an organization. But an organization does have characteristics unique to itself, and it must be evaluated as an organization. The principal aim in measuring the performance of an organization is to determine the overall quality of management, its leadership ability, and its capacity for effective achievements. The purpose is not to evaluate individuals *qua* individuals, but individuals within the context of the endeavor that shapes and inspires their actions, and to which they in turn contribute.

This section suggests some guidelines for quickly evaluating management and thus to gauge an organization's health, vitality, and ability to deliver results.[2]

Unifying Forces

The forces that hold any large complex organization together are (1) its objectives, policies, and operating principles; (2) the personal leadership of top management; and (3) the commitment of subordinates to the organization's goals.

Every governmental entity needs something to strive for, something to become, something to achieve. Sound, clear-cut, well-understood objectives are needed to attract and retain able people and motivate them to work together in attaining the purposes of the organization. But objectives alone are not enough. Top management must provide the personal leadership to marshal resources—especially its key personnel—into a well-knit, purposeful, and aggresive unit, moving in a clearly defined direction.

An ongoing evaluation can be conducted simply by asking a few executives in arbitrarily selected management positions and at various levels of management about the goals of the organization and of their own units. Vague and conflicting opinions of the agency's goals are strong indications of poorly defined and poorly communicated objectives. Orientation toward only a bureau or division rather than agency performance also reflects weaknesses in the understanding and acceptance of overall objectives.

If, on the other hand, executives describe the agency's goals and objectives in explicit and consistent terms and focus on achieving the agency's goals rather than just strengthening their own functions, it is reasonable to conclude that management has effectively formulated and communicated its goals and objectives. Where superior leadership is present, the professional goals of executives at all levels tend to coincide with the agency's objectives.

Strong leadership is also reflected in close cooperation within and between operating units. Evaluation of this sensitive area can be approached by asking various officials to describe examples of teamwork in the organization and to describe their relations with the agency head. If officials describe relations with the top man in an uncertain fashion and if there are hints that their relationships with other executives are not open, candid, and marked by mutual respect, there is probably good reason to doubt the strength of the top management's leadership.

Short- and Long-Range Plans

A thorough investigation of the planning process is essential. Long-range plans should be evaluated in light of overall knowledge of the organizational environment and the needs that the organization was established to fulfill. Does management have criteria to guide its programs? Are the agency's plans in harmony with foreseeable trends in the country? Is there sufficient evidence to show that the agency is capable of implementing its plans or is the agency vague or unrealistic? One key to evaluating an agency's long-range plans is to determine how well it has succeeded in the past.

The means of developing short-term or annual plans should also be investigated and some examples of the current year's plans checked. The following are some specific points to consider:

Are plans developed by those responsible for carrying them out and then consolidated, after careful evaluation, at higher levels of management?

Do programs set deadlines and fix responsibilities?

Are there explicit yardsticks for measuring progress against objectives?

Is current performance consistent with the requirements of the plan? (This question often provides a clue to the realism of long-range plans and forecasts.)

Another aspect of short-term planning that can represent an important plus is a philosophy of cost control. Such a philosophy includes more than the typical budgeting procedures and cost-reduction programs that are given lip service in government and are sometimes undertaken in a sporadic manner. Rather, it is an attitude that must be adopted to ensure every phase of an agency's operations is tightly managed. Many government agencies have reduced their spending through a philosophy of planned cost reduction designed to "look under every rock."

The extent of cost and results consciousness can be determined by asking various executives and supervisors to define their responsibilities. Supervisors who answer in terms of administering their activities—getting out the work, handling problems, keeping the process moving—are generally not oriented to real results and improvements. If improvement is a way of life in an agency, the supervisory personnel will think in terms of changing, upgrading, and improving, rather than simply maintaining their operations on a continuing basis. An excellent example of this type of improvement planning is found in one large government agency. The top officials of this agency require every executive to commit in advance to plans for improving his team's performance during the coming year and for reducing costs by a certain amount.

Effective Controls

Effective controls are, of course, necessary to ensure that plans are carried out. An official who is fully in control of his agency will have developed an effective information system on program progress and problems as well as a decision-making process based on facts and objectivity. Top officials of the agency must be able to act quickly and take corrective actions promptly in the fast-changing government environment.

To appraise an agency's management information capability, one might begin by discussing with different executives the uses and usefulness of one or two key reports. If people appear to find the formal reports fully adequate to provide them with timely, specific measures of progress against plans, and if they do not feel overburdened by reporting requirements, the system probably is soundly conceived and managed. But if there is evidence that line officials are compiling their own data rather than relying on the normal reports and conferences, this is a sign that the system is not functioning properly, if at all. Executives should also be asked to describe specific actions they have taken as a result of these reports and conferences. Their answers can provide further insight into the timeliness and usefulness of reports and the degree to which control is delegated throughout the organization.

To assess the agency's decision-making process, top officials should be asked to explain how one or two recent major decisions (such as introducing new legislation or developing a new policy initiative) were reached. Again, that should provide a good means of judging whether decision making is based on facts, objectivity, and rigorous analysis by those executives closest to the situation. Needless to say, decisions made more on the basis of opinion or intuition can be dangerous and are apt to be a sign of careless administration.

Organizational Soundness

The soundness of an organization plan is not easy to assess. After examining the organizational chart, various key executives should be questioned about their own duties, the responsibilities of others, and the coordination required. Top officials of the agency should also be asked to explain the agency's philosophy of organization. Why, for instance, is the agency organized by function rather than by divisions? The precision with which responsibilities are defined, the logic and soundness of the organizational philosophy, and the consistency of replies are good indications of the quality and acceptance of the organization plan.

Since sound performance is impossible without adequate management resources, it is important to determine the strength of management's "second team." At a minimum, there should be one competent executive and one capable backup man for each major function of the agency. Moreover, their background, experience, and philosophy should be appropriate to the future requirements of the agency. In industry, for example, IBM made its initial mark in computers because of its technological superiority; but management then saw that emphasis would have to shift to marketing and began to build up in this area to retain its leadership.

The factors outlined above are clearly not the only considerations in evaluating management or organization performance, nor are they intended as rigid guidelines. However, application of these appraisal factors, especially if combined with careful attention to the management-by-objectives process, can eliminate much subjectivity and result in far more accuracy and conviction in performance evaluation.

EVALUATING PROGRAM PERFORMANCE

The evaluation of governmental programs is a science unto itself. In its broadest and most important sense, the process of evaluation is intended to measure the overall effectiveness of programs in meeting objectives and the capacity of the objectives themselves to solve problems. If properly undertaken, evaluation permits government managers to make more judicious, objective decisions on new directions, allocation of resources, and modification of policies. It is beyond the scope of this book to assess the many analytical tools that can be used to evaluate programs; instead, we will focus here on the obstacles that stand in the way of program evaluation and ways that government managers can overcome them.

Despite its importance, program evaluation is usually done poorly or in many cases not at all. The top planning and evaluation official of the U.S. Office of Education concluded in 1974:

If we look back at the history of Federal efforts in the social program area . . . on up through the Great Society programs of the sixties, we are forced to acknowledge that virtually all the original decisions by the Congress and the Executive Branch of the Federal government to initiate programs in the areas of education, manpower, and poverty, and the later decisions to continue, expand, or terminate these programs, were taken with scarcely any knowledge of the size, character, and location of the problems, or the likely effectiveness of proposed programs to remedy them. Once instituted, such programs were only rarely subjected to rigorous objective evaluation.[3]

There are a number of difficulties that at least partially explain this traditional failure to evaluate. To start with, as we have seen, most federal programs have multiple, broad, ambiguous, and often conflicting or overlapping objectives. When government executives have no clear idea of what a program is supposed to accomplish, it is almost impossible to say whether the program is succeeding.

In business, results can be measured by the ultimate acceptance or rejection of a product or service in the competitive marketplace. The consumer is the final arbiter; it is his decision that spells the differences between success or failure of a business product. The marketplace thus serves as a built-in, impartial process of evaluation—and one that can work very efficiently.

When government develops a bad "product" or program, however, there is no rapid means of correcting the error. As we have seen in Chapter 8, even bad programs acquire constituencies, win champions in the legislative branch and the bureaucracy, and tend to become self-perpetuating. Further, because of the limited time horizons of elected and appointed officials of the executive branch, they are far more interested in associating their names with new initiatives than in evaluating how well an established program is serving the public's needs. While most programs, both good and marginal, breed strong constituencies with a vested interest in their growth and survival, few ever generate a countering constituency aimed at curbing their excesses. Far more people are interested in eating at the trough of governmental largesse than in watching over how the dollars are distributed.

A good example of the compulsion to rush ahead into new programs without adequate evaluation on the effects of these programs can be found in compensatory education. Early in the sixties, research revealed that 20 percent of the children in the country entered first grade with learning deficiencies, and the gap in their capacity for achievement tended to widen as they progressed through school. Many eventually dropped out of school and, because they were unskilled, never found steady employment. These disadvantages would then be passed on to their children, perpetuating the cycle of poverty and welfare problems. In response to this urgent problem, a number of important bills were enacted, including major compensatory education programs directed at early childhood. But in this rush to respond, no one asked whether or not the government really knew which programs or techniques would reduce the learning deficiencies of children. Not until the end of the decade were serious evaluations undertaken—the Westinghouse study in 1969 and the Wargo study in 1972—and they revealed that the results of the entire compensatory programs were poor and that, indeed, the government did not know what it was doing.

The attitudes of career program administrators reinforce the political appointee's tendency to neglect or avoid evaluation. These career administrators are largely concerned with recruiting qualified staffs, building their organizations, keeping people happy, avoiding budget cuts, developing a favorable public image, and wooing the interest groups. Under these conditions, the fulfillment of program goals frequently becomes of secondary concern, and evaluation of the program is often not even considered. In the rare instance where evaluation is carried out within an agency, it is very much a part-time business for the people involved and suffers from casual attention.

The problem is further complicated because the key issue

generally is not whether a given program is on the whole cost-beneficial but whether it is cost-effective on the margins; that is, should its budget go up or down and which techniques and approaches within the program are most and least cost-effective. Thus, the harried administrator with many other things on his mind is loath to tackle the complex evaluation that is required. He may instead fall victim to the syndrome, "We have a problem, we don't know exactly what it is and don't have time to think it through, so let's get a study to figure it out." Outside studies tend to be expensive documents, and frequently they wind up collecting dust on someone's bookshelves. Only the most aggressive management can ensure that full use is made of them.

The overall problem is summed up well by the findings of Carol Weiss, a psychologist:

> There is apparently something wrong with many of our social policies. . . . We do not know how to solve some of the major problems facing the society. Nor do we apply the knowledge that we have. We mount limited focus programs to cope with broad-gauge problems. . . . Above all, we concentrate attention on changing the attitudes and behavior of target groups without concomitant attention to the institutional structures and social arrangements that tend to keep them target groups.[4]

Fortunately, government is beginning to awaken to the needs of evaluating program results. Most agencies are in the process of building well-staffed evaluation offices. From 1968 to 1972, Congress wrote the requirement for program measurement into some forty laws, and the Congressional Budget and Development Control Act of 1974 provides a clear expression of interest in evaluating government programs through stringent analysis. Most recently enacted social programs, for example, have 1 percent of their funds set aside for evaluation. Given the limitations discussed earlier, this represents considerable progress, and there have been some real successes. For example, a 1971 study concluded that the risk of serious reaction and death from smallpox vaccination was greater than the risk from smallpox itself. The programs were ended, and subsequent study showed that the terminations, by reducing the costs of vaccination as well as illness caused by vaccination saved in excess of $60 million annually. But even though progress has been made, there are several additional measures that can and should be taken to come to grips with this vital area of government management:

Adequate funding needs to be made available for evaluation purposes, and stronger staffing should be developed across government at all levels. The funding can be obtained by ensuring that at least 1 percent of program funds is set aside to ongoing programs.

While evaluation should be made an important function of every line manager, each major agency of government should also have a complete, full-time staff to conduct in-depth evaluations of major programs.

At least part of the effort should be to evaluate and identify programs that should be abandoned. In fact, the zero-based budgeting approach recommended in the preceding chapter could result in a quantum leap forward in evaluation. It would be highly desirable if government agencies would put every one of its programs on trial for its life every few years, asking whether, with present knowledge, we would establish this program today if it did not exist.

A strategy of experimentation and demonstration should be more fully utilized to learn more about what works before massive investments are made and to forestall the political forces that fuel the growth of most programs once they are publicly launched. In this way, alternative approaches can be tested. If the results show that the approach or technique is defective, it is politically possible to abandon the pilot efforts and keep developing new approaches until a solution that really works is proven. If on the other hand the experiment proves successful, more massive resources can be committed with confidence that they will help to solve the problem in question. In contrast to the early-childhood compensatory education programs cited above, this experimental approach was used with the Follow Through program, whose purpose was to reinforce in secondary and high schools the gains that had been made in the early-childhood programs. The appropriation for this program was reduced from $120 to $15 million and evaluations were made on various approaches to compensatory education. The findings showed that some approaches resulted in larger gains than had even been experienced with compensatory education programs while other approaches yielded average results and some were counterproductive. Because of this evaluation effort, much greater benefits should now be derived as the Follow Through program is expanded in proved directions.

More comprehensive, integrated evaluations should be made not just of single programs but of the impact of all government programs on given social ills (e.g. poor health, unsatisfactory educational achievement, poverty). When a whole array of past program approaches has proven bankrupt, evaluation of one program at a time will not produce results that are timely or adequate.

To help accomplish more comprehensive evaluation, a significantly expanded and strengthened evaluation arm should be established in the Office of Management and Budget. This new office could lead or coordinate the interagency efforts required, serve as focal point for government evaluations, and act as a catalyst to inspire greater government-wide evaluation efforts.

Too often, evaluation is the neglected stepchild of government management. The political appointees find they can score more points with the public by proposing new ways to do things rather than finding what went wrong in the past.

Bureaucrats have a vested interest in protecting their empires and will not welcome meddlesome reviews by outsiders. Interest groups only reinforce these bureaucratic tendencies. The only one who really cares is the taxpayer, but until the problem is forcefully brought to his attention, he is blissfully ignorant of program performance. Even if the taxpayer were better informed, he is not organized to do anything about it.

If the programs themselves are faulty in conception, no amount of managerial effectiveness can make them serve the public interest. However, a more sensible and coherent organization of government, the subject of the next chapter, can help to sort out the bad from the good and establish a framework more conducive to many of the reforms called for in these chapters.

Chapter Ten

Organizing for Effective Government

Whenever the press, the Congress, or other elected officials discuss managerial improvements in government, they inevitably dwell on comprehensive, government-wide reorganization. Their focus, however, only serves to strengthen and perpetuate the myth that deep-seated substantive problems that cannot be solved in other ways can be cured by reorganizing.

In truth, the reorganizations that have been effected in government have seldom produced the lofty results anticipated. Many have featured form over substance, often degenerating into a sterile reshuffling of lines and boxes on organizational charts. They have been grossly oversimplified and have not combined real reform in management practices with reorganization. As Dean Acheson once stated: "Organization or reorganization in government can often be a trap for the unwary. The relationships involved in the division of labor and responsibility are far more subtle and complex than the little boxes which the graph drawers put on paper with their perpendicular connecting lines." [1]

Moreover, in recent years meaningful results from comprehensive organizational reform of the federal establishment have proven virtually unachievable. Most institutions of the executive branch are fixed by statute and can be altered only with congressional approval. Influenced by its own vested interests and by pressure from outside groups, Congress more often than not chooses to withhold this approval.

In spite of the limited results from past efforts, reorganization can play an important role in improving government's ability to deliver. Its effect, however, is not to reduce expenditures and achieve more economical government, as so often promised by politicians. Rather, the sole purpose can—and should be—better, more efficient government. As Franklin D. Roosevelt said, "We have to get over the notion that the purpose of reorganization is economy. . . . The reason for reorganization is good management." [2]

Without discounting the need for comprehensive, government-wide reorganization, this chapter will deal with more modest and practical efforts than can help make a government work more effectively and are within the reach of any elected chief executive or agency head.

PROBLEMS OF GOVERNMENT STRUCTURE

The federal government as it is constituted today is a hodgepodge of agencies with overlapping and conflicting missions. Over the years it has grown in a haphazard and piecemeal fashion. As we have seen, new agencies such as the Federal Energy Administration were established as problems were recognized or became politically "hot," regardless of how many existing agencies had pieces of the same responsibility. Moreover, little thought or attention was given to the way that problems interrelated or that new agencies would fit in with existing ones. Many large state and city government structures have experienced even more growth than the federal government and mirror its problems.

The result of this haphazard growth is that responsibility is highly fragmented. There is hardly a problem in our society that is within the purview of a single federal agency that has the sole authority to set goals and dedicate resources in a concerted effort to meet the problem. There are, for example, twenty-nine agencies of the federal government involved in education; fifteen agencies share responsibility for health matters; seven agencies provide assistance for water and sewer systems.

Fragmentation and confusion of roles even exist within single departments or agencies. For example, in 1974, the Department of Health, Education and Welfare (HEW) set forth rules to reimburse Medicare and Medicaid patients only for the cost of generic drugs, and not for the higher-priced "brand-name" drugs. They estimated a savings of about $48 million per year. Then another part of HEW, the Food and Drug Administration (FDA), determined that generic drugs are not always the same as their branded counterparts, so the FDA required generic manufacturers to demonstrate the effectiveness of their product, usually through a costly test process that substantially raised the price of those drugs and also added a new cadre of government inspectors. Thus, the savings that had been achieved by one hand of an agency were suddenly wiped out by the other hand of the same agency. And, in the opinion of many experts, the testing of the generic drugs was not really necessary. The overall result was that money that would have gone into drug research and other productive investments was used instead to hire more bureaucrats to solve a problem that didn't exist until other bureaucrats caused it.

The most severe problems emanating from the overlap and fragmentation of government organization can be categorized as follows:

Comprehensive strategies for the solution of our most pressing problems are discouraged and for the most part do not exist. No single agency, no matter how broad its perspective or enlightened its vision, can forge such a strategy when much of the information, resources, and authority for attacking a problem are distributed among other agencies. To this date, for example, the nation lacks a comprehensive approach to the welfare problem, in large part because responsibility for assisting the poor is divided between HUD (housing assistance), Labor (employment assistance and job training), Agriculture (food stamps), and HEW (cash payments for families with dependent children).

Even if a strategy were developed, this fragmentation would prevent coordinated attacks on most major problems. With the various authorities resting in different agencies, it is generally impossible to bring the agencies together in support of a unified campaign. In addition, great amounts of energy are directed inward to support bureaucratic struggles for "turf" instead of being used to further the public interest.

Accountability, which is elusive anyhow, is virtually destroyed by fragmentation. If no one person or agency is clearly charged with solving a particular problem, the chances are that it won't be solved. It is always convenient to "let the other guy" take responsibility for the tough jobs.

Efficiency is lost as agencies overlay each other's efforts. Duplication is commonplace to the point that different agencies have made grants to localities for the same purpose or even conflicting purposes. In other cases agencies with differing approaches to the same problem have found themselves spending most of their time in conflict rather than serving the needs of the public.

As competing offices find it impossible to resolve differences, decision making is generally pushed too high in the chain of command, creating additional burdens on the highest-level officials, causing delays, and forcing decisions by people not best equipped to make them.

Because of the fragmentation, a new layer of bureaucracy has been created within the executive branch of the government to oversee and coordinate activities of the different agencies. No less than 850 interagency committees have sprung into existence in recent years. In the process, bold and original approaches are sacrificed as differing agencies search for compromise solutions.

The extreme structural fragmentation and the inability to hold any one person or organization responsible for performance is the greatest organizational weakness within the government today. The most comprehensive reorganization effort since the 1930s (that of President Nixon to reorganize the executive branch) focused on this problem. The proposal was highly logical and would have been a major step forward. Unfortunately, resistance from the Congress, the bureaucracy, and various interest groups prevented any major changes. Moreover, the efforts devoted to this large-scale plan often crowded out less dramatic initiatives, many of which would have moved government toward consolidation and better-focused responsibility in high-priority areas. In his 1976 campaign, Jimmy Carter promised a fundamental overhaul of government organization, and in his first three months in office he won authority from the Congress to carry out his pledge and soon after was successful in creating a much needed Department of Energy. At the time of this writing, it was still too early to tell whether he would be any more successful than Johnson or Nixon overall.

What is clear from those earlier years is that the most promising results were obtained not from sweeping reorganizational efforts but from attention to selected initiatives on a smaller scale. The reorganization of the Food and Drug Administration and the creation of the Drug Enforcement Administration illustrate this more selective approach.

FOOD AND DRUG ADMINISTRATION (FDA)

In the fifteen years prior to 1969, the FDA experienced tremendous growth and diversification of its responsibilities.

This growth (from a $5.1 million budget in 1955 to a $72 million budget in 1969) had been accompanied by an equal growth in the number and severity of its problems. There was a large and growing backlog of new drug applications, many of which had lifesaving qualities but could not be marketed prior to FDA approval. At the same time, there were many food additives in use that were classified as "generally accepted as safe," but had not been tested. Evidence increasingly suggested that some of these additives were in fact not safe for human consumption. At the same time, consumers were beginning to exercise greater pressures for broader and more effective protection.

The Secretary of HEW, Robert Finch, directed me in 1969 to undertake a review to determine the managerial improvements necessary for the FDA to carry out its consumer protection responsibilities effectively. The FDA at this time was part of HEW's Consumer Protection and Environmental Health Service (CPEHS), which in turn reported to the Assistant Secretary of Health. Internally the FDA was organized into four bureaus for sciences, medicine, compliance, and veterinary medicine.

As a result of that review, which indicated that significant managerial and organizational deficiencies were contributing to the FDA's problems, significant changes were undertaken:

> The FDA's pressing regulatory functions, we found, were precluding its parent agency, CPEHS, from adequately fulfilling its own environmental mission. Moreover, CPEHS represented an unnecessary layer between FDA and the Secretary, making it more difficult for him to keep abreast of FDA's problems and preempting communications on some important, far-reaching decisions. To remedy this problem, the FDA was separated from CPEHS and became a fourth major health agency reporting directly to the Assistant Secretary of Health.

Under the existing FDA organization, authority and

responsibility for research, investigation, and compliance actions pertaining to any single drug or food product were fragmented. Three separate bureaus (science, medicine, and compliance) shared responsibility for studying and enforcing regulations on every single product. Because responsibility below the Commissioner of FDA was not pinned down, even minor decisions were forced up to his level. Finally, the divided responsibilities made it impossible to hold anyone accountable for expediting reviews, resulting in long delays that were harmful both to the drug industry and to consumers. To solve these problems, the three separate bureaus were abolished and replaced by a new Bureau of Foods, Pesticides, and Product Safety and a new Bureau of Drugs. Each of these two new bureaus had full responsibility and authority for all activity regarding foods and drugs from initial research to final regulatory action. With this change, responsibility for the product could be pinpointed.

Within each Bureau a single "product manager" was designated with responsibility for all activities relating to an application or product. Further, a planning and control system was created through which the commissioner could direct and monitor key research and investigative activities.

Executives with strong management skills and experience were recruited to the top positions in the FDA.

Over the course of the next several years, these reforms, while modest in scale, helped to speed up the processing of new drug applications, fostered more rapid compliance actions, and permitted greater guidance to and improved relations with industry.

DRUG ENFORCEMENT ADMINISTRATION (DEA)

By 1970 the drug addiction problem in the nation was growing at a terrifying rate. The number of heroin addicts jumped from an estimated 50,000 to 1960 to between 500,000 and 750,000 by 1970. To the administration, overcoming the drug threat became a matter of urgent priority. Its central plan was to curtail demand through treatment and rehabilitation and to reduce supply through concerted attacks on drug smuggling and strengthened domestic law enforcement.

On the supply side, however, federal law enforcement responsibilities were badly fragmented. Two agencies—the Bureau of Narcotics and Dangerous Drugs (BNDD) in the Justice Department and the Customs Bureau in Treasury—were each independently responsible for interdicting narcotics traffic. The Bureau of Customs drug mission was "to stop drug smuggling," which it interpreted to include all activities overseas preparatory to bringing drugs across the border and all subsequent distribution of the contraband material once it was in the United States. BNDD's mission was "narcotics law enforcement" whether overseas, at the border, or within the United States.

As the flow of heroin and cocaine increased, a Cabinet Committee on International Narcotics Control (CCINC) was created to coordinate policies on smuggling. In early 1972, motivated in part by the need to show some action in an election year, the President established the Office of Drug Abuse Law Enforcement (ODALE) within the Justice Department, and asked the new office to stop drug traffic at the street level. During that same period, an Office of National Narcotics Intelligence (ONNI) was established in Justice to coordinate information about drug traffic. In addition to this increase in organizations, the narcotics enforcement effort was reinforced by an elevenfold budget increase from $65 million in 1969 to $719 million in fiscal year 1974.

As a result of these concentrated efforts, drug arrests soon doubled in number, and seizures of heroin and cocaine increased more than sixfold in a three-year period. This success was accompanied, however, by a good deal of confusion and conflict, which threatened to undermine future drug enforcement efforts. The principal problems were between BNDD and Customs. Because of their overlapping missions both agencies felt the other to be poaching on its proper "turf" whenever the other did anything related to drug law enforcement. Competition between them became pervasive and counterproductive. Reports were rife of compromised evidence, kidnapping of suspects, shootouts between agents, and a complete lack of coordination in spite of a presidential directive identifying the Attorney General as the coordinator and director of what was to have been a unified "war on narcotics." In fact, their only common boss was the President.

In early 1973, as a result of thorough review, a Reorganization Plan was presented to the Congress aimed at strengthening drug enforcement organization. This plan aimed to rectify the problems of fragmented, overlapping authority and lack of accountability by consolidating all drug investigation and enforcement within the Justice Department. It also consolidated all immigration functions at ports of entry in Customs so as to eliminate the dual system of inspection of persons admitted into the United States. This step meant that three agencies within Justice—BNDD, ODALE, and ONNI—were consolidated into DEA, Customs lost its role of investigating drug smugglers and transferred five hundred agents to DEA, and the Immigration and Naturalization Service (INS) was to transfer about one thousand border inspectors to Customs. This new organization would provide a single agency with unbroken responsibility for investigation of drug cases from point of origin overseas to street-level distribution in the United States.

Under the President's reorganization authority, this plan would take effect after sixty days unless overruled by a majority vote of either house of Congress. However, there were three elements of resistance to the reorganization that had been severely underestimated by its creators and proponents. Officials within the Customs Bureau, from the Commissioner on down, deeply resented the loss of their drug investigation mission and, contrary to the President's instructions, urged members of Congress to disapprove the reorganization. They found a good deal of sympathy in members of Congress who had committee responsibilities related to the Treasury Department and who had been impressed with the work of Customs. These congressmen, led by Tom Steed, Chairman of the House Appropriations Subcommittee, which had jurisdiction over the Treasury and the White House, also mounted vigorous but expected opposition.

Completely unexpected opposition then arose from the American Federation of Government Employees (AFGE), an AFL–CIO affiliate representing the INS, which resented the loss of membership from the transfer of immigration inspectors. The AFGE had sufficient influence within the AFL–CIO so that the labor confederation made disapproval of the reorganization plan one of the year's handful of "must votes" and unleashed the full force of its lobbying efforts. Since the law at the time did not permit modifications to reorganization plans, we could not amend it to discard the INS provision. Overnight, as labor threw its weight onto the scales, supporters of the reorganization plan turned against it, and the House Government Operations Committee voted it down by a 20 to 16 margin. Since committee votes generally determine the vote of the full House, the plan appeared doomed.

Searching on the government's behalf for a solution to the dilemma, I negotiated an agreement with the AFL–CIO that the administration would support new legislation reversing the INS personnel transfer portion of the reorganization and would not transfer INS employees while waiting for its enactment. In return, the union withdrew its opposition, and in a rare reversal of a full committee, the Congress then voted in favor of the plan, and the new DEA was created. Angered by his defeat, Mr. Steed and his pro–Bureau of Customs allies in Congress later retaliated against the Office of Management and Budget (OMB), which had advocated and pushed the plan, by slashing OMB's own budget request by some 20 percent.

Unfortunately, the story does not end here. We experienced great difficulty in recruiting the right person for the top DEA post, due in part to the cloud that Watergate had cast over the administration. Severally ideally suited people declined, including James Thompson, then U.S. Attorney in Chicago and later Governor of Illinois. As a consequence, there was a five-month delay in the naming and confirmation of a permanent Administrator, and the new agency got off to a slow, rocky start.

The turbulence of the period further hindered the development and effectiveness of DEA. In its first two years of existence, the DEA lived with four different Attorney Generals, two Presidents and a White House staff whose attention was continually drawn elsewhere. As a result, strong management procedures were not instituted, a number of key positions remained unfilled for long periods or were filled by the wrong people, and some employees of the Bureau of Customs who were left unchecked spent a good portion of their time actively working against DEA and the concept of unified drug enforcement.

Therefore, in spite of the seemingly logical organization structure, DEA's effectiveness and the success of the nation's fight against drug abuse suffered during the first two years of DEA's existence. Success as measured by convictions and drug seizures actually declined during this two-year period, although arrests increased somewhat.

RECOMMENDATIONS FOR ORGANIZATIONAL REFORM

The conception, enactment, and organization of the Food and Drug Administration and the Drug Enforcement Administration illustrate a number of principles and pitfalls of government reorganization practices. The recommendations below are not intended as all-inclusive, nor is each applicable to every governmental situation. However, in the aggregate they do address the major problems of government organization.

Pinpoint Responsibility

As discussed earlier, fragmentation and a lack of pinpointed responsibility are the principal problems with existing government organization. Yet, as demonstrated again and again in the past, sweeping reorganization is not necessarily the best answer. Instead, consolidation and better-focused responsibility can usually be attained by a selective approach to reorganization in high-priority areas.

In the case of the Food and Drug Administration, the restructuring of an existing agency permitted full responsibility to be assigned to a single bureau for each and every food and drug considered by the agency, and it concentrated responsibility for each product in a single manager within the bureau. The creation of the Drug Enforcement Administration permitted the consolidation of four overlapping and conflicting entities and the fixing of responsibility for drug enforcement in one man—the head of the agency.

Contrary to the frustrations that have met most large-scale efforts to end fragmentation and pinpoint responsibility, these two examples show that a great deal can be achieved from the selective approach when the logic is sound and the need is great. It is also interesting to note that the restructuring of FDA was accomplished by order of the HEW Secretary and without the need for legislation. This suggests that there may be a great many additional opportunities that can be quickly seized by an administration willing to look beyond the more dramatic government-wide reorganization concepts.

Organize or Consolidate Around the Mission

As noted earlier, most government goals are broader than the resources and authorities of a single agency. Even if one agency tried, its ability to think with a broader national view would be seriously limited by the means and scope of its own authority. It is more likely that the proposals, if presented, would be solutions looking for problems.

Restructuring to create organizations that encompass entire missions of government is highly desirable. It was one of the principal aims of the Nixon reorganizational proposal. This goal was more successfully reached in the Truman years when the Army, Navy, and Air Force were brought under one umbrella. The Department of Defense has clearly developed techniques for establishing unified and cohesive goals and objectives and then devising the means for carrying them out. Before its creation, the process was often reversed: the goals of the national defense establishment were determined by the means (Army, Navy, or Air Force) or, more explicitly, the medium (land, sea, or air).

In the domestic area, the consolidation of four units into a single DEA organized around the mission of drug enforcement illustrates the type of improvement that is possible. Secretary Califano's 1977 reorganization of certain HEW functions is also an excellent illustration. With that move, the major medical financing programs (Medicare and Medicaid) were brought together into a single organization, federal welfare programs were consolidated into the Social Security Administration, and seven college-aid programs were consolidated into a new bureau of student financial assistance. Each of these changes should lead to a more coordinated approach and improve the management of these important social programs.

Despite the attractiveness of organizing around mission, it will not always be the answer, particularly when the ideal organization for one mission conflicts with what would be desirable for another. In the earlier cited example on drugs, for instance, reorganizing our international drug program around the mission would have involved merging elements from organizations as diverse as the Department of State, the Department of Agriculture, the CIA, and the Department of Defense. Obviously, an optimum organization for international narcotics control would have meant chaos for other important international missions. As a result, no true organizational consolidation of the international drug program was ever seriously contemplated. In such cases one has to decide which mission is most important, organize around it, and then establish some type of interagency coordinating mechanisms (e.g. the Cabinet Committee on International Narcotics Control) to manage the secondary missions. In any case, elimination of the constituency type of structure and consolidation of entities into broad mission-oriented agencies should remain a high priority of any reorganization planning.

Linking Organization with Management Improvements

The prime reason why many reorganizations fail to attain anticipated results is because their sponsors place too much credence in the value of the reorganization itself and neglect the need for accompanying management reform. Sound structure is only the start. Problems are not driven away simply by organizing around them. The rather disappointing results of the new DEA's first two years of operation give testimony to the fallacy of relying only on a sound and logical reorganization. In contrast, the reorganization of the FDA was accompanied by the injection of strong top management along with the establishment of improved management procedures. Consequently, the new FDA got off to a fast start, and improvements in its operations and the results it achieved could be seen within a few months.

For the entity to perform effectively, then, the structure must be staffed with able people, led with vigor and imagination, and managed firmly and systematically. Too many times the failure to meet these requirements has been incorrectly diagnosed as poor organization, and the real problems have not been tackled.

In his 1976 presidential campaign, by placing so high a value on the results of reorganization, Jimmy Carter may have raised public expectations to an unrealistic plane. At the same time, however, he recognized the need for more fundamental management reform:

> We must be as concerned with the progress of government as we are with its structure. . . . Moving boxes around on organizational charts, by itself, doesn't solve the whole problem. Part of our task is to keep the government out of areas it should not be in and to improve the way it works in those areas where government operation is necessary or desirable.[3]

Focus Attention and Make Decisions at the Appropriate Levels

One of the major problems of government highlighted in Chapter 8 is the large amount of routine that is forced to the top of any organization for resolution. Less frequently, as illustrated by the FDA case, the reverse is true—far-reaching, strategic decisions are made beneath the appropriate levels, too far removed from the policymakers.

Usually, any government issue brought to the attention of the chief executive and demanding his personal time would be better solved as a result. But the chief executive must deal with so many functions that a good management principle is to place responsibilities for every issue as far down in the organization as they can adequately be handled. Then the chief executive can reach into any one issue as he sees the need and can use his time on that, rather than having his time preempted when some low-level part of the organization is not able to resolve a problem with some other entity.

Given the fragmentation of government, this principle is quite difficult to follow, since the chief executive is often the only level of authority with purview over all the interacting elements of most initiatives. In the drug enforcement efforts described earlier, the fragmented entities and the conflicts between BNDD (Justice) and Customs (Treasury) forced even minor decisions up to the White House. The conflict was, in fact, the main impetus that led to the review and the ultimate consolidation of enforcement activities into DEA. This same desire to move trade-off decisions and coordination responsibilities for national defense out of the White House was a key motivation in consolidating the Army, Navy, and Air Force into the Department of Defense.

In spite of the needs for consolidation and greater decision making at the agency level, interest groups often lobby for more fragmentation so that their favorite cause can have a direct line to the President. In recent years, for example, education groups have vigorously advocated the separation of education functions from HEW, forming the nucleus of a new Department of Education. While this step might help to consolidate education functions, it would further fragment government responsibility in the broader human resources area, and the necessary responsibilities for resource allocation, policy, and operational coordination would simply be elevated from the cabinet level to the President. Thus, resistance to proposals that would result in further fragmentation or less efficient management is often just as important as launching positive reorganization initiatives.

Developing a Personal Organization

A fundamental problem of government organization is that far too many executives are supposed to receive direct supervision from a chief executive or major agency head. The

President, for example, has eleven cabinet departments, nine major agencies, and scores of minor agencies reporting directly to him. In the absence of a strong personal organization, his many other pressing responsibilities often force him to abrogate his supervision over his subordinates in the agencies since he does not have sufficient time to provide direction or follow the progress of so many units.

Most public affairs scholars argue against a strong White House staff, fearing that concentration of power can corrupt or result in inadequate consideration of many of the wide range of decisions dealt with. Most chief executives also start with the idea of limiting the power of the White House staff and delegating the maximum responsibility and widest latitude to strong and relatively independent cabinet members. Given the complexities of the chief executive's job, particularly the President, these are unassailable objectives. Cabinet delegation allows the President the maximum amount of discretion so that he can selectively address himself to those areas that have the greatest impact or where his presence will accomplish the most good. Moreover, it places authority in the hands of officials closer to the problem and with adequate staff resources to address the issues properly.

The problem with this approach, however, is that the fragmented organization of government mitigates against cabinet delegation by forcing a multitude of relatively minor interagency issues into the White House. In view of the fragmentation and breadth of government, the chief executive who overly depends on his agency heads will rapidly substitute informal lines of communications, directing some agencies through assistants, some through other agencies, some directly, and some not at all. This ad hoc approach will in turn result in fuzzy lines of authority and an erosion of cabinet authority.

The real issue, then, is whether the chief executive organizes according to a predetermined plan or simply lets the lines of communication develop in a haphazard fashion as problems become backed up at his door. The objective should be to develop a personal staff capacity to help coordinate government without weakening or diminishing the role of the line cabinet officials. There is nothing inconsistent with the concept of a strong cabinet working with a strong, active chief executive who orchestrates the whole government. Indeed, the very heart of organization in the executive branch is the working relationship within the chief executive's office and between the cabinet and the chief executive's staff. The workings of government can generally be enhanced far more by making this relationship function effectively than by any formal reorganization.

It is therefore imperative for a chief executive and also for his agency heads to develop personal staff arrangements that will permit them to communicate with, monitor, and otherwise influence the performance of key subordinates in a manner that is effective but unthreatening. While government leaders are generally restrained in bending department and agency structures to their style of management, they are given a high degree of freedom in modifying their own staff arrangements. Each chief executive and agency head should freely use this latitude to reorganize and adjust the units of his executive office to conform with his or her style and the priorities to be attacked in the term ahead.

One of the most interesting but unsuccessful attempts to achieve this objective of effective coordination occurred in early 1973. Frustrated by his inability to gain congressional action on his reorganization proposals, President Nixon decided to operate the government to the extent possible as if it had already been reorganized. This aim was to be accomplished by appointing five top assistants with responsibilities cutting across the whole spectrum of government. These five were accountable for administration of the White House office (Bob Haldeman), executive management (Director of OMB Ash), economic affairs (Secretary of Treasury Shultz), foreign affairs (Henry Kissinger), and domestic affairs (John Ehrlichman). The last three—Shultz, Kissinger, and Ehrlichman—were also to serve as line officers, and the heads of all other agencies and cabinet departments were to report to the President through them on most policy issues, except that the subordinated appointees were to work directly with the President on the most important policy matters.

To further the concept, the heads of three cabinet departments were to serve simultaneously as Counsellors to the President with coordinating responsibilities in areas similar to those that would have been formed by the reorganization. Thus, the Secretary of Agriculture became Counsellor for Natural Resources, the Secretary of HUD became Counsellor for Community Development, and the Secretary of HEW became Counsellor for Human Resources. In addition to their departmental offices, they also were given office space in the Executive Office Building that houses most of the President's staff.

The system worked extremely well in foreign affairs, moderately well in economic affairs, and very poorly in domestic affairs. The strength and excellence of the National Security Council staff ensured effective coordination of foreign affairs activities. The Office of Management and Budget, with a large and highly experienced staff, provided the support necessary for an improved approach to executive management and, along with the Council of Economic Advisors, also added support to the economic coordination role of Secretary Shultz.

In theory, the Counsellor approach should have permitted government to function in a less fragmented and more coordinated manner, much in the way it would be managed if a broad reorganization had been implemented. In practice, however, it was a failure and was abolished within five months. The reasons for this failure point up several pitfalls that a chief executive should guard against in planning his or her personal organization approach.

Assigning the Assistants to the President line authority over the cabinet and other agency heads created a great deal of resentment and resistance, particularly among heads of domestic departments and agencies whose direct access to the President was cut off. This resistance was also reflected among members of Congress whose major agency interests were in effect diminished.

The insertion of the Counsellors added another layer of bureaucracy between the agency heads and the President, thus delaying rather than facilitating decision making. The work of the Secretary of Interior, for example, was to be coordinated by the Counsellor for Natural Resources (Secretary of Agriculture), who in turn reported through the Assistant to the President for Domestic Affairs.

The Counsellors were expected only to coordinate and not to act as line officials. However, this coordinating role encroached upon the traditional responsibilities of the White House and OMB, and these latter staffs worked against and in competition with the Counsellors.

In an attempt to shortcut this extra layer, speed up decisions, and avoid reporting to a peer, cabinet officers found ways to work around the Counsellors and deal directly with the White House and OMB staff on certain issues. The result, of course, was further confusion brought on by multiple channels of communication and competing centers of coordination.

The Counsellors found the dual role of agency head and presidential adviser difficult to carry out. They were generally so pressed by duties of their own agencies that they had insufficient time to devote to the coordination effort, particularly since the vague nature of their authority made it so hard to impose their will.

Finally, the Counsellors were generally unable to divorce themselves from their departments and render completely unbiased and objective judgments. Decisions always seemed to favor the Counsellor's departments, and this only stiffened the resistance of other department and agency heads.

Despite the failure of the experiment, there are definitely inherent advantages in consolidating staff responsibilities around missions. Ideally, an answer could be found that captures all of the advantages while avoiding the problems noted above. A more workable approach would involve three to five assistants to the president whose responsibilities would correspond to the main missions of government (e.g. national security, economic affairs, human resources, community development, and natural resources). They would report directly to the President, but their staffs would be small and they would not be line officials. Rather, they would assist in the coordination of policy development that crosses agency lines (as most does), help to resolve minor interagency differences, and occasionally help to catalyze and coordinate major operational initiatives involving more than one agency. In this latter role, they would not attempt to lead, but would accomplish their ends through the use of task forces and the like led by appropriate cabinet officers. It is important to note that, under this arrangement, cabinet officers and other major heads would maintain full responsibility for the operation of their departments and would continue to report directly to the President. This type of staff arrangement would not only help the President keep abreast of key developments but would also move the government toward the more comprehensive and coordinated approach that is desired but does not seem to be achievable through reorganization.

Developing Organizational Relationships

As in any form of management, organization alone is not the answer, and there are additional steps a chief executive needs to take to build productive relationships between himself and his staff as well as the agency and department heads. Whatever personal organization he ends up with, the President can strengthen overall effectiveness by adopting the following principles:

He should look not to his White House staff but to his line officials for policy development. White House advisers should serve only to coordinate and review, ensuring that proposed policies are evaluated from a presidential rather than a more parochial department point of view. The key is to treat the cabinet as deputies to the President rather than inserting a layer of deputies above them. This approach is most likely to develop a team spirit among a group of strong and otherwise independent cabinet members and enhance their cooperation and support. It will also improve the prospect for the President to hear all sides of an issue and to receive objective analyses.

Insofar as possible, policy should be developed by those responsible for carrying it out, namely the cabinet and sub-cabinet officials. The line official who has developed the policy will be much more committed to its implementation than if the policy is imposed by someone else. Moreover, the line official is more familiar with operational capacity and thus is more likely to come up with policy that is practical and durable. Presidential scholar Stephen Hess adds: "Presidents have no difficulty obtaining advice. . . . But those who can implement administration policies are extremely few in number. . . . The history of the modern Presidency indicates that the White House staff is not an effective implementer." [4]

The chief executive should avoid the temptation of taking on too many problems in the White House. To do so undercuts the cabinet he wants to strengthen. Moreover, the practice of drawing the White House into operational responsibilities, once started, is likely to become steadily more prevalent and lead to further growth of the

White House staff, which in turn further encroaches on cabinet responsibilities.

The chief executive should not take loyalty for granted and should actively work at courting his cabinet. No matter what kind of commitment is made at the start of a term, strong independent people (those with the records of accomplishment likely to qualify for the cabinet) are not going to meekly follow the President's lead over an extended period. They must be led, listened to, communicated with, and respected by the chief executive if he expects them to work consistently as dedicated members of his team.

LIMITATIONS OF REORGANIZATION

While significant opportunities for improvement do exist, a chief executive should proceed very cautiously with any reorganization efforts. In the past, too many attempts at government reorganization have been nothing more than window dressing. Most political managers seriously overestimate the impact of organization structure and naively resort to reorganization as a kind of miracle drug. Few seem to recognize that establishing the right organization structure is not performance itself, but rather a prerequisite to performance. As President Eisenhower stated: "Organization cannot make a genius out of an incompetent. . . . On the other hand, disorganization can scarcely fail to result in inefficiency and can easily lead to disaster." [5]

Presidents and their appointed managers have too often reorganized just for the sake of creating a flurry of action and favorable press reports. This tendency has been particularly true where there has been a growing public awareness of a problem and an administration has been under pressure to demonstrate its concern and response. In the earlier DEA example, the Office of Drug Abuse Law Enforcement and the Cabinet Committee on International

Narcotics Control were both created partly for cosmetic effect in the face of growing national concern. Later, a difficult consolidation had to be brought about to reduce the overlapping responsibilities of the various drug enforcement units. The Federal Energy Administration, discussed in Chapter 1, was also created in large part as a political response to an urgent national issue. A "final solution" for HEW's organizational mess has been proposed every year for the last twenty years.

The problem with reorganizing for public relations purposes is that it achieves no substantive good and often results in a new proliferation of agencies, considerable overlap, diffused responsibilities, wasted money, and, ultimately, public disillusionment. As was the case with the Federal Energy Administration, these liabilities are rather quickly perceived and undo any temporary political value of the reorganization.

The message, then, is not to avoid reorganization in government. Rather, move deliberately and very selectively, recognizing that, in most instances, efforts to reorganize should be subordinated to more fundamental reforms such as setting direction, developing a system or framework for managing, and providing adequate evaluation of results. Further, when organization structure does appear to be a problem, recognize that a clear definition of objectives and strategy should define the type of structure needed; reorganization should not be viewed as an end in itself.

Barriers to Effective Reorganization

Even when an administration devises a sound, feasible plan for reorganization, it will often find the road blocked by vested interests. Time and again, past administrations have butted their heads against a stout wall of resistance. The political obstacles only underline the importance of proceeding with care and selectivity.

Opposition to reorganization generally emanates from the

three sides of the iron triangle described in Chapter 8. As the National Academy of Public Administration commented in a recent report: "It's difficult to eliminate duplication of responsibilities, reduce the federal role, rationalize programs, attack excess staffing or phase out unnecessary programs. The same alliances which got the programs passed in the first place fight to keep the programs intact." [6] In the case of the Drug Enforcement Administration, as we have seen, all of these opposition forces were at work: the Customs bureaucracy, a congressional subcommittee with a long association and deep interest in the Customs Bureau, and a powerful interest group (the AFL–CIO) representing employees of the Immigration and Naturalization Service. The power of this opposition was sufficient to change a key provision of the plan. In addition, the political price paid by the President and the Office of Management and Budget was quite steep, since a key subcommittee and its chairman were alienated and needed budgetary resources were lost.

The bureaucracy, as we have seen, also has a natural aversion to change. When this change means a shifting or relinquishing of responsibility, as it did with the Customs Bureau, its aversion turns to granite resistance. Even if overcome and the reorganization is implemented, the infighting and backbiting from that segment of the bureaucracy that has lost the argument can greatly inhibit the effectiveness of the new organization. The subtle undermining of DEA's efforts by certain Customs employees played a major role in limiting DEA's effectiveness, thus helping to fulfill Customs' original prophecy that the organization would fail.

Congressional motives in opposing change are due in the main to the same considerations motivating the bureaucracy: unwillingness to relinquish power. Senior members invest many years in gaining familiarity with the intricacies of a certain agency's operations, getting to know the ranking career officials, arguing for appropriations, and in some cases learning to enjoy the privileges of close association with that agency. It is not surprising, therefore, that they develop strong loyalties to these agencies. Nor is it surprising that they look askance at any move that will diminish or liquidate their favorite agency. What seems like a streamlining of government to the White House looks like a loss of power to senior members of Congress.

Many anomalies in the structure of the executive branch are in fact attributable to the unorthodox committee structure of Congress and the unwillingness of powerful congressional members to give up jurisdiction over the substance or appropriations of certain agencies. For example, every President since Herbert Hoover has recognized the need to consolidate the water resource responsibilities of the Department of Interior, the Army Corps of Engineers, and the Department of Agriculture. However, three powerful congressional committees—the Interior Committee, the Public Works Committee, and the Agriculture Committee, respectively—are loath to give up jurisdiction in an area so loaded with pork.

Unfortunately, the best studies of reorganization to date have addressed the executive branch alone without casting the same penetrating eye on the Congress. While this book has intentionally skimmed over the role of Congress in making government work more effectively, reorganization of Congress must be a high priority, not only to improve the effectiveness of the Congress itself, but also to enhance the chances of meaningful executive branch reorganization. Initial results from the overhaul of the budget process in the Congress suggest that further congressional reorganization could be highly fruitful.

The difficulties of reorganizing the executive branch in face of congressional and bureaucratic opposition were summed up well in a *Wall Street Journal* editorial just prior to President Carter's inauguration:

The federal bureaucracy is generally viewed as a self-sustaining, impermeable mass cloaked with the protection of Congress, which is itself a self-sustaining impermeable mass. The combination endures presidential reorganization efforts as easily as a hippopotamus lives with flies, submerging into the morass on those rare occasions when it feels discomfort.[7]

Against this background, any chief executive must take a somewhat skeptical and highly selective approach to reorganization, weighing its benefits against other possible initiatives and an exhaustive supply of executive energies. When he does decide to pursue a reorganization initiative, however, there are several techniques that are likely to raise his chances of success.

Timing

The most important consideration is successfully implementing a plan of reorganization is timing. The failure of President Nixon to gain serious congressional consideration of his comprehensive proposal was mostly due to the fact that government mismanagement was simply not a burning public issue at the time. Consequently, the administration was unable to generate the necessary support from the public, special-interest groups, and the Congress. Moreover, the plans were so dramatic that they were received as unsettling shock waves by those affected. It generally makes more sense to start more modestly with easily digestible proposals and evolve an overall organization plan over a period of time as confidence and support is gained.

The creation of the Environmental Protection Administration (EPA) in 1970 illustrates the positive impact of timing in achieving reorganization. Faced with growing problems of pollution and increasing public interest in the environment, a broad coalition was enlisted to support the transfer of functions from HEW and other agencies to form a new agency, which became the cutting edge of government's fight against pollution.

President Carter also utilized a good sense of timing in directing his initial reorganization efforts to a fairly popular proposal to form a new Department of Energy. As of this writing, President Carter enjoyed the most propitious timing of all recent Presidents for winning support of comprehensive organizational reform. Congress itself is in a state of transition. Many key leadership positions have changed as long-term committee chairmen have retired or been deposed (e.g. Congressmen Patman, Mills, and Herbert). The average age of Congress has dropped, and the new and younger members seem more disposed to change. The combination of the President's interest and his advantageous timing augur well for constructive reorganization in the Carter years.

Involvement

The problems of resistance can be reduced by involving the bureaucracy and the Congress early on in any deliberations and studies concerning organizational reform. In most cases the career officials themselves have a well-developed sense of structural weaknesses that blur authority and responsibility, and their insights can represent an important contribution. Participation by career officials will also provide greater assurance that all points of view are adequately considered before acting. Moreover, the very act of enlisting them in the effort will certainly soften any opposition and in some instances will even preclude it. The most desirable means of gaining their involvement is to utilize the task force approach to studying organizational problems and their possible solutions. This technique was used successfully in the reorganization of the Food and Drug Administration and to an extent in the formation of the Environmental Protection Administration.

It is less likely that members of Congress and their staffs will be as well acquainted with the intricacies of organization, focusing as they do on policy and appropriation issues. However, their involvement and understanding of the problems and needs is also likely to increase their receptivity to the desired changes. Their participation should proceed with a sincere flexibility and willingness to compromise on certain points in order to generate broad support for the overall plan. Revising the plan on the drug agency, for instance, was not desirable in itself, but it was a perfectly acceptable price to pay for neutralizing union opposition and gaining approval of the overall effort.

Sound organization is necessary for better government, but by itself it will not make government work. Essential though it is, its value is generally overstated, and the barriers to reorganizing are great. Nevertheless, there are severe problems in the structure of government today, and chief executives should not be totally discouraged in their efforts by the failures of their predecessors. The chief executive who does not unreasonably raise expectations and is willing to invest in low-profile but substantively important initiatives can make government work better by first ensuring that his own office is effectively organized and then, on a selective basis, seeking organizational reform in areas of high priority.

Chapter Eleven

Making Government Work: A Summing-Up

This book began with the central proposition that government does not work well because it is not managed well. As we have seen, there are enormous impediments to the efficient, responsible operation of the government. These impediments have mitigated against effective government for some time, and many will persist for years to come. If these impediments were removed, if political leaders became more attuned to the problems and their solutions, and if other reforms were undertaken so that the government reflected the very best techniques of modern management, then the government would perform much more effectively.

Yet the question must also be raised whether a managerial revolution, standing alone, would be enough to make government "work." Would it assure prompt and efficient delivery of services? Would it reduce the inflationary impact of government policies? Would it end the cynicism and distrust that pervades so much of what government does? And, would it enhance the prospects for human freedom and happiness at the end of the twentieth century and beyond?

Unhappily, the answer is no. Managerial reform alone will not be enough to wipe out all the problems of government ineffectiveness that have been accumulating over the past several decades. The maladies afflicting modern government in the United States spread far beyond and far deeper than matters of management, so that the remedies prescribed in this book, while they will help the patient to walk again, will not restore total vigor and good health.

A fundamental problem that has developed in Washington is that we have piled too many responsibilities upon the government's shoulders, and we are continuing to add to the burden. For the first century or more of our nation's existence, the prevailing ethos in the United States was that our government should be severely limited in its powers and that the citizenry should have the right—as well as the responsibility—to look after itself. In the late nineteenth century, however, as industrial giants began to emerge in the private sector, as the public began to blame the volatile ups and downs of economic life upon the robber barons of industry, and as writers such as Upton Sinclair and Lincoln Steffens exposed the darker sides of the industrial revolution, people began turning to the government as a protector and shield from the vicissitudes of modern life.

The first wave of government reform in the early years of the twentieth century significantly strengthened the powers of the central government, and then along came the First World War and the Depression, giving the country a mighty shove toward government centralization. By the middle of the 1930s, observers such as Walter Lippmann were writing that the underlying philosophy of American life had undergone a revolution. In *The Good Society*, Lippmann wrote:

> The older faith, born of long ages of suffering under man's dominion over man, was that the exercise of unlimited power by men with limited minds and self-regarding prejudices is soon oppressive, reactionary and corrupt. In the new age, however, this tested wisdom is submerged under a world-wide movement which has at every vital point the support of vested interests and the afflatus of popular hopes. . . . The predominant teachings . . . are that there are no limits to man's capacity to govern others and that, therefore, no limitations ought to be imposed upon government.

Lippmann was profoundly unhappy with this changing philosophy and he clung to the older, "liberal" view. In conclusion, he observed:

> Men may have to pass through a terrible ordeal before they find again the central truths they have forgotten. But they will find them again, as they have so often in other ages of reaction, if only the ideas that have misled them are challenged and resisted.[1]

When he wrote back in the thirties, Lippmann was not expressing a popular view, but today his perspective is shared by an increasing number of Americans who are concerned with the even more dramatic shift of power to Washington in the intervening years. With each succeeding crisis—and energy is only the latest example—we have loaded new responsibilities on Washington because we have not had enough faith in the private marketplace or in personal self-reliance.

Theoretically, it should be possible for government to concentrate on a single issue and solve it magnificently. It could clean up the environment, for instance. It could rebuild our cities. It could replace our inadequate housing. It could reform the welfare system and put an end to poverty. It could explore the farthest reaches of the universe. It could ensure that enough energy is available for our future needs. And it could defend our national security. Any one of these things a well-managed government could presumably do well. But when government tries to do all of these things and do them simultaneously, as it does today, then it begins to break down under the load. It becomes not just muscular but muscle-bound. As Peter Drucker wrote in *The Age of Discontinuity:* "There is mounting evidence that government is big rather than strong; that it is fat and flabby rather than powerful; that it costs a great deal but does not achieve much. . . . Indeed, government is sick—and just at the time when we need a strong, healthy and vigorous government."[2]

The indices of government's growth and intrusion into the private sector come easily to hand:

Federal spending in the past fifteen years has quadrupled, and federal, state, and local government spending as a share of GNP has grown from 12 percent in the early 1930s to approximately 35 percent today.

The number of people working for government at some level has grown to one out of every six members of the labor force.

Government taxes have become the fastest-growing item in family budgets, and for the average family now consume more than the first four months of annual pay.

Government regulations have spread over almost every major segment of American industry. Today the Code of Federal Regulations constitutes a stack of books fifteen feet high and containing over sixty thousand pages.

It is this final extension of government power—the power to regulate—that may have brought government centralization to a crest. Opposition to government regulators has now become intense, running the gamut from Kennedy Democrats to Reagan Republicans and encompassing segments of the academic as well as the business community. Perhaps this opposition will help turn the tide, and government may become a more modest force in our society. There is no guarantee of that outcome, but at least there is hope.

While government regulations are as old as the government itself, it has only been in the past decade and a half that there has been such an explosion of regulatory agencies and regulatory edicts. During this period much of the decision making in American industries has been shifted from their owners or professional managers to a vast cadre of government regulators.

This acceleration of federal controls has coincided with, and actually reinforced, a slowing of productivity growth, a faltering standard of living, and the worst siege of inflation and unemployment in many generations. Today, the additional costs brought about by federal regulation are an important source of inflation. Industries such as the airlines, trucking, and medical services are all thought to be charging significantly higher prices to consumers because of regulatory constraints. Moreover, regulation has also been identified as one of the chief reasons why energy industries such as oil and natural gas are producing fewer supplies today than they were a few years ago.

Ironically, there is an iron triangle buttressing government regulations just as there is for domestic assistance programs. As pointed out in a recent article in *Fortune,* the iron triangle of regulation

> refers to a three-sided entente that tends to form among a regulatory agency, the Congressional committees with jurisdiction over it, and the industry it regulates. These three parties defend regulation because it confers power on the regulators, gives political benefits to the Congressmen, and provides shelter for the businessmen who prefer the comfort of their gilded cage to the rigors of competition.[3]

Fortunately, there has been some evidence in the mid-seventies that the iron triangle of regulation is beginning to corrode. As this chapter is written, a considerable movement is afoot to reduce control by the Civil Aeronautics Board over airline prices and routes. There are also growing hopes for lifting government restrictions on services offered by banks, for cutting back on the ossified rulings of the ICC, for ending regulation of new natural gas, and for curtailing FCC restrictions on cable television. Support is also building for sunset laws or other legislative devices that would compel periodic reviews of the regulatory agencies.

While each of these efforts may differ on the merits, there can be little question but that the overall thrust toward paring back and rationalizing the crazy patchwork of current regulations is a healthy sign for the future. It is this kind of effort, along with tax reform, welfare reform, educational reform, judicial reform, medical reform, and all the other domestic areas in need of overhaul, that must accompany reform of management if government is to work. Better management is a vital component of any effort to make government more effective and responsive; unless managerial improvements are made, all else will be relatively futile. But there is no sense pretending that better management alone is a panacea for what Lippmann once called "the sickness of an overgoverned society."

SUMMARY ANALYSIS AND RECOMMENDATIONS

So, then, the fundamental problem is that government tries to do so much that it does very little well—and it chokes off individual initiative in the process. For the most part, this book has accepted government for what it is and has searched for ways to make "what it is" work more effectively and deliver closer to its full potential.

Several problems have persisted as themes throughout these chapters. The first is the unalterable fact that most government chief executives, especially Presidents, enter office with inadequate preparation for making government work effectively. While in most respects the development of political skills remains the best preparation for the presidency— sensing the national mood, bringing people together, forming a vision of the future, building the consensus necessary for progress—it is for the most part antithetical to the development of managerial capabilities and understanding. This is not likely to change, nor should it, in view of the other imperative responsibilities of the presidency.

However, because of the growing complexity of government, its increasing inability to deliver effective results, and the public's growing disaffection with democratic institutions, another imperative of government leadership has developed—that of making government work through improved managerial leadership.

What is called for first is improved understanding in the highest circles of government of what management really is and what it can accomplish. Most elected political leaders and most appointed cabinet members have only a fuzzy view of management, and those who give it any thought generally conceive of it in terms of logistics, housekeeping, computers, personnel systems, and the like.

Undeniably, these administrative support activities have a role, but the heart of managing is the entire process of systematically running an organization to obtain desired results. True management means setting goals, developing policies and plans in objective fashion, selecting the best people, molding the people into an effective team, and leading the team toward a realization of the ultimate goals. An understanding of what really comprises this management process is a prerequisite for practicing it effectively.

A second theme traced through most of this work is the continuous battle between political and substantive considerations. As we have seen, it is extraordinarily difficult to evaluate the performance of high government officials as managers or the way they achieve other substantive results. It is easier and much more common for their report cards to be based on political standards—the stance taken on a particular issue, their ability to communicate with vigor and appeal, their relationships with Congress, their stated philosophies. Because of the desire to be appreciated and receive high marks—apparent in any walk of life but especially deep in politics—there is a strong tendency in the upper echelons of government to subjugate the policy that is substantively responsible to one that is politically expedient. Among the many examples we have seen have been the tendency of the chief executive to ignore management, the political influences that govern many personnel appointments, and the unwillingness of political appointees to tackle issues that lack political sex appeal, such as the development of a fair, rational system for compensating career government executives. This disturbing inclination has also been seen in the reluctance of government to plan beyond the next election, the failure to set and stick to precise objectives that necessarily choose between competing priorities, and the failure to follow through on the implementation of important initiatives to ensure that bold pronouncements lead to substantive achievements. Finally, the subordination of substantive to political concerns has shown up in government's stubborn refusal to pare back useless or outmoded expenditures in order to make way for the new and needed, and by its orientation toward flashy reorganization proposals as opposed to more fundamental management reform.

A final theme that emerges in every chapter is the lack of any "system of management" in the government that is comparable to what exists in the private sector. There are no handles in government that a new executive can quickly grasp and transform the mysterious problems of the bureaucracy into logical, effective management. A good system of management in the government should include an established method for finding and attracting the best people to public service and for developing and utilizing the career people who are already there. Most importantly, it should include a framework within which long-term planning becomes an integrated part of everyday business, methods are established for allocating budgetary resources to the most urgent priorities, clear objectives are regularly agreed upon, and then objectives are used to provide direction and coherence to the everyday operation of government.

These, then, are the three major themes that frame the problems covered in this book:

1. The inadequate preparation of top government officials for managerial responsibilities

2. The subordination, once in office, of considerations of substance to political needs

3. The lack of a readily identifiable "system of management" within the government

The initiative for corrective action in all three of these areas must start at the top with the President. Given the many other urgent demands on his time, we cannot expect and indeed would not want management to become the first priority of the President. But a President—even though he may lack any executive background—can exert managerial leadership with only a limited investment of his time by (1) setting a tone of high ethical standards, basing decisions on a factual foundation, rewarding people for results, and imparting a sense of urgency to the bureaucracy; (2) devoting his personal efforts to the selection of the most able people; (3) developing a personal organization suited to his style and his goals; (4) providing clear guidance to department and agency heads on their direction and expected accomplishments; and (5) making clear to all his subordinates his insistence on sound management and solid leadership and inspiration to the career employees of government.

One of these tasks, selection of people, deserves special consideration, especially at the earlier stages of an administration, because of the enormous impact those selections will have on all else that follows. A prerequisite to choosing high-quality people is a perception of the unique qualities needed in the complex governmental environment. An executive with an excellent track record in the private sector may fall flat on his face in government, and vice versa, simply because government service demands different personal strengths. At every turn, the government executive must contend with a constant glare of publicity, the powerful influence of public opinion, the need to win congressional support for important initiatives, the sheer diversity and dispersion of government programs, the need to make an early impact and achieve results within a limited time span, the lack of management competence and divided loyalties throughout government, the propensity to avoid risks, and the extreme difficulty in evaluating executive performance or program results.

Because of these demands, the successful government executive must bring to his post, or quickly cultivate, qualities that in many instances are opposed to those that fostered success in the private sector. Certainly he must be an exceptional manager because all the traditional management tools are required in government. Beyond that, however, he must also have a keen ability to communicate so that he can convince and persuade the public, the press, the Congress, special-interest groups, and his own bureaucracy to support new initiatives. In addition, he requires sufficient sensitivity and awareness to understand the real motives of those other players and to judge in advance how they will react to his actions. He further needs the determination and patience to endure the slow pace and tortuous turns of government, the flexibility to alter course and compromise in order to achieve at least part of his objective, and the resiliency to endure criticism and defeat but bounce back with good humor.

It is a major challenge to any administration to find and attract men and women who possess these extra dimensions. Unfortunately, most administrations fail in this regard as they start from scratch in devising methods of talent search, resorting to subjective and rather primitive methods of recruiting, confining themselves to a narrow universe from which to make selections, and failing to hold appointees long enough to gain a real payoff from their services.

The solution to this personnel challenge is to develop within the administration a professional ,executive search capability that can call upon the assistance of a wide network of sources and reach out systematically to recruit the most talented candidates in the country for each individual position. The identification of appealing candidates can also mitigate against the appointment of unqualified people whose only strength is their political pull. This approach to recruiting can be aided and given a much faster start in a new administration if an institutional, professional recruiting arm were established in the Executive Office of the President. The selection process would also be enhanced by greater use of expert panels set up to advise Presidents on personnel decisions. Perhaps the greatest personnel improvement would be realized if chief executives put a stop to the revolving-door syndrome of top appointees and insisted on a four-year commitment from every person appointed.

But reforming the personnel selection processes is only part of the change needed. Equally important is the handling of the career bureaucracy. Political appointees must break down the barriers to trust and confidence by an open, straightforward, communicative approach that involves career people in key projects and recognizes their contributions. Resistance to change and avoidance of risk within the bureaucracy must be minimized by encouraging people to stick their necks out, by demonstrating a willingness to accept an occasional failure, and by flattening organization structures so that there can be more face-to-face communication and better understanding of organizational problems by top management. Rigid personnel systems and narrow career patterns should be eliminated by combining federal personnel systems, providing flexibility within the system, and requiring regular job rotation for rising career executives.

Further development of career executives should be achieved by devoting added resources to graduate education fellowships in management and by requiring developmental experiences as a precondition of advancement to the higher levels of government. Finally, outmoded and ineffective pay practices should be replaced by a system guaranteeing adequate salaries at the top, periodic pay increases across the board, bonuses for outstanding performance, and a faster promotion system that recognizes and advances outstanding civil servants before they are lured away by the private sector.

Selecting the right people and stimulating performance of the bureaucracy will lay the foundation for effective government, but it is equally important to build upon that base. In particular, it is essential to decide carefully upon the goals of the government. The focus of the political executive is generally short-term, or at least not beyond his term of office. Because of this perspective and because of the pressing urgency of other problems and issues, government as a whole notoriously neglects long-term planning, especially in the domestic areas. Government leaves much to chance and fails to ensure that the policies of today are consistent with the needs of tomorrow.

To correct this deficiency, the top line officials of government must become more personally involved in strategic planning and treat planning as an important element of their jobs. To assist them, and to provide conceptual stimulation for the planning process, a strategic planning office should be formed within the Executive Office of the President, preferably through a revitalization of the Domestic Council. This office, along with the other agencies of government, should be held accountable by the Congress for developing long-range plans, and these plans should be carefully reviewed as a key part of the budget process. To ensure that long-range planning is of a high caliber, a greater effort must also be made to bring into government conceptual thinkers of keen intellect and with a broad view of the country's direction and needs.

If long-range planning is properly done, it can be vitally helpful in the annual budgeting process, providing top executives with a useful framework as they choose between competing priorities. The problem with the current budget process is that money for new initiatives and even for the expansion of productive programs is almost impossible to obtain because (1) laws already on the books dictate an inexorable rise in spending for existing programs, placing them outside the year-to-year control of the executive branch or the Congress; (2) existing programs are seldom pared down but instead develop strong constituency-based pressures for more and more spending; and (3) even outmoded, ineffective programs are perpetuated as iron triangles of the bureaucracy, congressional committees, and industry beneficiaries fight to keep their favorite programs alive.

Since Congress is unlikely to halt the rise of uncontrollable expenditures, the executive branch must apply stringent criteria in vigorously attacking wasteful programs in order to permit funding of truly urgent priorities. It should do this by approaching reduction targets selectively and sequentially, by working ever more closely and constructively with the Congress and the bureaucracy, and by mounting large-scale communications efforts to inform the public and gain their support. In addition, selective use should be made of zero-based budgeting so that every program is scrutinized at least once every five years. Finally, the executive branch should seek to move more spending decisions from the federal government to state and local levels where these decisions can be made by officials who are closer to the problems and are directly accountable for their solution.

The management of human resources forms the first stage, while long-range planning and allocation of resources, working in tandem, form the second stage of what we might term "a system of managing"—that is, the development of procedures that any executive can use to set the wheels of government in motion. What is needed next is a third stage to guide the executive in his day-to-day work.

Several striking failures in government management make it clear that top executives need a framework for their daily operations. Most top government officials reign but do not rule. They do not really gain control over their organizations because they lack a means of providing systematic direction and evaluating results on a consistent basis. Further, they tend to focus only on a few highly visible issues and problems, failing to follow up on the implementation of new initiatives. Finally, officials in government have no meaningful way of measuring individual performance or program results on a consistent basis.

These problems can be ameliorated by the third stage of our "system of management"—management by objectives. Under MBO, clear objectives for each unit must be enunciated at the start, objectives must be stated in terms of end results to be achieved, and there must be simple plans or milestones for attaining the objectives. Further, each subordinate should be required to set objectives that support those of the next higher level of the organization, pyramid-fashion.

Management by objectives ensures that each unit of government has a clear sense of direction and establishes clear and precise goals; focuses the attention of top officials on these goals all the way through to completion; mitigates against the diversions of fire fighting; and enables senior officials to monitor progress and ensure that these goals are achieved. It is also extremely useful as a communications device in gaining understanding of priorities throughout an organization.

Finally, MBO provides a solid means of assessing the performance or achievement of an individual or an organization because at the end of each year top management can determine how much progress has been made toward their stated goals. Moreover, by periodically checking progress against the objective's milestones, it is possible to detect emerging problems while they are still correctable and before they become crises. It must be added that if management by objectives is to succeed, it demands the full commitment of people up and down the line as well as the personal involvement of top executives.

The fourth and final stage in erecting a system of management is the evaluation of government programs. Program evaluation today is done poorly, if at all, because of the serious difficulties in assessing programs that have vague or ambiguous purposes and because of the disinterest of executive branch and congressional leaders. There are no pat solutions to the need for improved program evaluation, but progress can be made by ensuring adequate staff support for that purpose, by exerting pressure on department and agency heads for regular follow-up efforts, and by adopting a strategy of experimentation and demonstration prior to full-scale funding of new programs.

Implicit in all of this discussion is the need for a sound organization structure. While reorganization has been much overrated as a means to strengthen performance, and few attempts at comprehensive reorganization have succeeded, good organization is a prerequisite to good management. Reorganization is inherently difficult, but there are approaches that can mitigate against the fragmented and overlapping structure of government. For instance, the executive branch can reform individual agencies on a selective basis, organizing them around a central mission or modifying them so that decisions are focused at the optimum level. Selective reorganization is also needed within the congressional committee structure. Of key importance, top government officials must act with flexibility in developing a personal organization and a set of working relationships that encourage better team efforts and smooth the resolution of policy issues.

As stated earlier, management reform alone will not solve all of the ills of government, but it will make government work far better than it does today. It can and will bring government far closer to delivering the level of services expected by the American taxpayer.

To accomplish this, however, requires a national "will to manage." It requires a will on the part of the electorate to look past the surface, to demand improved performance, and to hold elected politicians accountable for their substantive accomplishments. Even more importantly, it requires a realization and an understanding on the part of political leaders and their appointees of the potential for improvement—and the will to take advantage of opportunities.

The realization, the understanding, and the will have been absent too often in the past, and are not much in evidence today. But this condition does not have to persist. The need is with us, the possibilities abound. It is long past a due time for political will to match national need in the urgent mission of making government work.

Appendix A

Development of Presidential Appointment Talent Bank for Postelection Staffing

INTRODUCTION

This paper outlines the procedures for developing a talent bank of two hundred clearly superior PA and PAS candidates to be used in the staffing of those positions that will be vacated after the reelection of the President.

This effort is brought about by the realization that many of the present appointees will be leaving the administration to return to their former positions. By planning now, we will have time to conduct a nationwide search for approximately two hundred highly qualified individuals that have the substantive skills and the motivation to either serve in the administration or on high-level task forces. A network of key sources, covering a wide range of professions, will then be interviewed and evaluated and, if qualified, will become part of the talent bank.

The approach for this effort is discussed in three sections:

1. Development of Key Sources
2. Profile of Candidates
3. Screening and Evaluation

DEVELOPMENT OF KEY SOURCES

The effectiveness of this program hinges to a large extent on our ability to identify and utilize sources from a wide range of professions. The majority of the sources will be from the business community. However, sources will also be developed within the academic, scientific, medical, and environmental fields, as well as from state and local governments.

Sources should be selected on their ability to identify the high-caliber type of candidate we need. They should not be selected solely for their national prominence or senior position. It is important that a geographic spread be maintained so that candidates will not come primarily from one section of the country or have similar backgrounds. Obviously, these sources should have a loyalty to the President and a strong willingness to help in the staffing of his administration.

From our past recruiting efforts, approximately 150 key sources have already been developed. This list must now be enlarged upon and new names carefully cultivated to bring us to a total source list of approximately 250 names. We will seek new sources from knowledgeable administration officials such as Schultz, Stans, Flanigan, and Peterson, as well as from our own contacts in the business community. Finally, we will use Ed David and Sid Marland as key sources in the scientific and academic communities respectively, with the assignment of developing candidates in their fields. From these efforts, a final approved list will be prepared and the program started.

The sources will then be contacted and briefed on the program and their active participation encouraged. Appropriate follow-up and thank yous will ensue. To a large extent, the success of this program will rest on our ability to motivate the sources to be of active and continuous help.

PROFILE OF CANDIDATE

Although highly specialized backgrounds will be required for certain positions, e.g. Comptroller, Department of Defense; Assistant Secretary for Science and Technology, Department of Commerce; Assistant Secretary for International Affairs, Department of the Treasury; there are certain minimum—extremely stiff—general requirements that each candidate must meet.

First, they must be good managers who are able to make things happen—synthesizers—able to get projects finished, decisions made, and programs pushed ahead. They should possess a high capability to master and understand complex programs; have the people skills and sensitivities that are effective in a large organization; be tough enough to accept constant and frequently hostile surveillance; have sufficient flexibility to survive the political environment; and possess charisma. Finally, and most importantly, they should be totally loyal and dedicated to job performances and achievement, rather than glory or other self-aggrandizement.

Generally speaking, candidates will be between the ages of thirty-two and fifty, and will have a proven track record of success. They will have achieved a compensation level that will allow them to leave their present positions and move to Washington for at least two years. They must be supportive of the President's programs (this does not exclude registered Democrats) and motivated toward public service.

Candidates need to be developed from the following functional fields:

A. *Management Generalist*   Broad-spectrum people who possess professional management skills that can be used in a variety of situations. These individuals will usually have an area of functional strength, i.e. finance, marketing, manufacturing, consulting, but the overall strength will be their ability to see the large picture, manage complex situations, and handle people.

B. *Legal Profession* (1) Those whose interests and skills are broad and can be used in positions other than those requiring a strictly legal background. (2) Specialists in law, whose interest and experience best fit positions requiring special training, e.g. antitrust, criminal, and tax laws.

C. *Labor Relations* People whose philosophy in labor and management relations support the administration's point of view.

D. *Transportation* Recognized authorities in the field: (1) air, (2) railroads, (3) trucking, (4) mass transit.

E. *International* Individuals whose knowledge and experience are in any of the following: (1) foreign trade, (2) international finance, (3) international relations.

F. *State and Local Government* Young comers whose interests are in politics, urban affairs, and problems surrounding local government.

G. *Medicine and Health* Specialists whose talents and training can be utilized in specialized areas of HEW and other agencies. This category will include environmentalists. Dr. DuVal of HEW and Russell Train will be asked to assist in these categories by contacting sources and developing candidates.

H. *Education* Leaders in the academic community who are in the forefront of their fields. We will lean heavily on Commissioner of Education Sid Marland to develop an initial list here.

I. *Science/Engineering/Research* The Office of Science and Technology will be asked to undertake a broad search project in these areas, identifying and evaluating the leaders and recommending final candidates for inclusion in the talent bank.

Additional fields from which to develop candidates will be determined after the study of upcoming vacancies is completed.

SCREENING AND EVALUATION

We will need approximately eight hundred résumés on suggested candidates. These résumés will be carefully screened and evaluated. Those who survive the screening (an estimated four hundred) will be phoned so that the need can be explained and their interest determined. After interest is established, further research and referencing will be conducted. If they pass this screening, a personal interview will be arranged to further determine their suitability. If this meeting reveals that the individual is of truly high caliber, he will be added to the talent bank for later contact. If the candidate is reluctant to serve, we will attempt to persuade him either now or after a specific job is identified for him.

Many of the candidates interviewed will not meet our strict requirement for incorporation in the talent bank. However, their skills and abilities will be well above average, qualifying them for a level just below that of a presidential appointment. These names will be referred to the ongoing candidates list in the WHPO. All qualified persons contacted will be utilized as an avenue of information for additional sources and candidates.

The accompanying table shows the timing and the steps involved in the screening and evaluation process. This effort will be the full-time endeavor of one man. No additional staffing is anticipated. However, as the program progresses, if additional manpower is required for a timely completion, personnel will be made available.

The internal control and retrieval of pertinent data on the candidates will be through the use of a functional control

Steps and Target Start/Completion Dates

Step	Start Date	Completion Date
Contact all sources (approximately 250)	May 1	May 31
Obtain results of contacts (approximately 800 names)	May 15	July 31
Screen and evaluate names	June 1	August 31
Contact and determine interest	June 15	August 31
Conduct reference checks	July 1	September 15
Complete personal interviews	August 1	October 31
Submit final names for talent bank (approximately 200)	October 1	October 31

card like those now being used in the White House recruiting operation. Since it is anticipated that no more than two hundred candidates will be developed, it will not be necessary to computerize the talent bank.

Appendix B

Federal Government Objectives

DEPARTMENT OF AGRICULTURE

Maintain high levels of farm income while increasing the supplies of agricultural commodities to meet domestic and export demands and relieve the inflationary pressures of recent excessive increases in farm product prices.

Maintain exports at not less than $10 billion and achieve an annual rate of $11.5 billion by the end of FY 1974, subject to the availability of adequate domestic supplies at acceptable prices.

Reappraise and develop a comprehensive strategy for improving the effectiveness of USDA's marketing program.

Bring the Screwworm Barrier program to an initial operational status in Mexico.

Develop a plan for preventing the entry of Foot and Mouth Disease into the U.S. from South America when the Pan American Highway is completed.

Develop a comprehensive USDA policy position on child nutrition including more cost-effective programs and draft legislation if appropriate.

Modify the Food Stamp Program to include (1) new eligibility criteria that will focus on true individual income assistance needs at reduced costs, and (2) administrative improvements that strengthen enforcement.

Develop, install, and evaluate a system for proceeding with the Rural Development Act of 1972, including

(1) coordination under Section (603) and (2) implementation of the Special Rural Development program in the FY 1974 budget.

Achieve the National Forest timber sales target for 1973, and, consistent with environmental constraints, develop a program to achieve the full allowable cut by the end of FY 1976.

Meet existing commitments for identifying National Forest acreage for inclusion in wilderness areas.

Complete plans and initiate a nationwide Land Inventory and Monitoring Program as required by Section 302 of the Rural Development Act of 1972.

Develop and implement specific affirmative-action plans for minority employment and promotion that are consistent with budget, program, and personnel constraints.

DEPARTMENT OF COMMERCE

Eliminate, reduce, or reorient ineffective or marginal programs, provide adequate support of high-priority programs, redesign management structures and systems.

Provide and report against resource and program performance measures for approximately 1500 budget-line items.

Provide monthly reports on all major objectives and on progress in implementing new programs and redirecting existing programs.

Mount an effort to increase the exports of the 250 largest U.S. exporters. Contribution to exports: $250M.

Identify and reduce domestic obstacles to export and participate in efforts to increase U.S. access to foreign markets.

Broaden the export base by getting U.S. companies to export and participate in efforts to increase U.S. access to foreign markets.

Assist U.S. companies in capturing specific export sales opportunities by providing 500 major export project leads and 18,000 smaller trade opportunities.

Stimulate and assist U.S. companies to enter the markets of Eastern Europe, the USSR, and China.

Analyze requirements for export incentive programs and help identify objectives for FY 75 and beyond.

Provide key information on the competitiveness and trade position of the U.S. in world markets.

Work toward the ratification of the Patent Cooperation Treaty and completing negotiations, and presenting to Congress a Trademark Registration Treaty.

Increase foreign exchange earnings from tourism by $167 million and foreign visitor arrivals by 334,000 over levels which would result from normal growth.

Reduce the gap between domestic and foreign shipyard productivity and reduce subsidy rates from 39 percent by June 1973 to 35 percent by June 1975.

Reduce or eliminate ship operating subsidies and reduce the base ship crew for bulk ships supported by subsidy to 24 by January 1975.

Evaluate the costs and benefits of revitalizing the U.S. Merchant Marine, and propose implementing legislation.

Encourage direct foreign investment in the U.S., for the purpose of improving the U.S.'s balance-of-payments position.

Develop supply needs, fuel substitute data, timing, price effects, problems, and possible federal actions for U.S. industries impacted by new energy policies.

Preserve and enhance the competitiveness of industries dependent on oil, by insuring that they are treated equitably under the new license-fee oil import program.

Provide federal policymaking officials with balance-of-payments data on consequences of current and possible future energy policies.

Publish NBS energy conservation methods for buildings; stimulate industry use of best current energy conservation practices, and identify additional energy conservation opportunities in government.

Meet ship and port needs for energy material imports.

Analyze potential U.S.-Soviet LNG projects to determine energy and balance-of-payments impact as well as technical and economic feasibility.

Establish the costs of producing oil and natural gas, including exploration and development costs.

Increase minority business ownership; assist minority businessmen in obtaining procurement contracts worth $300 million; and take steps to reduce failure rates.

Determine the value of the return on the federal investment in minority business enterprise.

Develop planning and reporting system for SBA minority business enterprise programs and for the OMBE program.

Reduce the economic and social disruption of natural disasters by improved warning and prediction systems.

Provide measurement methods, standards and data required for monitoring and controlling environmental pollution.

DEPARTMENT OF DEFENSE

Develop additional strategic force employment options suitable for approximate nuclear parity between the U.S. and USSR.

Maintain strategic, tactical, and support forces, modernized and properly deployed.

Ensure that forces based in the United States are capable of responsive deployment overseas.

Sustain the All-Volunteer Force by recruiting and retaining the number and the quality of personnel required.

Improve force structure, capability, and manpower supply of the National Guard and Reserve to better meet mission and readiness requirements.

Reduce the material portion of grant aid (MAP) on a country-by-country basis by substituting foreign military commercial sales.

Improve NCA command and control of operational forces through development of the World-Wide Military Command and Control System (WWMCCS) and improvement of its intelligence support.

Reduce the personnel (military and civilian) of headquarters staffs and support activities.

Realign the DoD domestic and overseas base support structure consistent with projected force levels and requirements.

Attain greater efficiencies and economies in information collection and evaluation and intelligence dissemination through the restructuring of DoD intelligence activities.

Ensure that research and development programs are designed to produce cost-effective systems that take into greater account real need and cost as well as technological improvement.

Improve DoD capability to estimate the real costs of weapons systems so as to reduce underfunding in the FYDP and avoid costly schedule and procurement quantity changes.

Increase logistics systems compatibility and integration within the Department of Defense.

Provide effective economic adjustment assistance to communities impacted by DoD base realignments.

Assure that equal-opportunity criteria are applied in all activities of the Department of Defense and assure that the FY 1974 program is achieved.

Reduce drug and alcohol abuse by service people to levels below those of comparable age and economic groups in society at large.

Increase the recruitment of women for the military

services by 25 percent over planned FY 1974 accessions and the number of civilian women in professional positions throughout the DoD by 10 percent.

Reduce DoD consumption of energy by 7 percent.

Account for all those missing in action throughout Indochina.

Ensure the public release of the maximum amount of information about DoD plans, programs, and activities consistent with DoD Principles of Public Information, Executive Order 11652, and the Freedom of Information Act.

Provide Congress all information necessary and appropriate for its deliberations.

Improve public understanding of the purposes and programs of the Department of Defense in support of the nation's vital interests and well-being.

DEPARTMENT OF HEALTH, EDUCATION AND WELFARE

Develop, submit and secure passage of the administration proposal for National Health Insurance.

Develop a new approach to welfare reform in conjunction with HUD, VA, DOL, and Agriculture.

Improve the administration of the Aid to Families with Dependent Children Program by (1) issuing more effective regulations, and (2) determining and reducing the magnitude of the ineligibility and overpayment rates by 3 percent and 5 percent respectively.

Improve health-care cost control and reduce medical inflation by (1) cutting the annual growth rate in hospital charges and doctors' fees to 6 percent and 2.5 percent respectively, and (2) saving $100 million in Medicare and $200 million in Medicaid through a reduction in unnecessary utilization.

Decentralize all departmental programs and support functions.

Prepare an operational plan for the effective implementation of the National Cancer Program from both a management and a scientific point of view.

In conjunction with the private sector, develop an effective national system for blood-collection distribution and utilization; use existing regulatory authority to reduce health hazards; increase the available supply of safe blood.

In conjunction with the states, provide assistance to an additional 6.2 million aged and disabled persons under the expanded Social Security Act.

Develop policy options for restructuring the federal role in postsecondary-education student aid with emphasis on minimum and controllable costs.

DEPARTMENT OF HOUSING AND URBAN DEVELOPMENT

Secure passage of the Better Communities Act (BCA) for community development revenue sharing.

Assure an efficient, equitable phase-out of seven existing categorical grant programs for community development.

Promote readiness by state and local governments for the advent of the Better Communities Act (BCA).

Complete a major study of federal housing policies and programs and develop recommendations.

Develop policies that will preserve federally insured/subsidized housing properties, reduce mortgage deficits, and improve overall administration.

Secure passage of the Disaster Assistance Act of 1973.

Secure passage of the Flood Insurance Act of 1973.

Assimilate OEP's disaster assistance functions into HUD pursuant to Reorganization Plan No. 1.

Prepare and secure passage of the Responsive Governments Act.

Develop and administratively implement changes to HUD's planning and management assistance program.

Develop an overall federal policy for providing technical assistance to state and local governments.

Prepare a report on "National Growth Policy" for submission to Congress.

Evaluate the existing HUD field structure and develop alternatives consistent with the department's changing responsibilities.

Improve internal management systems to enhance accountability and produce desired results.

Develop and install improved evaluation and research methods.

Further the cause of equal opportunity in national programs relating to housing and community development.

Develop and secure passage of legislation creating a Department of Community Development.

DEPARTMENT OF INTERIOR

Obtain Deepwater Port, Gas Deregulation, and Trans-Alaska Pipeline legislation, and issue a permit for the TAP.

Complete Outer Continental Shelf lease sale targets on an accelerated schedule that is consistent with the President's energy message.

Develop new analytical and operational capabilities for energy conservation and nonnuclear R&D, and implement the President's short-term conservation goal.

Pass legislation to strengthen tribal government.

Redirect Indian programs to strengthen tribal government.

Take specific actions to involve Indian people in tribal government.

Secure passage of the Land Reform legislation package with emphasis on the Mined Area Protection Act, the Land Use Policy and Planning Assistance Act and the National Resource Lands Management Act.

Transmit legislation recommending additions to or the creation of units of the National Park, Forest, Wildlife Refuge, and Wild and Scenic Rivers Systems in Alaska.

Submit the Nationwide Outdoor Recreation Plan to the Congress.

Determine new administration water resource policies.

Develop an optimum water resource construction strategy for the 17 western states.

Develop a five-year land acquisition and development plan for authorized areas of the National Park System.

Strengthen the department's regulatory, inspection, and enforcement authority for metal and nonmetal mine and health safety.

DEPARTMENT OF JUSTICE

Reduce the impact of organized crime.

Effectively implement the reorganization of the federal drug enforcement program.

Seek enactment and implementation of a Revised Criminal Code.

Reduce the size of the illegal alien population.

Reduce prison overcrowding and improve treatment programs.

Develop a national criminal statistics system.

Reorganize the department to improve its management direction on program effectiveness.

Improve the prosecutorial and managerial effectiveness of the U.S. attorneys' offices.

Secure passage of special revenue sharing for law enforcement grant programs administered by LEAA.

Develop a plan for a comprehensive management information system for the legal divisions and the U.S. attorneys.

Implement the lead-agency concept for law enforcement telecommunications policy.

Increase the narcotics information disseminated by the FBI to the appropriate drug enforcement agencies.

DEPARTMENT OF LABOR

Design and install a form of manpower revenue sharing within existing statutory authority.

Improve Work Incentive Program operations at all government levels in order to provide for the most effective methods for securing employment for AFDC recipients.

Plan and implement that phase of the "black lung" compensation program which involves medical benefit payments and liability on the part of responsible mine operators.

Develop and implement a system for setting goals and monitoring agency progress relative to affirmative-action activities by government contractors.

Achieve an integrated system of federal-state occupational safety and health enforcement.

Reach administrative agreements to achieve comprehensive occupational safety and health coverage for the U.S. work force and develop appropriate legislative recommendations.

DEPARTMENT OF TRANSPORTATION

Draft a National Transportation Policy Statement that fully considers (1) the proper role of federal, state, and local governments; (2) long term economic efficiency through the use of competition; (3) the reduction of economic regulation to a level consistent with public interest; and (4) the relationship to other national objectives such as energy, environment, and safety.

Enact industry regulatory reform legislation for all

modes of transportation with emphasis on the northeastern railroad problem in the rail sector.

Participate in regulatory agency proceedings to achieve maximum flexibility in adapting to changing technological and market conditions.

Develop an internal coordinating and control structure to handle urban systems, policies, and issues as a whole.

Improve intermodal planning procedures through the development of state and local transportation planning and programming capability related to community development.

Develop criteria for evaluating urban transportation investments for all modes.

Determine effective approaches to handling the transportation needs of the disadvantaged in both urban and rural areas.

Improve the effectiveness of UMTA through (1) reorganization, (2) management assistance to transit operations, (3) rationalizing an approach to the capital grant process, and (4) developing a program to explore noncapital-intensive means for urban transportation.

Enact and implement the 1973 Highway Act with provisions for increased flexibility in the use of federal funds and reduced federal restraints on transportation investment decisions by state/local officials.

Study modifications to the federal-aid highway program including user taxes to reflect changing national priorities and increased control by states and local communities, and initiate the development of appropriate legislative proposals.

Enact and implement legislation to restructure the northeastern rail system.

Institute revised administrative user charges designed to recover personnel and aircraft licensing/certification costs, and perform the Airport and Airway Cost Allocation

Study required by Congress to determine more equitable recovery through user charges.

Increase airport and airway productivity by improved ATC automation, more selective safety inspections, and better rule-making procedures to achieve an annual 2 percent reduction in FAA service-unit operating costs.

Analyze airport and airway operational alternatives and their respective cost-effectiveness.

Develop an approach for formally appraising energy consequences in the DoT grant approval process.

Improve automotive transportation energy efficiency.

Improve aircraft operating procedures to reduce the consumption of aircraft fuels.

Develop a computer simulation model and provide reports to other agencies on refinery deep-water port locations.

Initiate studies on transportation patterns and develop alternatives to induce users to shift to lower energy-consuming modes.

Develop alternative plans to reduce accident and fatality rates for highway as well as other modes of transportation.

Determine the feasibility of establishing national accident reduction goals and take implementation steps as appropriate.

DEPARTMENT OF THE TREASURY

Develop, negotiate, and secure acceptance of an outline agreement for reforming the international monetary system by the IMF.

Provide trade policy support by (1) securing enactment of the President's Trade Bill, (2) developing the U.S. position and working with GATT bodies to prepare for multilateral trade negotiations, and (3) administering the Trade Agreements Program.

Develop a U.S. position on international investment policy and the role of the multinational corporation.

Develop a program for management of U.S. participation in the international financial institutions.

Develop U.S. positions on the effectiveness and role of financial mechanisms available to promote U.S. exports.

Secure removal of the Interest Equalization Tax and other foreign-currency restraints.

Secure enactment and implement the Federal Financing Bank Act of 1973.

Secure enactment of legislation from the President's Commission on Financial Structure and Regulation (the Hunt Commission).

Enhance the taxpayer's ability to comply with the law by (1) improving the quality and convenience of local IRS services, and (2) simplifying tax forms and instructions through administrative changes and legislative revisions to the Internal Revenue Code.

Develop and carry out the Economic Stabilization Program under the guidelines of Phase IV.

Decrease the availability of narcotics and dangerous drugs to addicts by reducing smuggling and disrupting distribution and financing systems.

Evaluate revenue-sharing compliance through field office audits and investigations.

Notes

Chapter 1. A Government That Doesn't Deliver (pp. 1–16)

1. Amerada Hess, *Wall Street Journal*, March 27, 1975, p. 17.

2. "Federal Energy Administration Regulation, Report of the Presidential Task Force," American Enterprise Institute, April 1977, p. 146.

Chapter 2. The Chief Executive as Manager (pp. 17–38)

1. *Washington Post*, March 27, 1976, p. A3.

2. The White House had decided upon a tax cut in late 1975, and the President wished to announce it in a public address. He called David R. Gergen of Treasury Secretary Simon's staff to work on this. Gergen had headed the Nixon speech-writing operation and was forced out of the White House shortly after Ford came into office. The first collaboration between the President and Gergen was successful, and Gergen was called in again. Eventually, he was brought back into the White House.

3. Gerald R. Ford, quoted in *Parade*, October 31, 1976, p. 7.

4. Quoted in "Presidents Spend Too Much Time on Foreign Issues," *Washington Post*, October 17, 1976, p. C4.

5. David Broder, *Washington Post*, May 16, 1976, p. C7.

6. Patrick Caddell, "Initial Working Paper on Political Strategy," December 10, 1976, p. 36.

7. Robert Wood, "When Government Works," *The Public Interest,* no. 18 (Winter 1970), p. 41.

Chapter 3. The Government Executive (pp. 39–59)

1. As quoted by John McDonald, "The Businessman in Government," *Fortune,* July 1954, p. 69.
2. Portions of this chapter were originally contained in an article I wrote, entitled "Mr. Executive Goes to Washington," *Harvard Business Review,* September/October 1972, pp. 63–68.

Chapter 4. Attracting the Finest (pp. 60–89)

1. Stephen Hess, *Organizing the Presidency* (Brookings Institution, 1976), p. 162.
2. Karen Elliott House, *Wall Street Journal,* February 2, 1977, p. 1.
3. Karen Elliott House, *op. cit.*
4. Harold Laski, *The American Presidency* (Harper, 1940).
5. Joseph A. Califano, Jr., *A Presidential Nation* (Norton, 1975), pp. 195–96.
6. Mr. Zarb lived up to his advance billing, later becoming Associate Director of the Office of Management and Budget and then Administrator of the Federal Energy Administration.

Chapter 5. Making the Bureaucracy Work (pp. 90–117)

1. Stephen Hess, *Organizing the Presidency* (Brookings Institution, 1976), p. 9
2. Robert Semple, *Playboy,* September 1971.
3. Joel D. Aberbach and Bert A. Rockman, "Clashing Bureaucracy, the Executive Branch: The Nixon Administration Bureaucracy," *American Political Science Review* 70 (June 1976) pp. 458 and 467.
4. Duncan Spencer, *Washington Star,* Feb. 13, 1974, p. 1.

5. *Op. cit.*

6. Portions of this section were originally contained in an article I wrote, entitled "The Development of Public Executives—Neglect and Reform," *Public Administration Review*, May/June 1974, pp. 230–33.

7. George F. Will, *Washington Post*, November 14, 1976, p. C7.

Chapter 6.   Long-Range Planning: Shaping Our Destiny (pp. 118–140)

1. "Forging America's Future: Strategies for National Growth and Development," Report of the Advisory Committee on National Growth Policy Processes to the National Committee on Supplies and Shortages (U.S. Government Printing Office, 1977), p. iii.

2. Quoted in David Broder, "A Lack of Strategy in the Carter Camp," *Washington Post*, June 8, 1977, p. A23.

3. Elliot Richardson, *The Creative Balance* (Holt, Rinehart & Winston, 1976), p. 190.

4. Quoted in Brandt Ayers, "Defining America's Goals," *Washington Post*, December 21, 1976.

5. Stephen Hess, *Organizing the Presidency* (Brookings Institution, 1976), p. 160.

6. Russell Train, "The Challenge of Scarcity," *Cry California: The Journal of California Tomorrow*, 1976, p. 6.

7. Quoted in "Forging America's Future: Strategies for National Growth and Development," Report of the Advisory Committee on National Growth Policy Processes to the National Committee on Supplies and Shortages (U.S. Government Printing Office, 1977), p. iii.

8. Dwight D. Eisenhower, quoted in *Time*, Oct. 6, 1952.

Chapter 7.   Providing New Direction to Government (pp. 141–166)

1. Richard E. Neustadt, *Presidential Power* (John Wiley & Sons, 1960).

2. Quoted in Richard Rose, *Managing Presidential Objectives* (Free Press, 1976), p. 70.

3. Peter F. Drucker, "What Results Should You Expect," *Public Administration Review,* January/February 1976, p. 13.

4. Appendix B contains the actual objectives for the eleven cabinet departments that were finally submitted to and approved by the President, except for the State Department, whose submission was classified secret.

5. Rodney Brady, "MBO Goes to Work in the Public Sector," *Harvard Business Review,* March/April 1973, p. 72.

6. Peter Drucker, "What Results Should You Expect," *Public Administration Review,* January/February 1976, p. 13.

Chapter 8. Putting Federal Money to Work (pp. 167–191)

1. Nick Thimmisch, *Saturday Evening Post,* January/February, 1977, p. 66.

2. *Washington Post,* March 29, 1977, p. D8.

3. Aaron Wildavsky, *The Politics of the Budgetary Process* (Little, Brown, 1964), p. 14.

4. David A. Stockman, "The Social Pork Barrel," *The Public Interest,* Spring 1975.

5. Quoted in *Nation's Business,* November, 1976, p. 53.

6. Senator Edmund Muskie, quoted in *Business Week,* April 11, 1977, p. 128.

Chapter 9. Evaluating Results (pp. 192–213)

1. Quoted in Richard Rose, *Managing Presidential Objectives* (Free Press, 1976), p. 62.

2. Many of these observations on evaluating organizations were originally recorded in "Assessment of Management Quality: A Guide for Outsiders," an article I wrote that appeared on pages 23 through 28 in the April 1968 issue of *Business Horizons* (Graduate School of Business, Indiana University) which focused on

private corporations. After experience in government, I was struck by the applicability of many of these same evaluation techniques to government organizations.

3. John W. Evans, Invitational address presented at the Annual Meeting of the American Educational Research Association, Chicago, Illinois, April 18, 1974.

4. Carol H. Weiss, "Where Politics and Evaluation Research Meet," *Evalaution,* January 3, 1973, p. 44.

Chapter 10.   Organizing for Effective Government
(pp. 214–242)

1. Dean Acheson, "Thoughts about Thoughts in High Places," *New York Times Magazine,* October 11, 1959.

2. Quoted in Richard Polenberg, *Reorganizing Roosevelt's Government* (Harvard University Press, 1966), p. 8.

3. Quoted in the *Wall Street Journal,* November 26, 1976, p. 8.

4. Stephen Hess, *Organizing the Presidency* (Brookings Institution, 1977), p. 207.

5. Dwight D. Eisenhower. *The White House Years: Mandate for Change, 1953–56* (Doubleday, 1963), p. 114.

6. Albert R. Hunt, *Wall Street Journal,* March 11, 1977, p. 16.

7. *Wall Street Journal,* November 26, 1976, p. 8.

Chapter 11.   Making Government Work: A Summing-Up
(pp. 243–258)

1. Walter Lippmann, *The Good Society* (written 1933 to 1937): Smith, Peter (Universal Library), or Grosset 1956.

2. Peter Drucker, *The Age of Discontinuity* (Harper & Row, 1968), p. 212.

3. Paul H. Weaver, "Unlocking the Gilded Cage of Regulation," *Fortune,* February 1977, p. 179.

Index